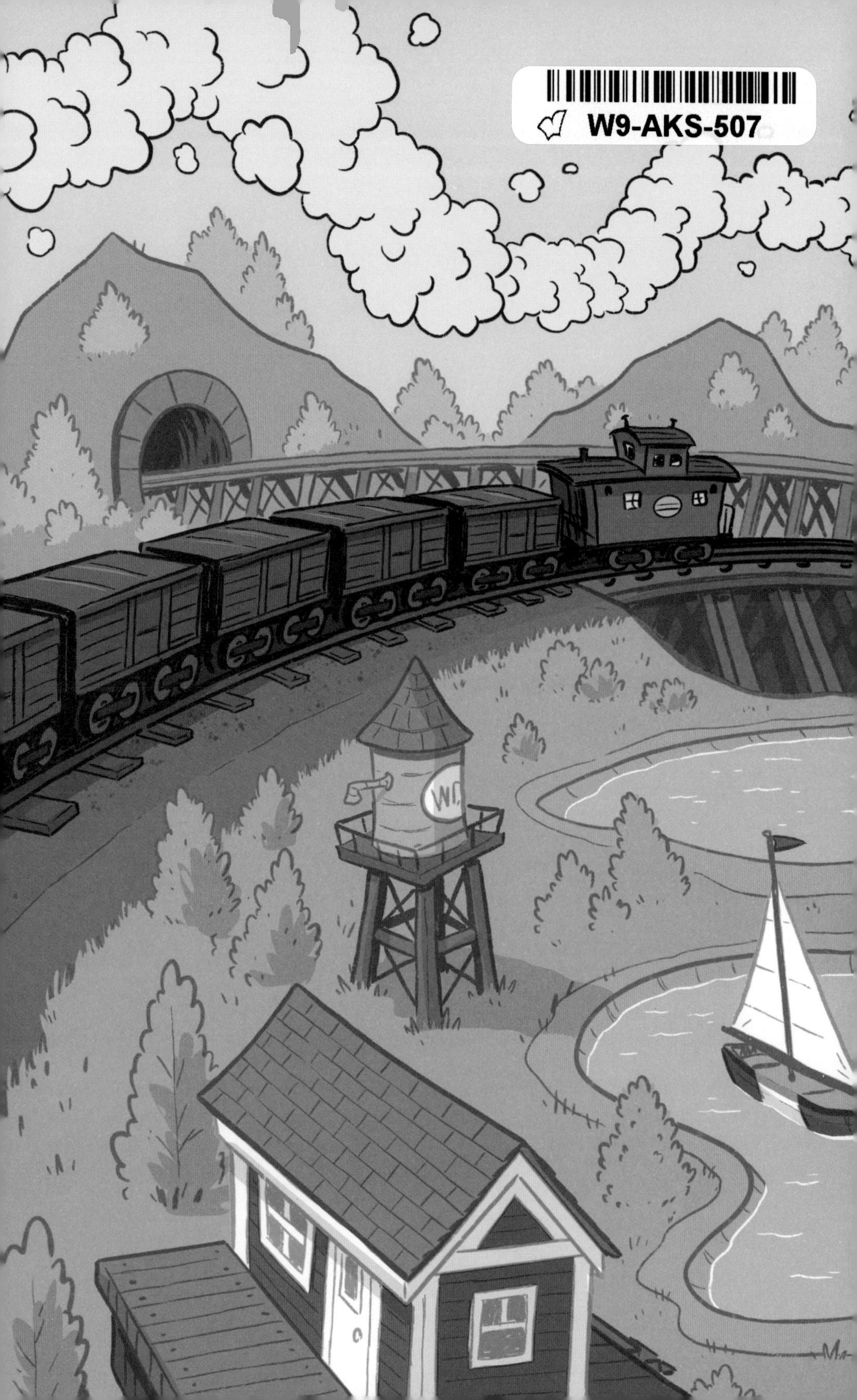

SHOW ME HISTORY!

WALT Disney

The MAGICAL INNOVATOR!

BY
MARK SHULMAN

ILLUSTRATED BY
OTIS FRAMPTON

LETTERING & DESIGN BY
COMICRAFT

COVER ART BY
IAN CHURCHILL

PORTABLE
PRESS

SAN DIEGO, CALIFORNIA

Portable Press
An imprint of Printers Row Publishing Group
10350 Barnes Canyon Road, Suite 100, San Diego, CA 92121
www.portablepress.com • mail@portablepress.com

Correspondence regarding the content of this book should be addressed to Portable Press, Editorial Department, at the above address. Author or illustrator inquiries should be addressed to Oomf, Inc., www.oomf.com.

Publisher: Peter Norton
Associate Publisher: Ana Parker
Developmental Editor: Vicki Jaeger
Senior Product Manager: Kathryn C. Dalby
Production Team: Jonathan Lopes, Rusty von Dyl

Created at Oomf, Inc., www.Oomf.com
Director: Mark Shulman
Producer: James Buckley Jr.

Author: Mark Shulman
Illustrator: Otis Frampton
Colorist: Tracy Bailey
Lettering & design by Comicraft: John Roshell, Forest Dempsey, Sarah Jacobs & Drewes McFarling
Cover illustrator: Ian Churchill

Library of Congress Cataloging-in-Publication Data

Names: Shulman, Mark, 1962- author. | Frampton, Otis, illustrator.
Title: Walt Disney: the magical innovator! / by Mark Shulman; illustrated by Otis Frampton; lettering & design by Comicraft: John Roshell; cover art by Ian Churchill.
Description: San Diego, CA: Printers Row Publishing Group, 2020. | Series: Show me history! | Audience: Ages 8-12. | Audience: Grades 4 to 6.
Identifiers: LCCN 2019018371 | ISBN 9781645170754 (book / paper over board--unjacketed hc)
Subjects: LCSH: Disney, Walt, 1901-1966--Comic books, strips, etc.--Juvenile literature. | BISAC: JUVENILE NONFICTION / Comics & Graphic Novels / Biography. | JUVENILE NONFICTION / Performing Arts / Film. | JUVENILE NONFICTION / Art / Cartooning. | JUVENILE NONFICTION / Biography & Autobiography / Performing Arts.
Classification: LCC NC1766.U52 D5615 2020 | DDC 741.5/8092 [B]--dc23
LC record available at https://lccn.loc.gov/2019018371

Printed in China

24 23 22 21 20 1 2 3 4 5

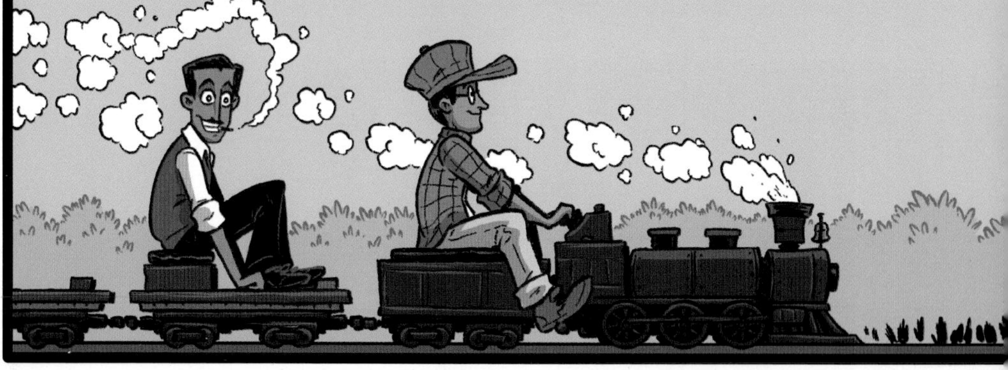

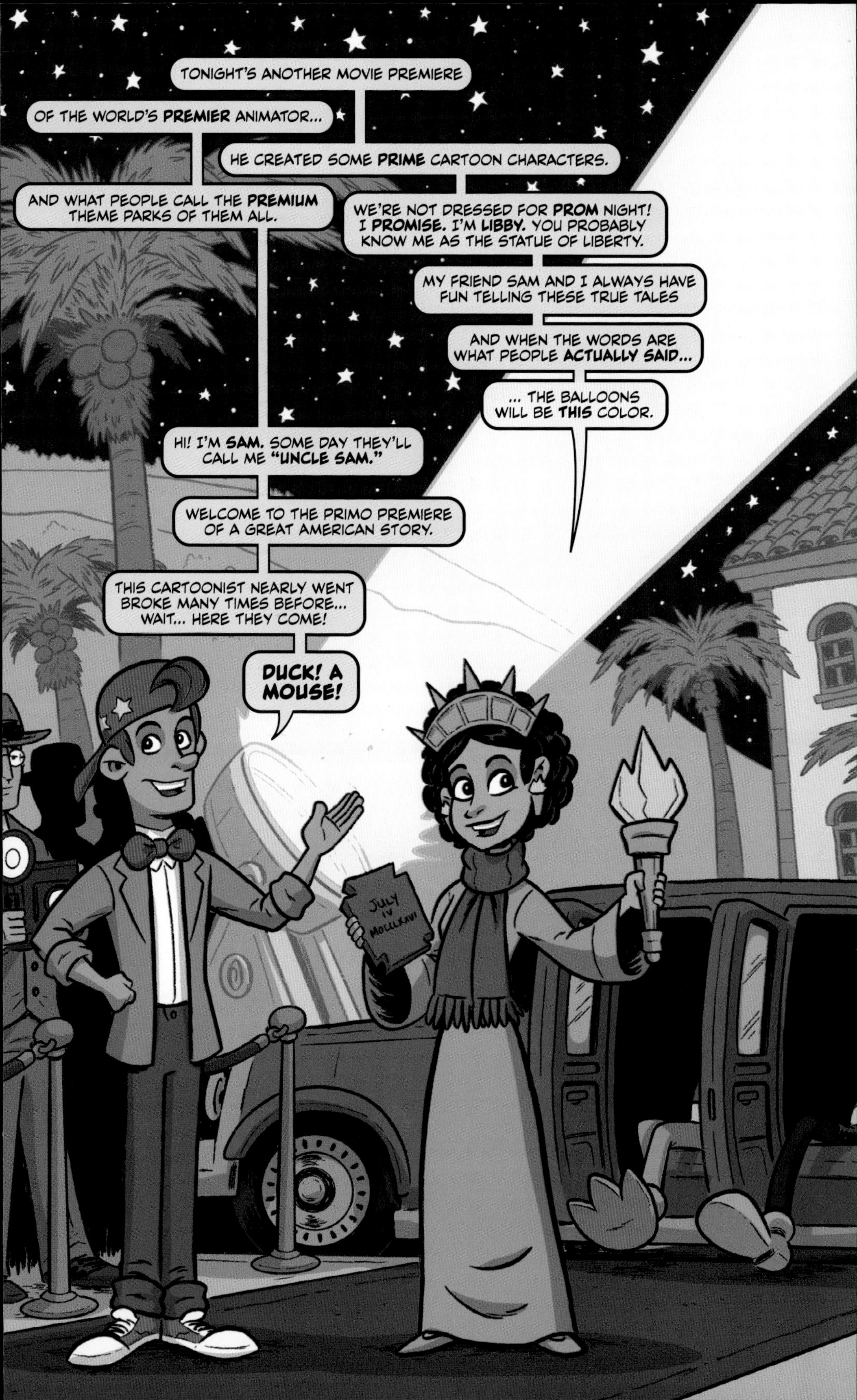
TONIGHT'S ANOTHER MOVIE PREMIERE
OF THE WORLD'S PREMIER ANIMATOR...
HE CREATED SOME PRIME CARTOON CHARACTERS.
AND WHAT PEOPLE CALL THE PREMIUM THEME PARKS OF THEM ALL.
WE'RE NOT DRESSED FOR PROM NIGHT! I PROMISE. I'M LIBBY. YOU PROBABLY KNOW ME AS THE STATUE OF LIBERTY.
MY FRIEND SAM AND I ALWAYS HAVE FUN TELLING THESE TRUE TALES
AND WHEN THE WORDS ARE WHAT PEOPLE ACTUALLY SAID...
... THE BALLOONS WILL BE THIS COLOR.
HI! I'M SAM. SOME DAY THEY'LL CALL ME "UNCLE SAM."
WELCOME TO THE PRIMO PREMIERE OF A GREAT AMERICAN STORY.
THIS CARTOONIST NEARLY WENT BROKE MANY TIMES BEFORE... WAIT... HERE THEY COME!
DUCK! A MOUSE!
JULY IV MDCCLXXVI

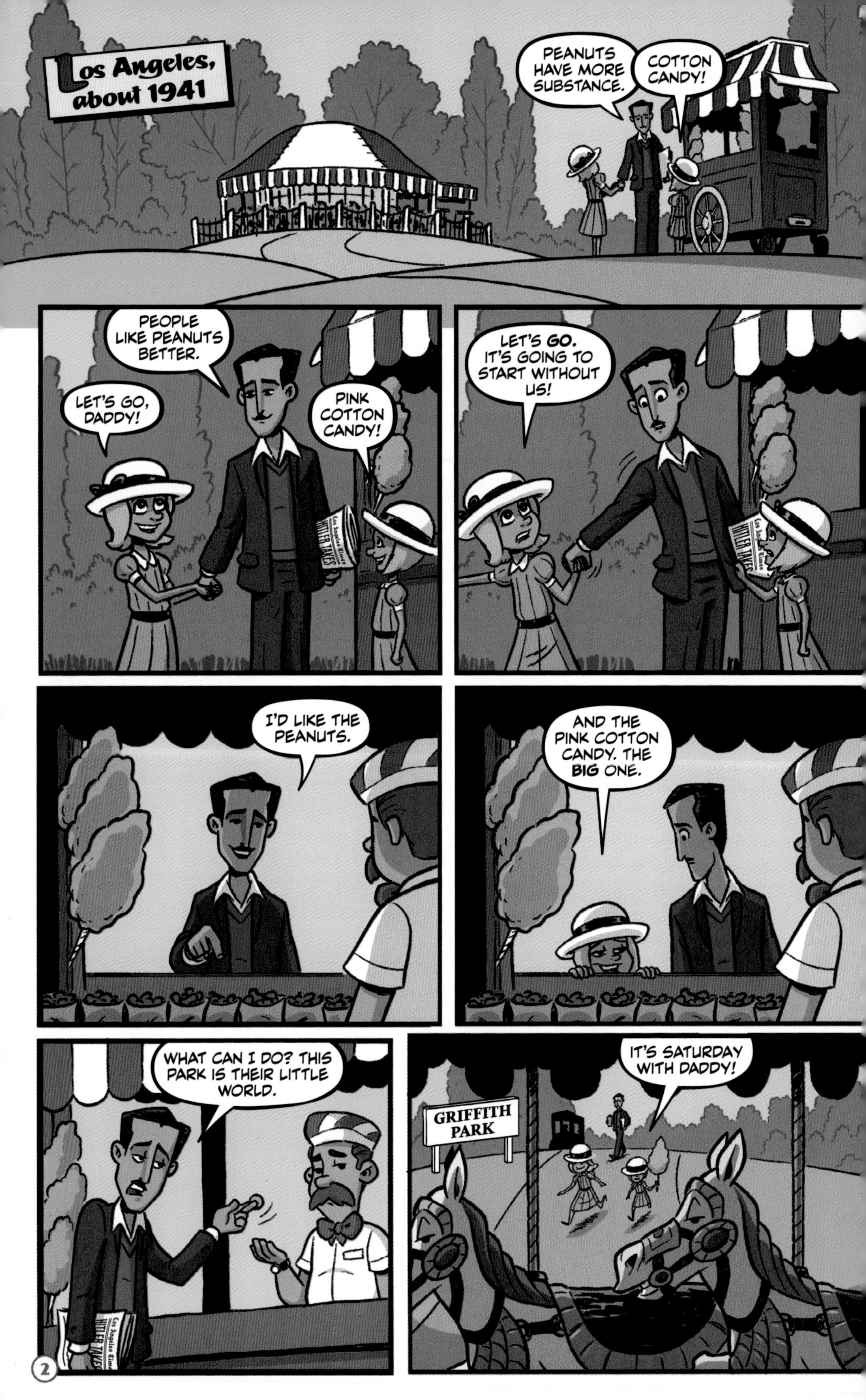
Los Angeles, about 1941
PEANUTS HAVE MORE SUBSTANCE.
COTTON CANDY!
PEOPLE LIKE PEANUTS BETTER.
LET'S GO, DADDY!
PINK COTTON CANDY!
Los Angeles Times
HITLER TAKES
LET'S GO. IT'S GOING TO START WITHOUT US!
I'D LIKE THE PEANUTS.
AND THE PINK COTTON CANDY. THE BIG ONE.
WHAT CAN I DO? THIS PARK IS THEIR LITTLE WORLD.
IT'S SATURDAY WITH DADDY!
GRIFFITH PARK

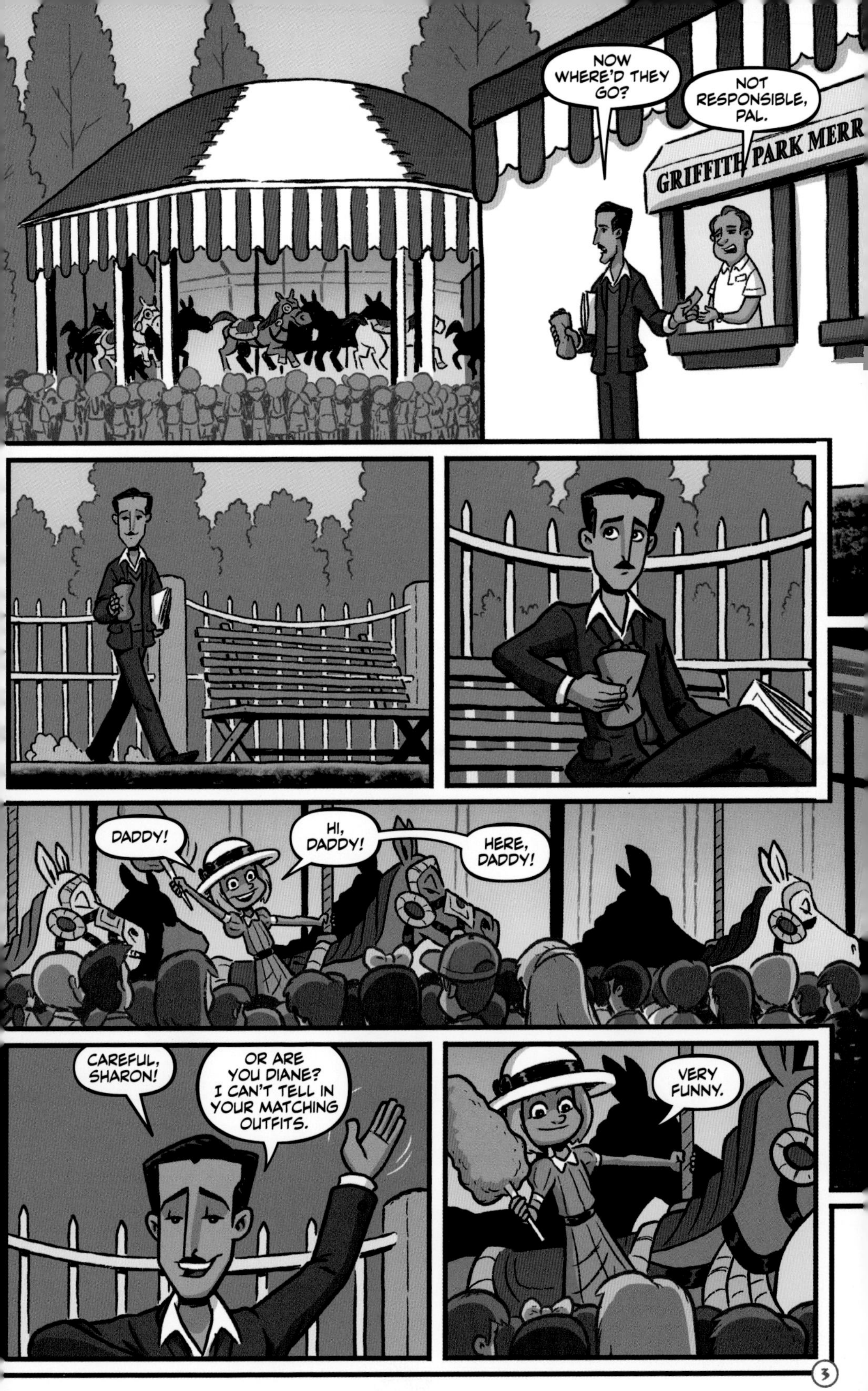
NOW WHERE'D THEY GO?
NOT RESPONSIBLE, PAL.
GRIFFITH PARK MERR
DADDY!
HI, DADDY!
HERE, DADDY!
CAREFUL, SHARON!
OR ARE YOU DIANE? I CAN'T TELL IN YOUR MATCHING OUTFITS.
VERY FUNNY.

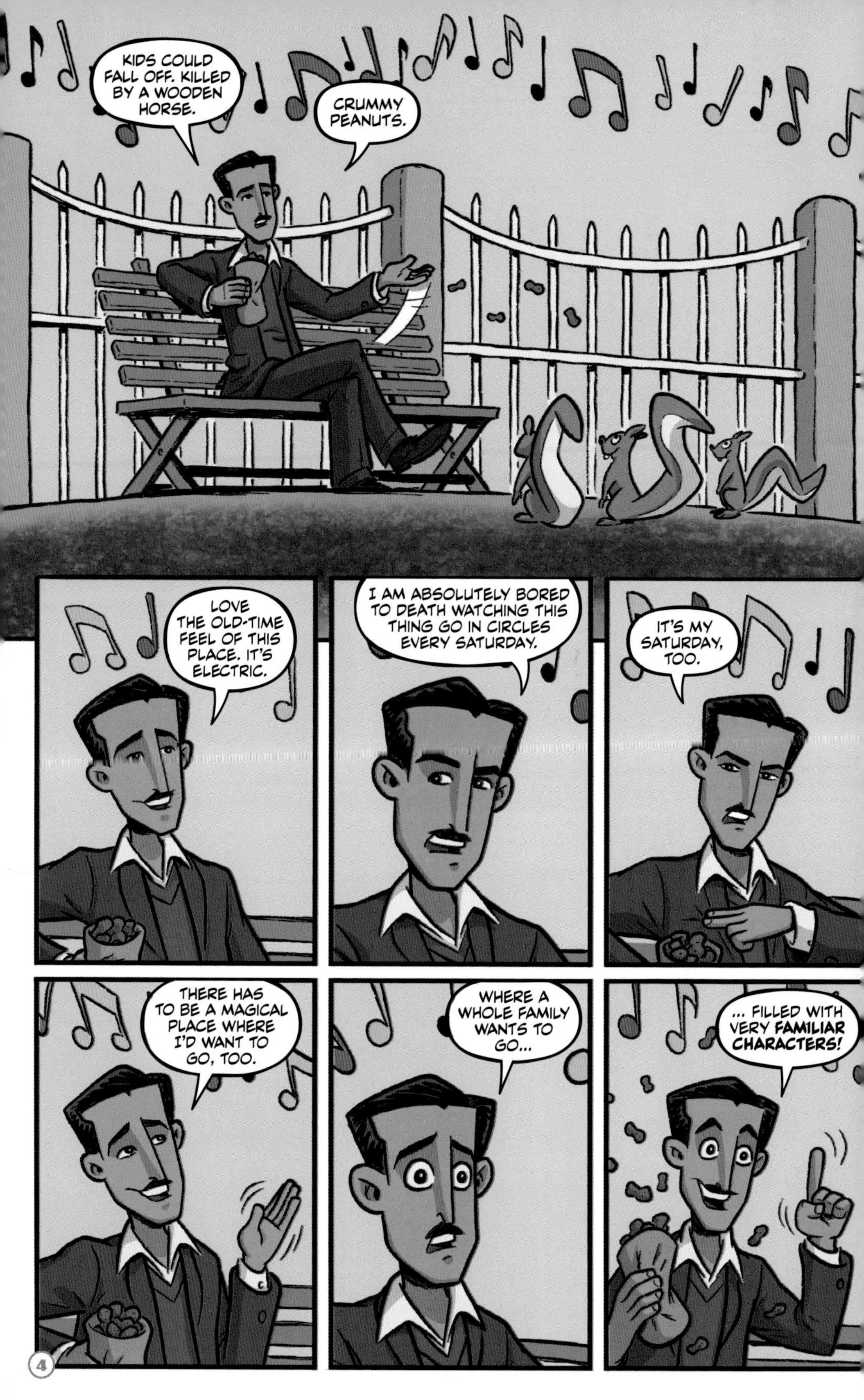
KIDS COULD FALL OFF. KILLED BY A WOODEN HORSE.
CRUMMY PEANUTS.
LOVE THE OLD-TIME FEEL OF THIS PLACE. IT'S ELECTRIC.
I AM ABSOLUTELY BORED TO DEATH WATCHING THIS THING GO IN CIRCLES EVERY SATURDAY.
IT'S MY SATURDAY, TOO.
THERE HAS TO BE A MAGICAL PLACE WHERE I'D WANT TO GO, TOO.
WHERE A WHOLE FAMILY WANTS TO GO...
... FILLED WITH VERY **FAMILIAR CHARACTERS!**

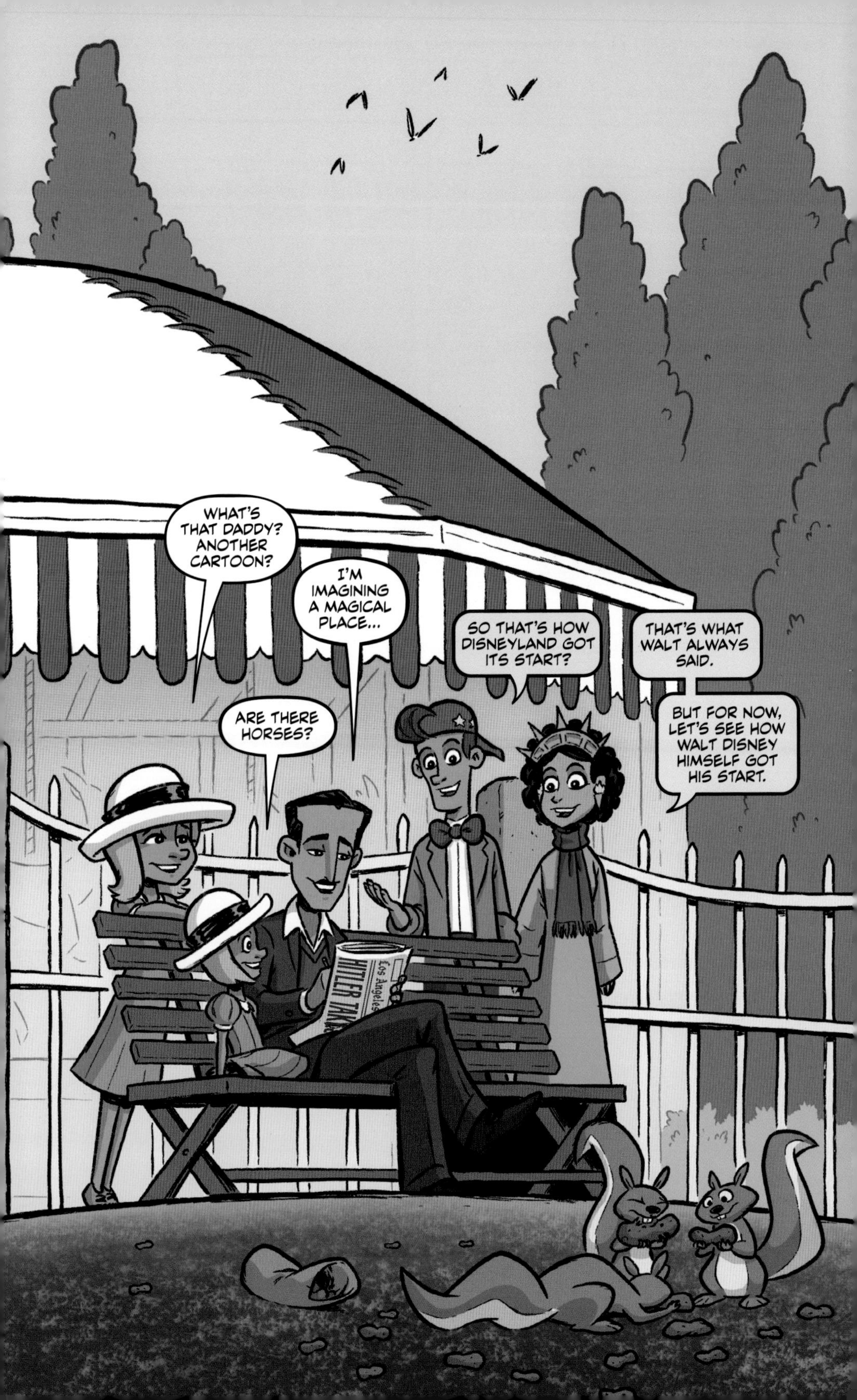
WHAT'S THAT DADDY? ANOTHER CARTOON?
I'M IMAGINING A MAGICAL PLACE...
ARE THERE HORSES?
SO THAT'S HOW DISNEYLAND GOT ITS START?
THAT'S WHAT WALT ALWAYS SAID.
BUT FOR NOW, LET'S SEE HOW WALT DISNEY HIMSELF GOT HIS START.
Los Angeles

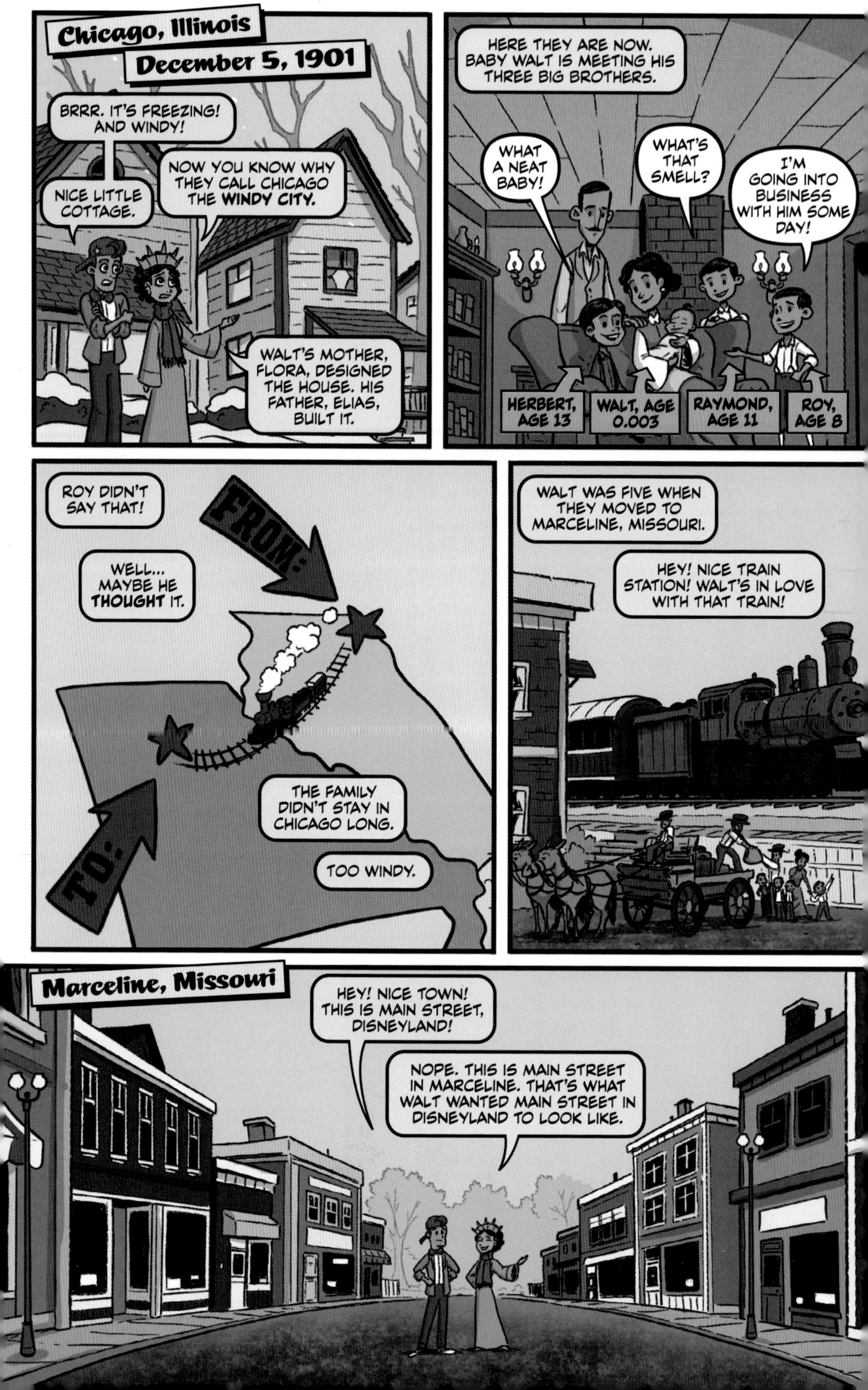
Chicago, Illinois
December 5, 1901
BRRR. IT'S FREEZING! AND WINDY!
NICE LITTLE COTTAGE.
NOW YOU KNOW WHY THEY CALL CHICAGO THE WINDY CITY.
WALT'S MOTHER, FLORA, DESIGNED THE HOUSE. HIS FATHER, ELIAS, BUILT IT.
HERE THEY ARE NOW. BABY WALT IS MEETING HIS THREE BIG BROTHERS.
WHAT A NEAT BABY!
WHAT'S THAT SMELL?
I'M GOING INTO BUSINESS WITH HIM SOME DAY!
HERBERT, AGE 13
WALT, AGE 0.003
RAYMOND, AGE 11
ROY, AGE 8
ROY DIDN'T SAY THAT!
WELL... MAYBE HE THOUGHT IT.
FROM:
TO:
THE FAMILY DIDN'T STAY IN CHICAGO LONG.
TOO WINDY.
WALT WAS FIVE WHEN THEY MOVED TO MARCELINE, MISSOURI.
HEY! NICE TRAIN STATION! WALT'S IN LOVE WITH THAT TRAIN!
Marceline, Missouri
HEY! NICE TOWN! THIS IS MAIN STREET, DISNEYLAND!
NOPE. THIS IS MAIN STREET IN MARCELINE. THAT'S WHAT WALT WANTED MAIN STREET IN DISNEYLAND TO LOOK LIKE.

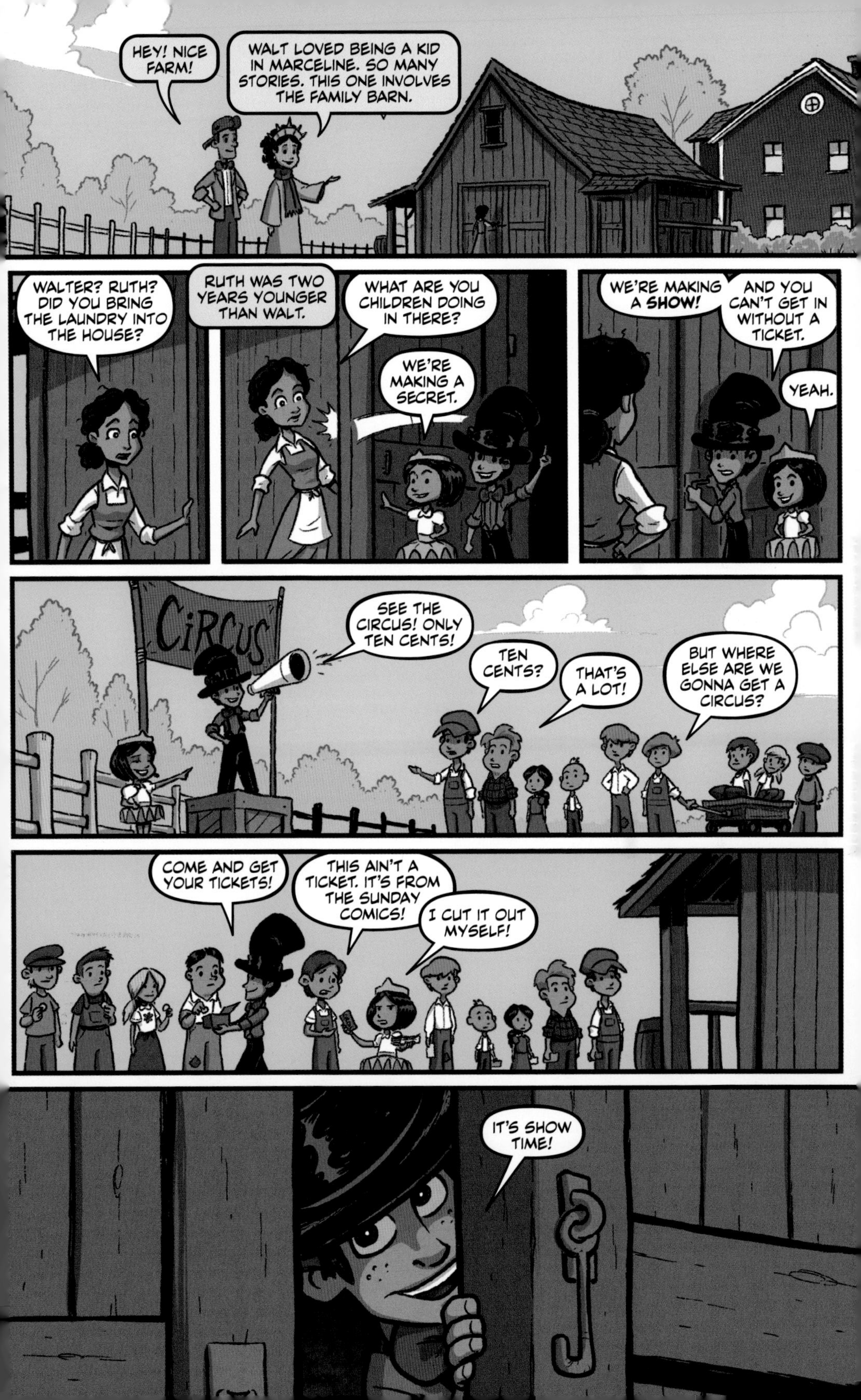
HEY! NICE FARM!
WALT LOVED BEING A KID IN MARCELINE. SO MANY STORIES. THIS ONE INVOLVES THE FAMILY BARN.
WALTER? RUTH? DID YOU BRING THE LAUNDRY INTO THE HOUSE?
RUTH WAS TWO YEARS YOUNGER THAN WALT.
WHAT ARE YOU CHILDREN DOING IN THERE?
WE'RE MAKING A SECRET.
WE'RE MAKING A **SHOW!**
AND YOU CAN'T GET IN WITHOUT A TICKET.
YEAH.
CIRCUS
SEE THE CIRCUS! ONLY TEN CENTS!
TEN CENTS?
THAT'S A LOT!
BUT WHERE ELSE ARE WE GONNA GET A CIRCUS?
COME AND GET YOUR TICKETS!
THIS AIN'T A TICKET. IT'S FROM THE SUNDAY COMICS!
I CUT IT OUT MYSELF!
IT'S SHOW TIME!

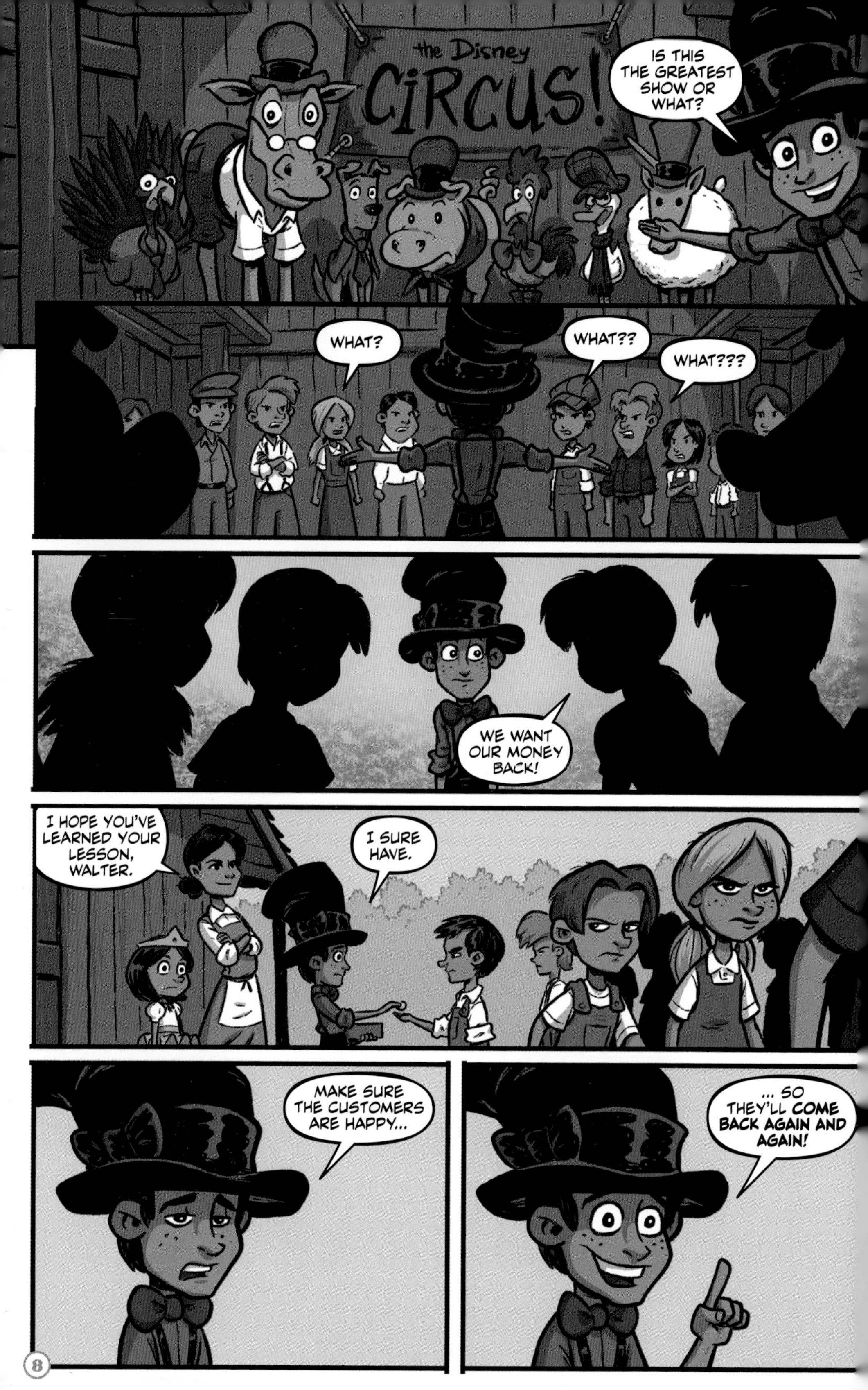
the Disney CIRCUS!
IS THIS THE GREATEST SHOW OR WHAT?
WHAT?
WHAT??
WHAT???
WE WANT OUR MONEY BACK!
I HOPE YOU'VE LEARNED YOUR LESSON, WALTER.
I SURE HAVE.
MAKE SURE THE CUSTOMERS ARE HAPPY...
... SO THEY'LL **COME BACK AGAIN AND AGAIN!**

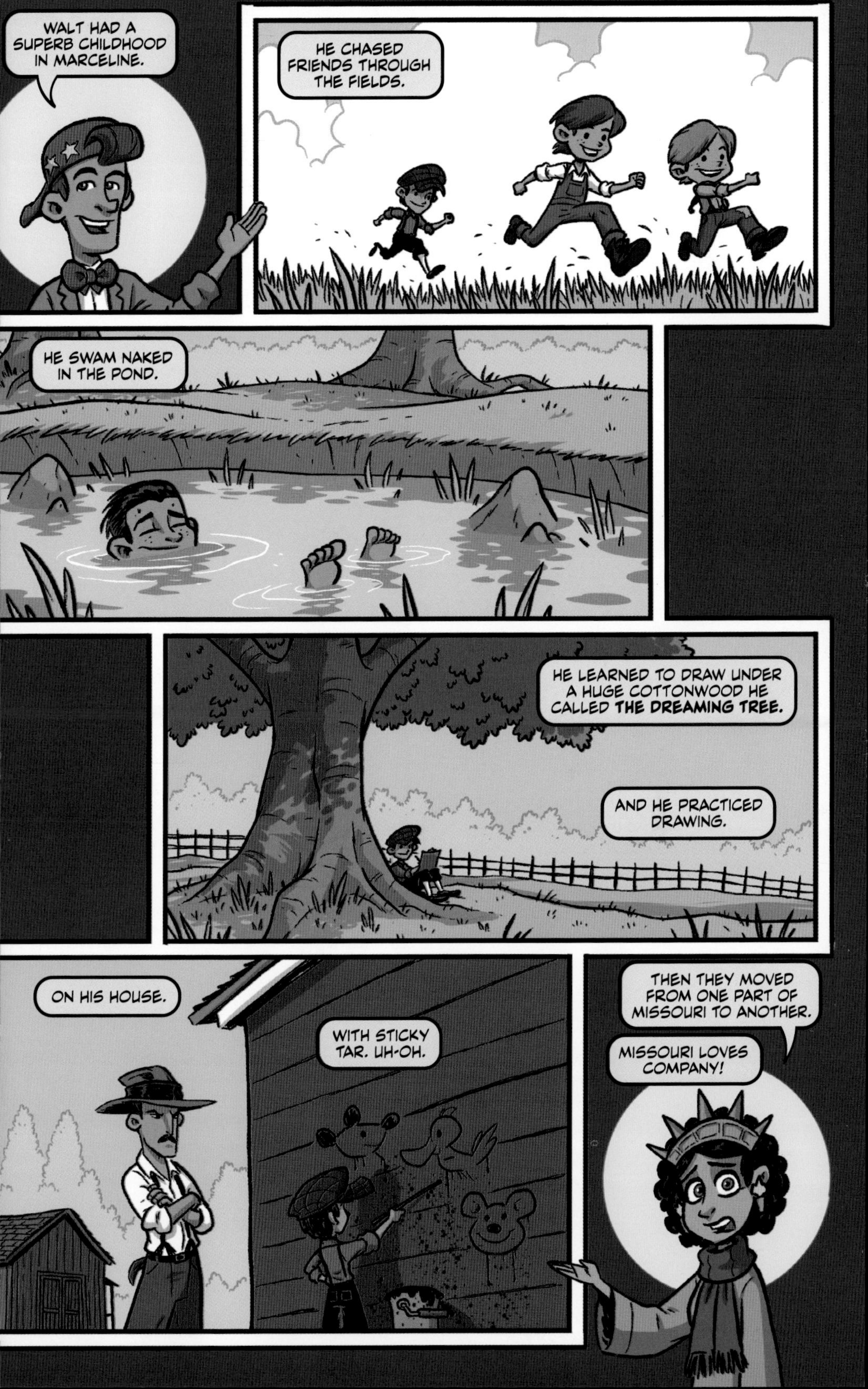
WALT HAD A SUPERB CHILDHOOD IN MARCELINE.
HE CHASED FRIENDS THROUGH THE FIELDS.
HE SWAM NAKED IN THE POND.
HE LEARNED TO DRAW UNDER A HUGE COTTONWOOD HE CALLED **THE DREAMING TREE.**
AND HE PRACTICED DRAWING.
ON HIS HOUSE.
WITH STICKY TAR. UH-OH.
THEN THEY MOVED FROM ONE PART OF MISSOURI TO ANOTHER.
MISSOURI LOVES COMPANY!

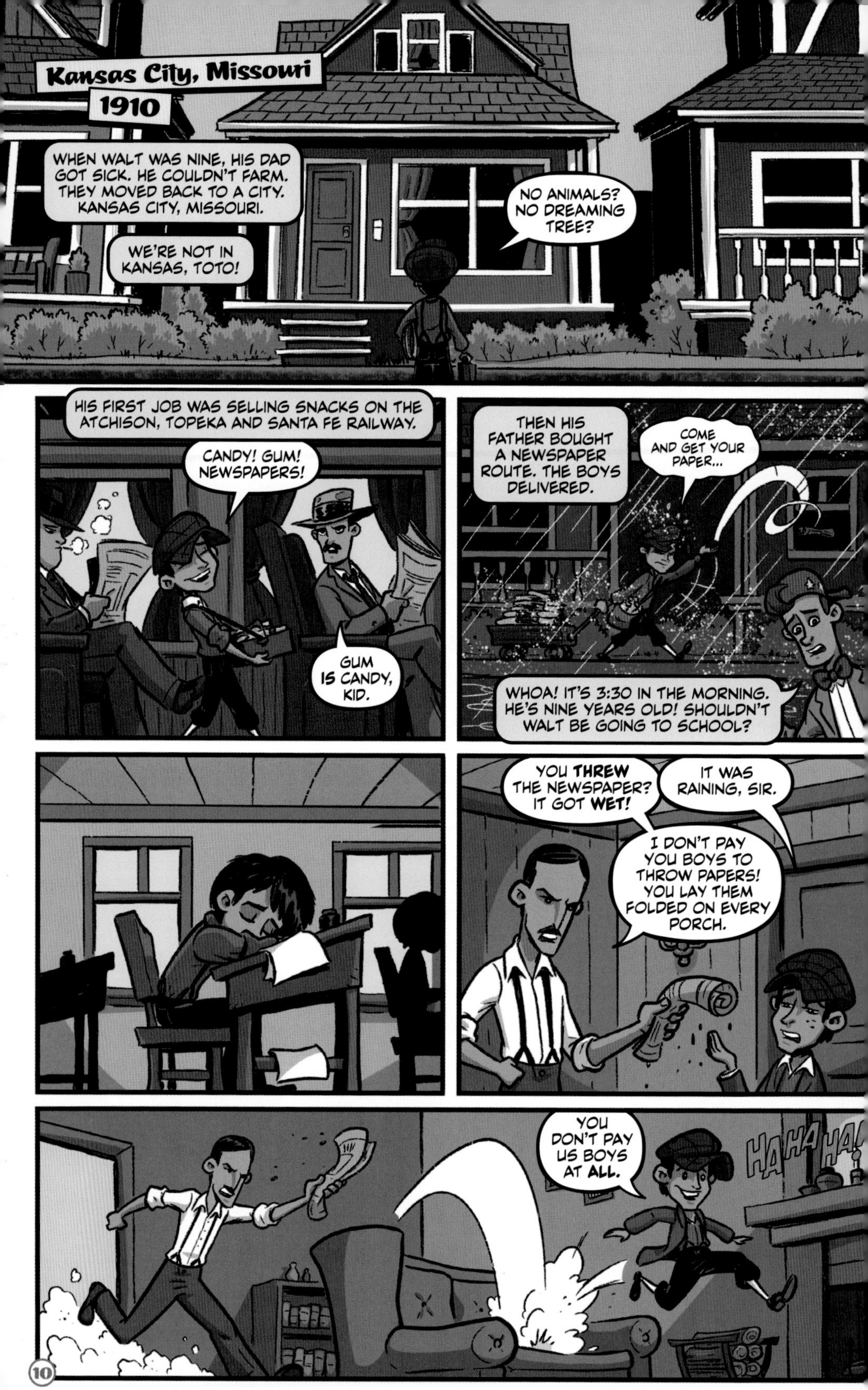
Kansas City, Missouri
1910
WHEN WALT WAS NINE, HIS DAD GOT SICK. HE COULDN'T FARM. THEY MOVED BACK TO A CITY. KANSAS CITY, MISSOURI.
WE'RE NOT IN KANSAS, TOTO!
NO ANIMALS? NO DREAMING TREE?
HIS FIRST JOB WAS SELLING SNACKS ON THE ATCHISON, TOPEKA AND SANTA FE RAILWAY.
CANDY! GUM! NEWSPAPERS!
GUM IS CANDY, KID.
THEN HIS FATHER BOUGHT A NEWSPAPER ROUTE. THE BOYS DELIVERED.
COME AND GET YOUR PAPER...
WHOA! IT'S 3:30 IN THE MORNING. HE'S NINE YEARS OLD! SHOULDN'T WALT BE GOING TO SCHOOL?
YOU THREW THE NEWSPAPER? IT GOT WET!
IT WAS RAINING, SIR.
I DON'T PAY YOU BOYS TO THROW PAPERS! YOU LAY THEM FOLDED ON EVERY PORCH.
YOU DON'T PAY US BOYS AT ALL.
HA HA HA!

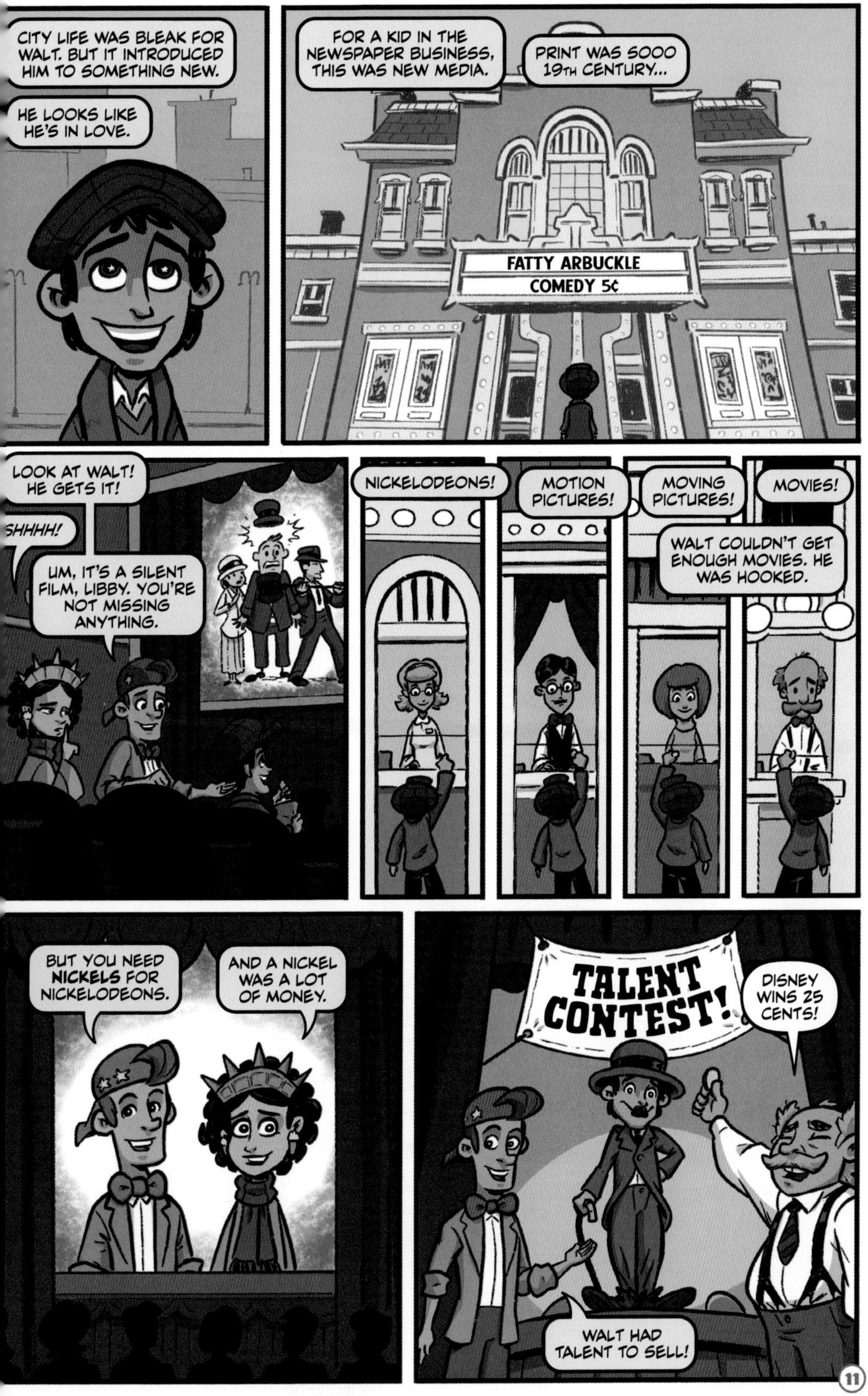
CITY LIFE WAS BLEAK FOR WALT. BUT IT INTRODUCED HIM TO SOMETHING NEW.
HE LOOKS LIKE HE'S IN LOVE.
FOR A KID IN THE NEWSPAPER BUSINESS, THIS WAS NEW MEDIA.
PRINT WAS SOOO 19TH CENTURY...
FATTY ARBUCKLE
COMEDY 5¢
LOOK AT WALT! HE GETS IT!
SHHHH!
UM, IT'S A SILENT FILM, LIBBY. YOU'RE NOT MISSING ANYTHING.
NICKELODEONS!
MOTION PICTURES!
MOVING PICTURES!
MOVIES!
WALT COULDN'T GET ENOUGH MOVIES. HE WAS HOOKED.
BUT YOU NEED **NICKELS** FOR NICKELODEONS.
AND A NICKEL WAS A LOT OF MONEY.
TALENT CONTEST!
DISNEY WINS 25 CENTS!
WALT HAD TALENT TO SELL!

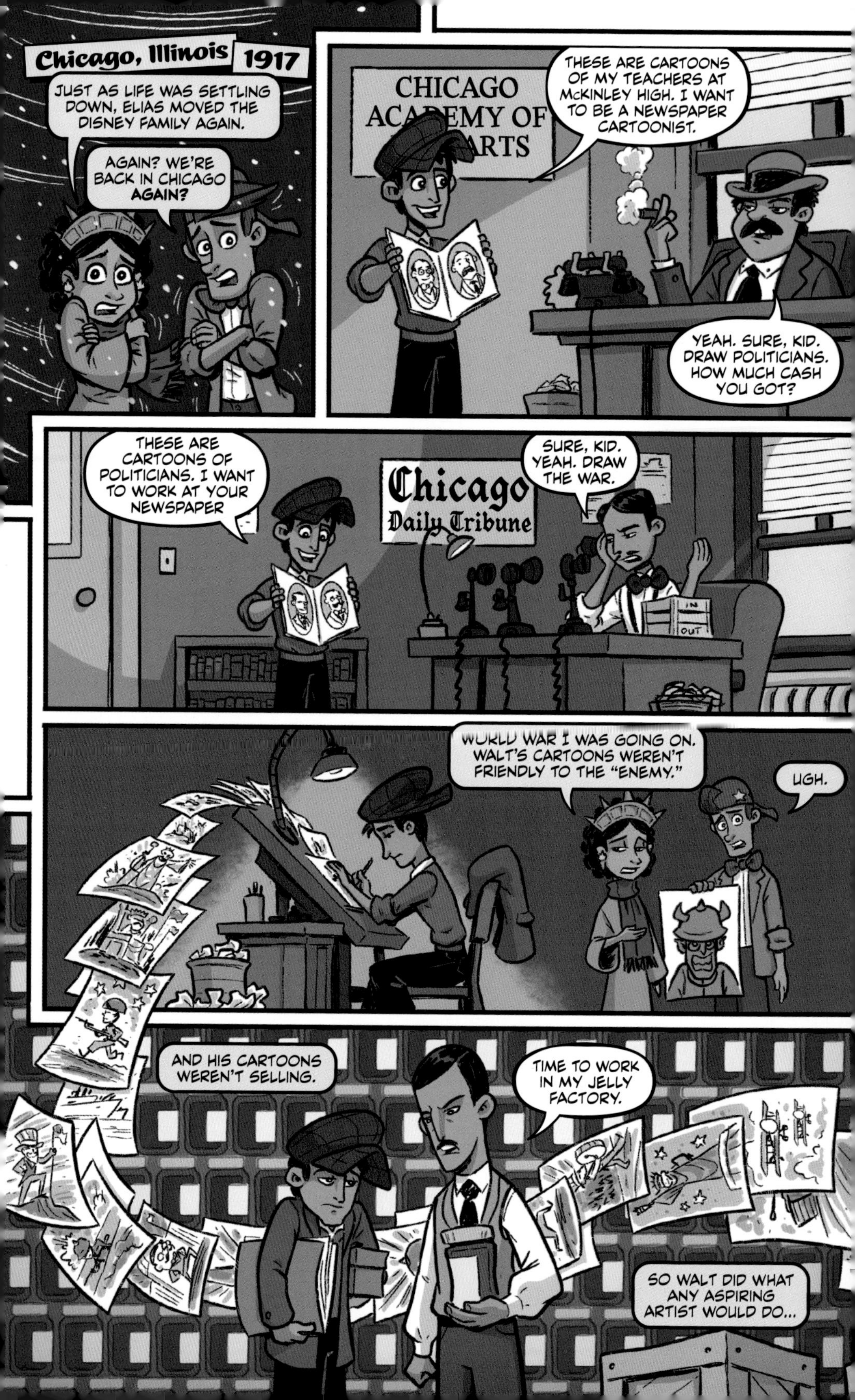
Chicago, Illinois 1917
JUST AS LIFE WAS SETTLING DOWN, ELIAS MOVED THE DISNEY FAMILY AGAIN.
AGAIN? WE'RE BACK IN CHICAGO AGAIN?
CHICAGO ACADEMY OF FINE ARTS
THESE ARE CARTOONS OF MY TEACHERS AT McKINLEY HIGH. I WANT TO BE A NEWSPAPER CARTOONIST.
YEAH. SURE, KID. DRAW POLITICIANS. HOW MUCH CASH YOU GOT?
THESE ARE CARTOONS OF POLITICIANS. I WANT TO WORK AT YOUR NEWSPAPER
Chicago Daily Tribune
SURE, KID. YEAH. DRAW THE WAR.
IN
OUT
WORLD WAR I WAS GOING ON. WALT'S CARTOONS WEREN'T FRIENDLY TO THE "ENEMY."
UGH.
AND HIS CARTOONS WEREN'T SELLING.
TIME TO WORK IN MY JELLY FACTORY.
SO WALT DID WHAT ANY ASPIRING ARTIST WOULD DO...

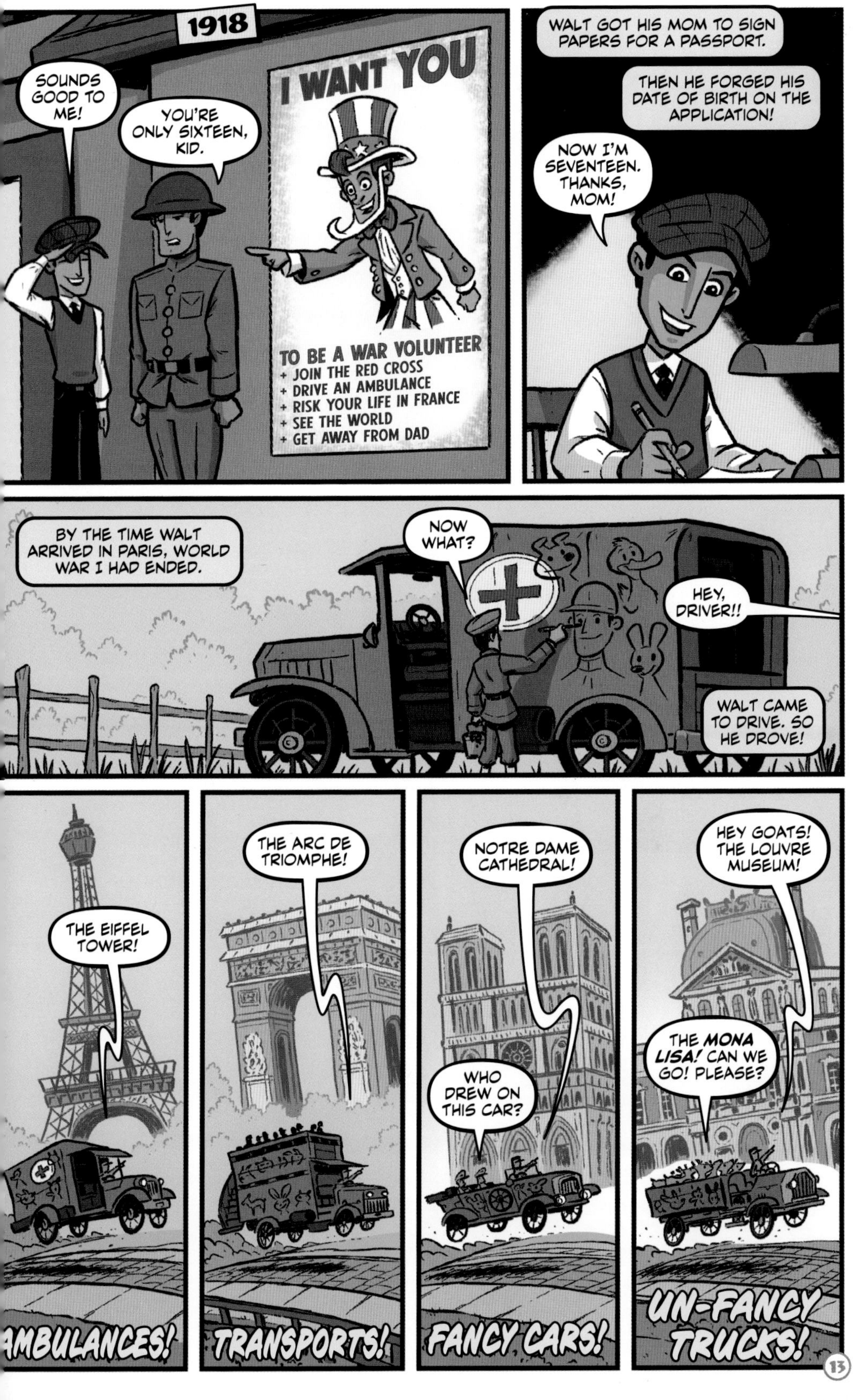
1918
SOUNDS GOOD TO ME!
YOU'RE ONLY SIXTEEN, KID.
I WANT YOU
TO BE A WAR VOLUNTEER
+ JOIN THE RED CROSS
+ DRIVE AN AMBULANCE
+ RISK YOUR LIFE IN FRANCE
+ SEE THE WORLD
+ GET AWAY FROM DAD
WALT GOT HIS MOM TO SIGN PAPERS FOR A PASSPORT.
THEN HE FORGED HIS DATE OF BIRTH ON THE APPLICATION!
NOW I'M SEVENTEEN. THANKS, MOM!
BY THE TIME WALT ARRIVED IN PARIS, WORLD WAR I HAD ENDED.
NOW WHAT?
HEY, DRIVER!!
WALT CAME TO DRIVE. SO HE DROVE!
THE EIFFEL TOWER!
AMBULANCES!
THE ARC DE TRIOMPHE!
TRANSPORTS!
NOTRE DAME CATHEDRAL!
WHO DREW ON THIS CAR?
FANCY CARS!
HEY GOATS! THE LOUVRE MUSEUM!
THE MONA LISA! CAN WE GO! PLEASE?
UN-FANCY TRUCKS!

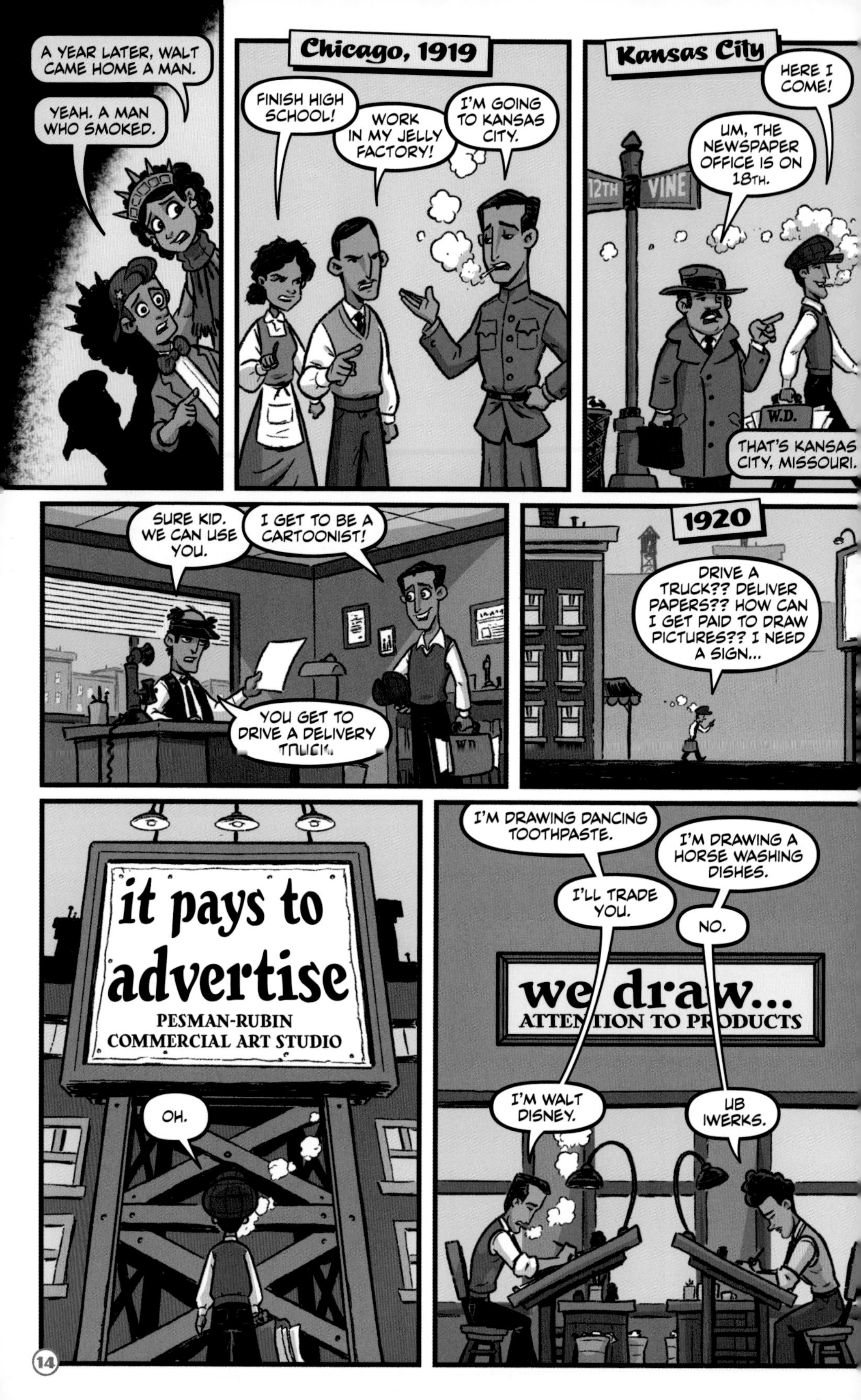
A YEAR LATER, WALT CAME HOME A MAN.
YEAH. A MAN WHO SMOKED.
Chicago, 1919
FINISH HIGH SCHOOL!
WORK IN MY JELLY FACTORY!
I'M GOING TO KANSAS CITY.
Kansas City
HERE I COME!
12TH
VINE
UM, THE NEWSPAPER OFFICE IS ON 18TH.
W.D.
THAT'S KANSAS CITY, MISSOURI.
SURE KID. WE CAN USE YOU.
I GET TO BE A CARTOONIST!
YOU GET TO DRIVE A DELIVERY TRUCK.
1920
DRIVE A TRUCK?? DELIVER PAPERS?? HOW CAN I GET PAID TO DRAW PICTURES?? I NEED A SIGN...
it pays to advertise
PESMAN-RUBIN
COMMERCIAL ART STUDIO
OH.
I'M DRAWING DANCING TOOTHPASTE.
I'M DRAWING A HORSE WASHING DISHES.
I'LL TRADE YOU.
NO.
we draw...
ATTENTION TO PRODUCTS
I'M WALT DISNEY.
UB IWERKS.

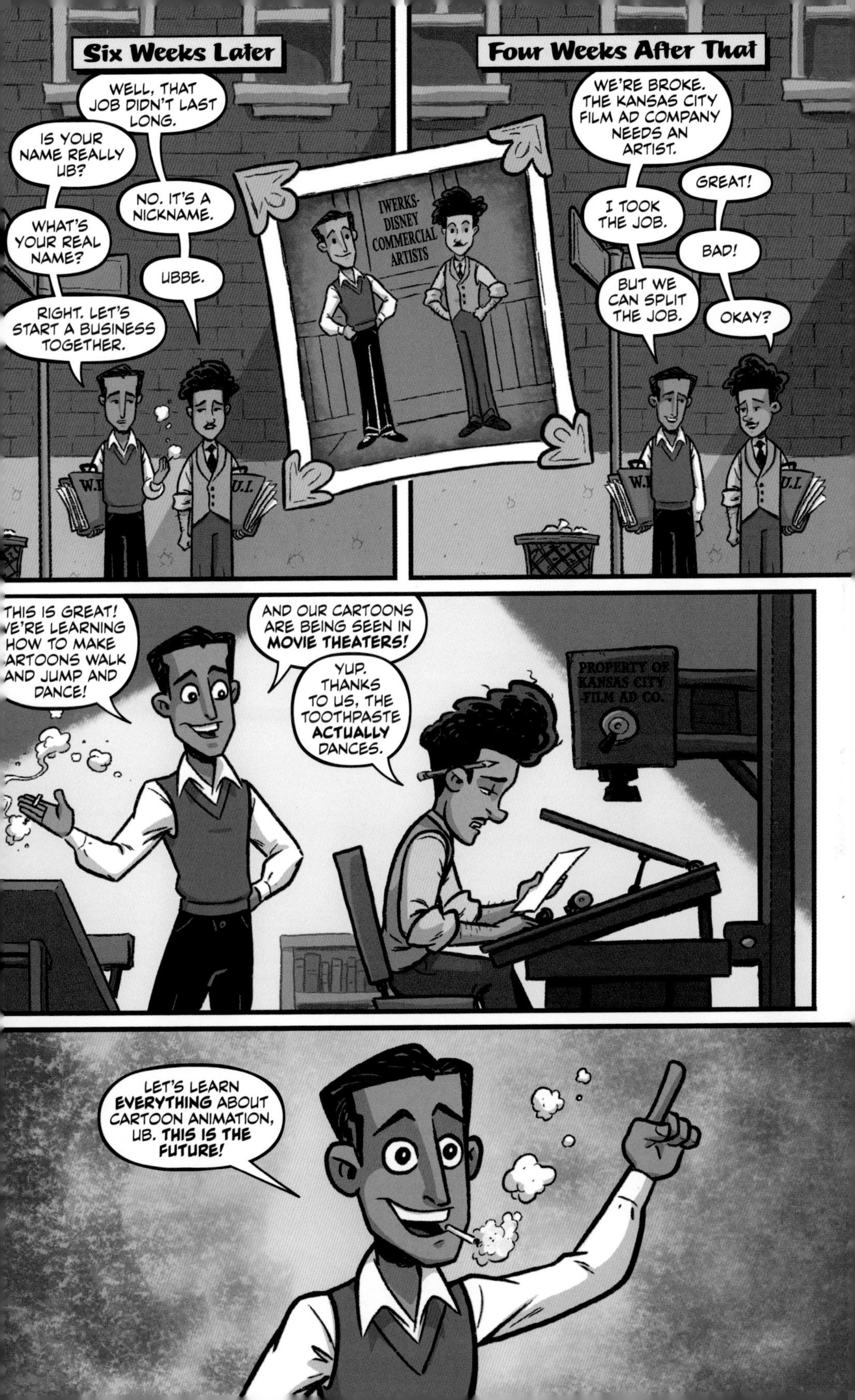
Six Weeks Later
WELL, THAT JOB DIDN'T LAST LONG.
IS YOUR NAME REALLY UB?
NO. IT'S A NICKNAME.
WHAT'S YOUR REAL NAME?
UBBE.
RIGHT. LET'S START A BUSINESS TOGETHER.
IWERKS-DISNEY COMMERCIAL ARTISTS
Four Weeks After That
WE'RE BROKE. THE KANSAS CITY FILM AD COMPANY NEEDS AN ARTIST.
I TOOK THE JOB.
GREAT!
BAD!
BUT WE CAN SPLIT THE JOB.
OKAY?
THIS IS GREAT! E'RE LEARNING HOW TO MAKE ARTOONS WALK AND JUMP AND DANCE!
AND OUR CARTOONS ARE BEING SEEN IN **MOVIE THEATERS!**
YUP. THANKS TO US, THE TOOTHPASTE **ACTUALLY** DANCES.
PROPERTY OF KANSAS CITY FILM AD CO.
LET'S LEARN **EVERYTHING** ABOUT CARTOON ANIMATION, UB. **THIS IS THE FUTURE!**

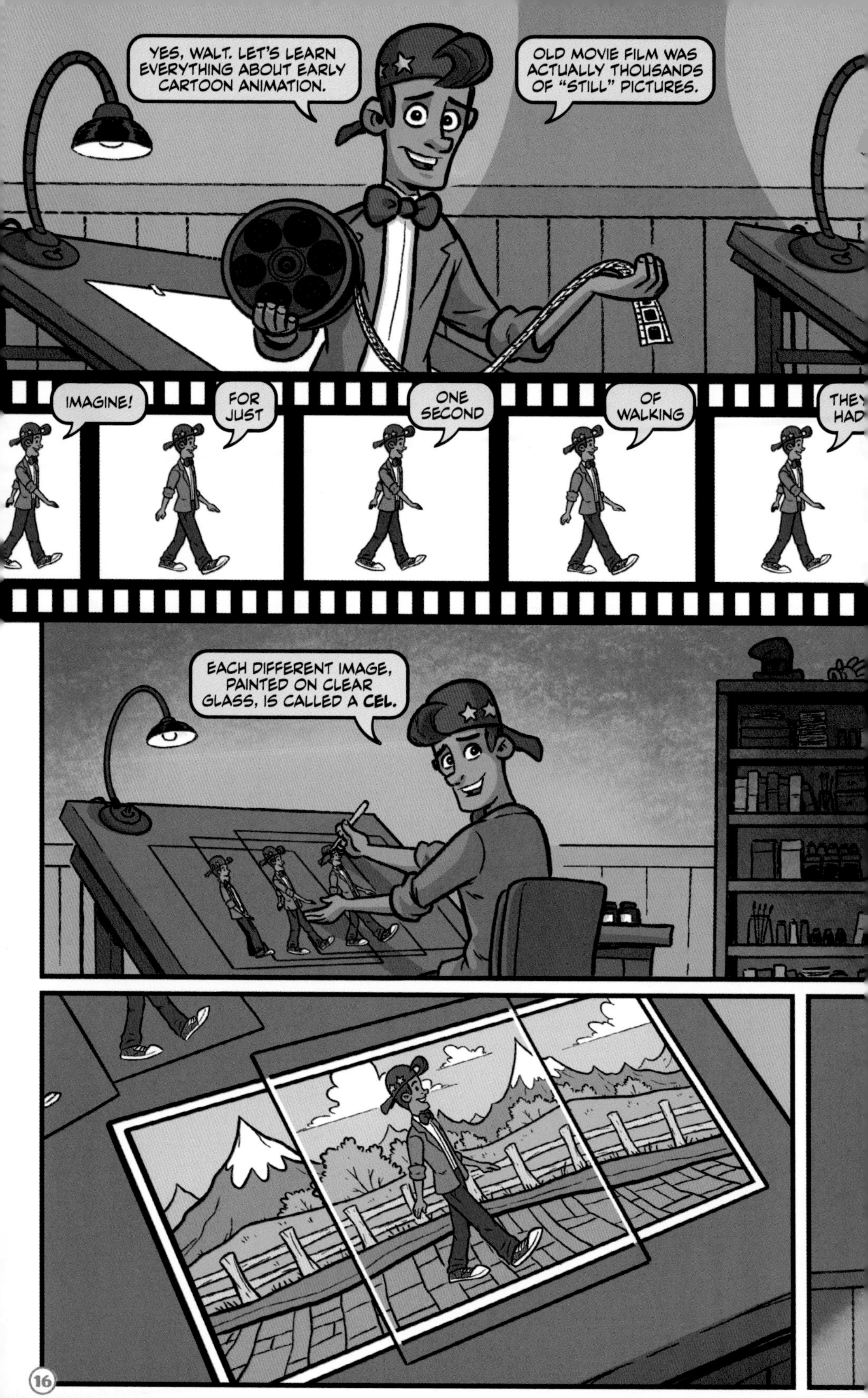
YES, WALT. LET'S LEARN EVERYTHING ABOUT EARLY CARTOON ANIMATION.
OLD MOVIE FILM WAS ACTUALLY THOUSANDS OF "STILL" PICTURES.
IMAGINE!
FOR JUST
ONE SECOND
OF WALKING
EACH DIFFERENT IMAGE, PAINTED ON CLEAR GLASS, IS CALLED A **CEL.**

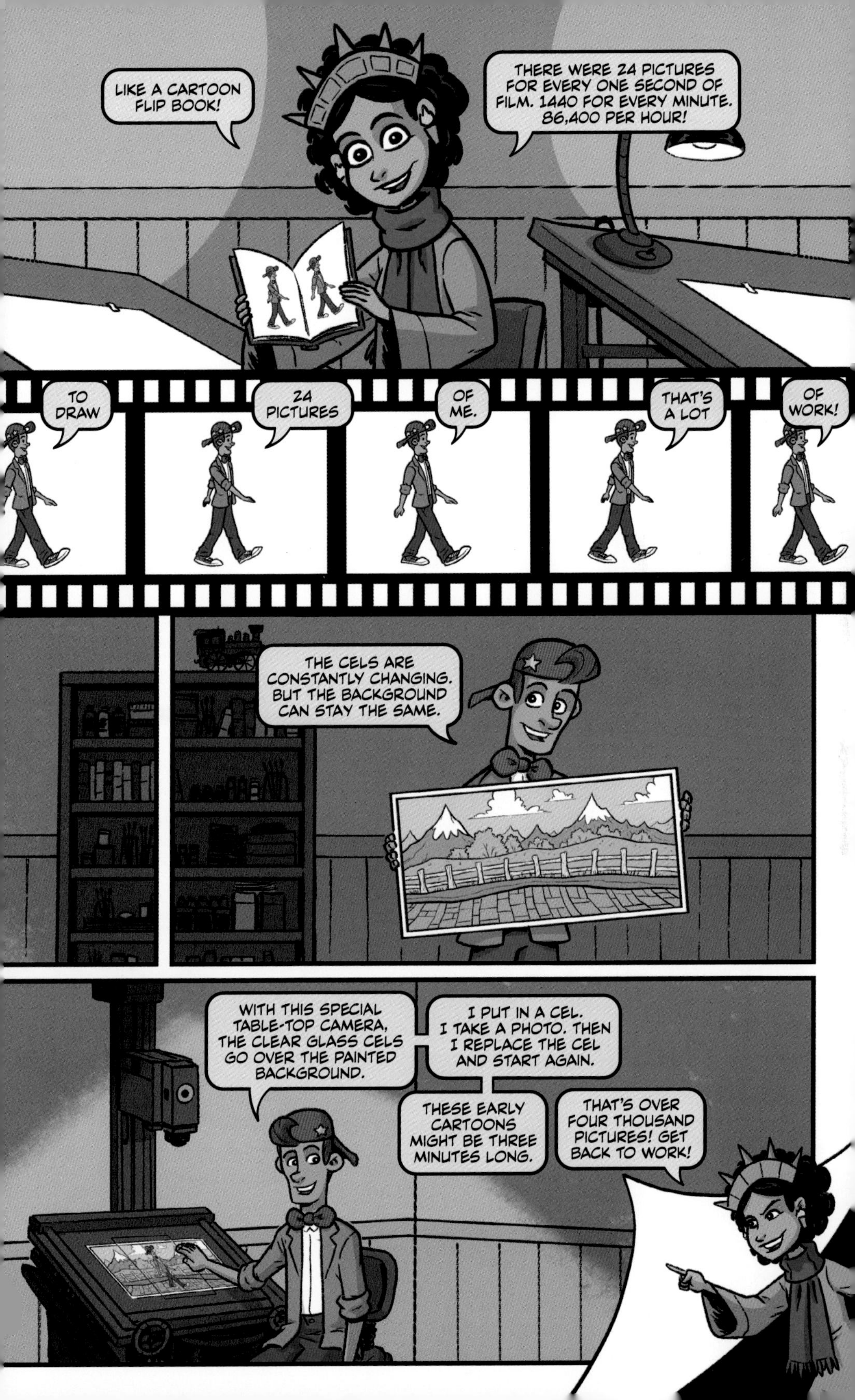
LIKE A CARTOON FLIP BOOK!
THERE WERE 24 PICTURES FOR EVERY ONE SECOND OF FILM. 1440 FOR EVERY MINUTE. 86,400 PER HOUR!
TO DRAW
24 PICTURES
OF ME.
THAT'S A LOT
OF WORK!
THE CELS ARE CONSTANTLY CHANGING. BUT THE BACKGROUND CAN STAY THE SAME.
WITH THIS SPECIAL TABLE-TOP CAMERA, THE CLEAR GLASS CELS GO OVER THE PAINTED BACKGROUND.
I PUT IN A CEL. I TAKE A PHOTO. THEN I REPLACE THE CEL AND START AGAIN.
THESE EARLY CARTOONS MIGHT BE THREE MINUTES LONG.
THAT'S OVER FOUR THOUSAND PICTURES! GET BACK TO WORK!

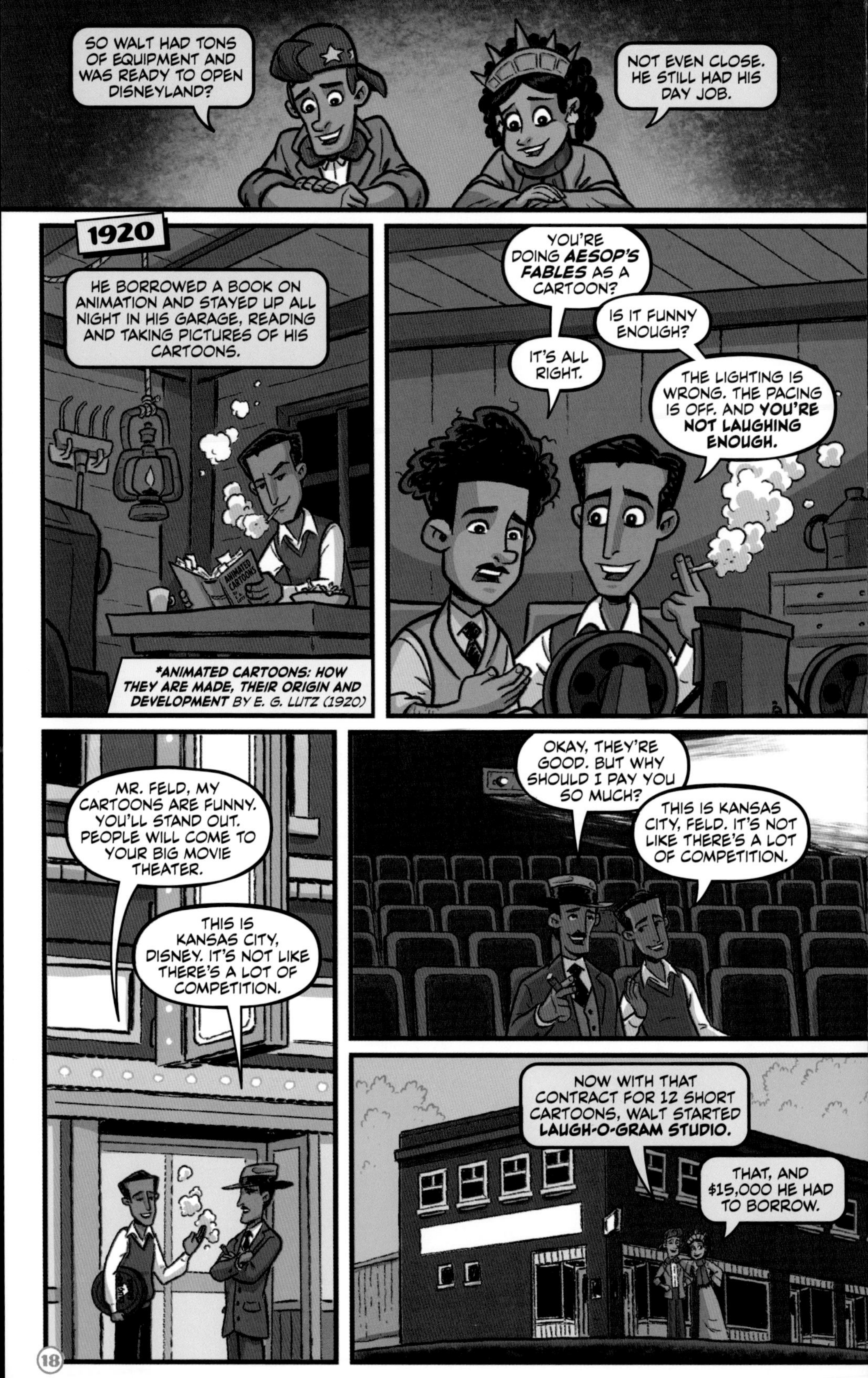
SO WALT HAD TONS OF EQUIPMENT AND WAS READY TO OPEN DISNEYLAND?
NOT EVEN CLOSE. HE STILL HAD HIS DAY JOB.
1920
HE BORROWED A BOOK ON ANIMATION AND STAYED UP ALL NIGHT IN HIS GARAGE, READING AND TAKING PICTURES OF HIS CARTOONS.
ANIMATED CARTOONS
*ANIMATED CARTOONS: HOW THEY ARE MADE, THEIR ORIGIN AND DEVELOPMENT BY E. G. LUTZ (1920)
YOU'RE DOING AESOP'S FABLES AS A CARTOON?
IS IT FUNNY ENOUGH?
IT'S ALL RIGHT.
THE LIGHTING IS WRONG. THE PACING IS OFF. AND YOU'RE NOT LAUGHING ENOUGH.
MR. FELD, MY CARTOONS ARE FUNNY. YOU'LL STAND OUT. PEOPLE WILL COME TO YOUR BIG MOVIE THEATER.
THIS IS KANSAS CITY, DISNEY. IT'S NOT LIKE THERE'S A LOT OF COMPETITION.
OKAY, THEY'RE GOOD. BUT WHY SHOULD I PAY YOU SO MUCH?
THIS IS KANSAS CITY, FELD. IT'S NOT LIKE THERE'S A LOT OF COMPETITION.
NOW WITH THAT CONTRACT FOR 12 SHORT CARTOONS, WALT STARTED LAUGH-O-GRAM STUDIO.
THAT, AND $15,000 HE HAD TO BORROW.

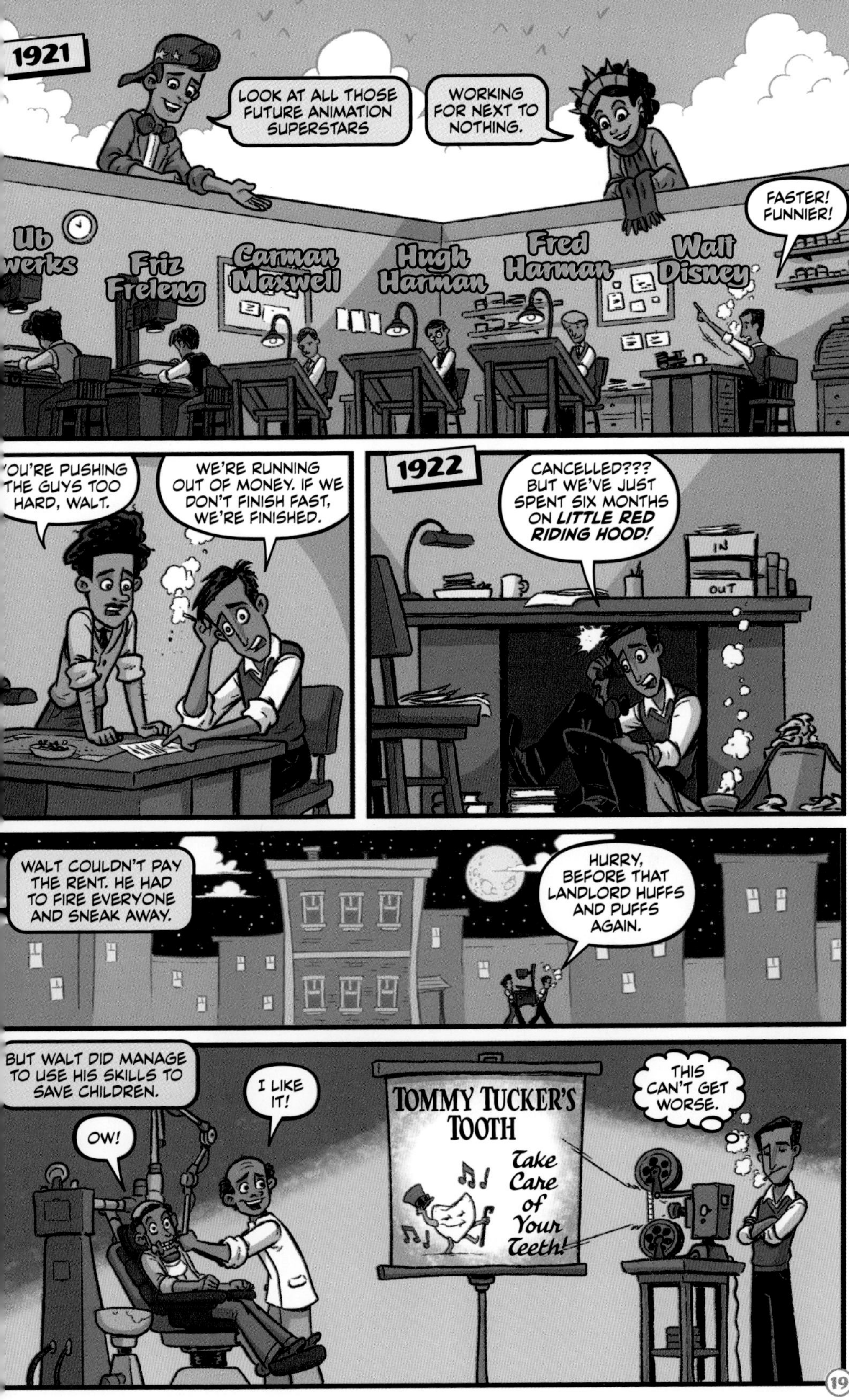
1921
LOOK AT ALL THOSE FUTURE ANIMATION SUPERSTARS
WORKING FOR NEXT TO NOTHING.
Ub Iwerks
Friz Freleng
Carman Maxwell
Hugh Harman
Fred Harman
Walt Disney
FASTER! FUNNIER!
YOU'RE PUSHING THE GUYS TOO HARD, WALT.
WE'RE RUNNING OUT OF MONEY. IF WE DON'T FINISH FAST, WE'RE FINISHED.
1922
CANCELLED??? BUT WE'VE JUST SPENT SIX MONTHS ON *LITTLE RED RIDING HOOD!*
IN
OUT
WALT COULDN'T PAY THE RENT. HE HAD TO FIRE EVERYONE AND SNEAK AWAY.
HURRY, BEFORE THAT LANDLORD HUFFS AND PUFFS AGAIN.
BUT WALT DID MANAGE TO USE HIS SKILLS TO SAVE CHILDREN.
OW!
I LIKE IT!
TOMMY TUCKER'S TOOTH
Take Care of Your Teeth!
THIS CAN'T GET WORSE.

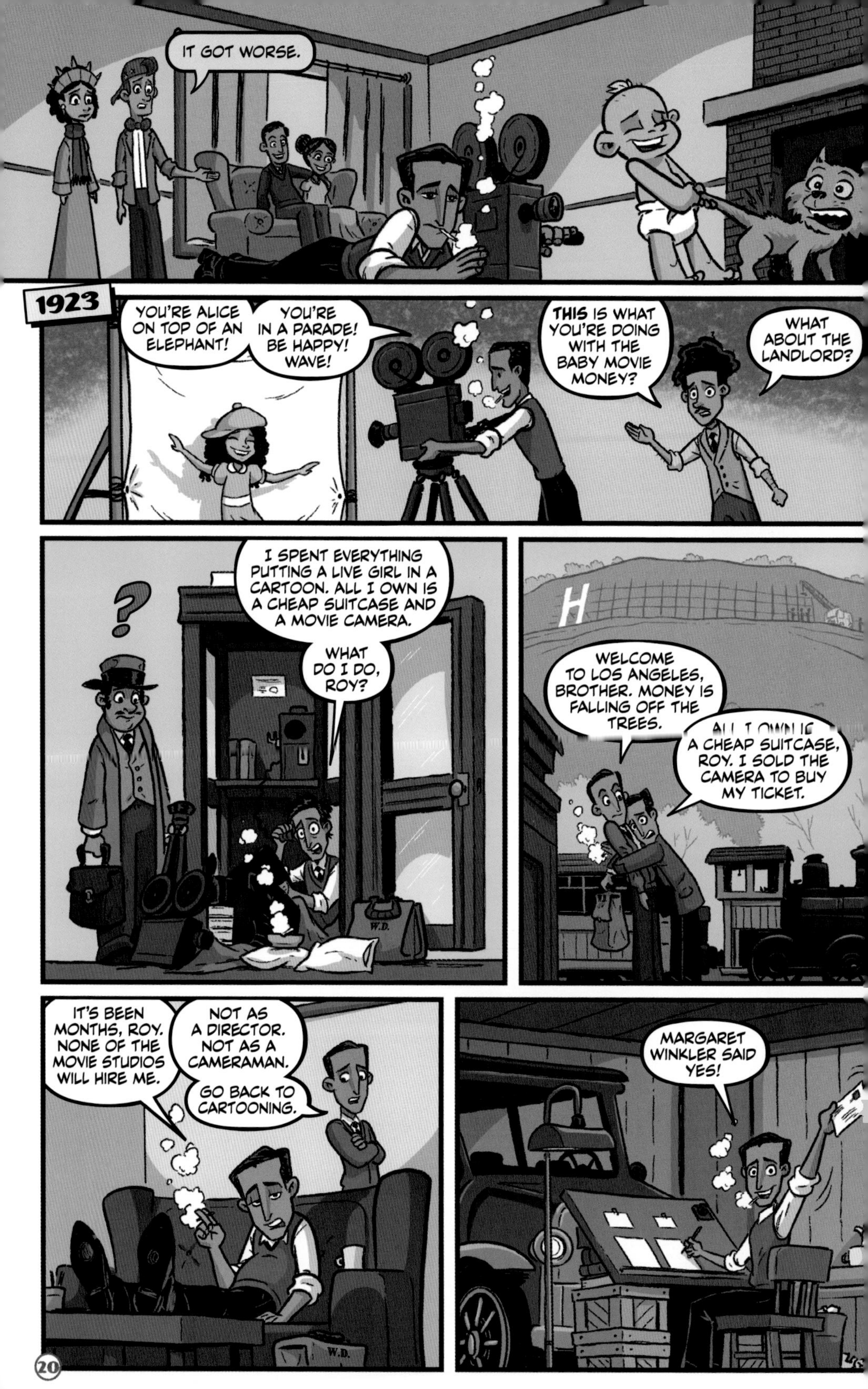
IT GOT WORSE.
1923
YOU'RE ALICE ON TOP OF AN ELEPHANT!
YOU'RE IN A PARADE! BE HAPPY! WAVE!
THIS IS WHAT YOU'RE DOING WITH THE BABY MOVIE MONEY?
WHAT ABOUT THE LANDLORD?
?
I SPENT EVERYTHING PUTTING A LIVE GIRL IN A CARTOON. ALL I OWN IS A CHEAP SUITCASE AND A MOVIE CAMERA.
WHAT DO I DO, ROY?
W.D.
H
WELCOME TO LOS ANGELES, BROTHER. MONEY IS FALLING OFF THE TREES.
A CHEAP SUITCASE, ROY. I SOLD THE CAMERA TO BUY MY TICKET.
IT'S BEEN MONTHS, ROY. NONE OF THE MOVIE STUDIOS WILL HIRE ME.
NOT AS A DIRECTOR. NOT AS A CAMERAMAN.
GO BACK TO CARTOONING.
W.D.
MARGARET WINKLER SAID YES!

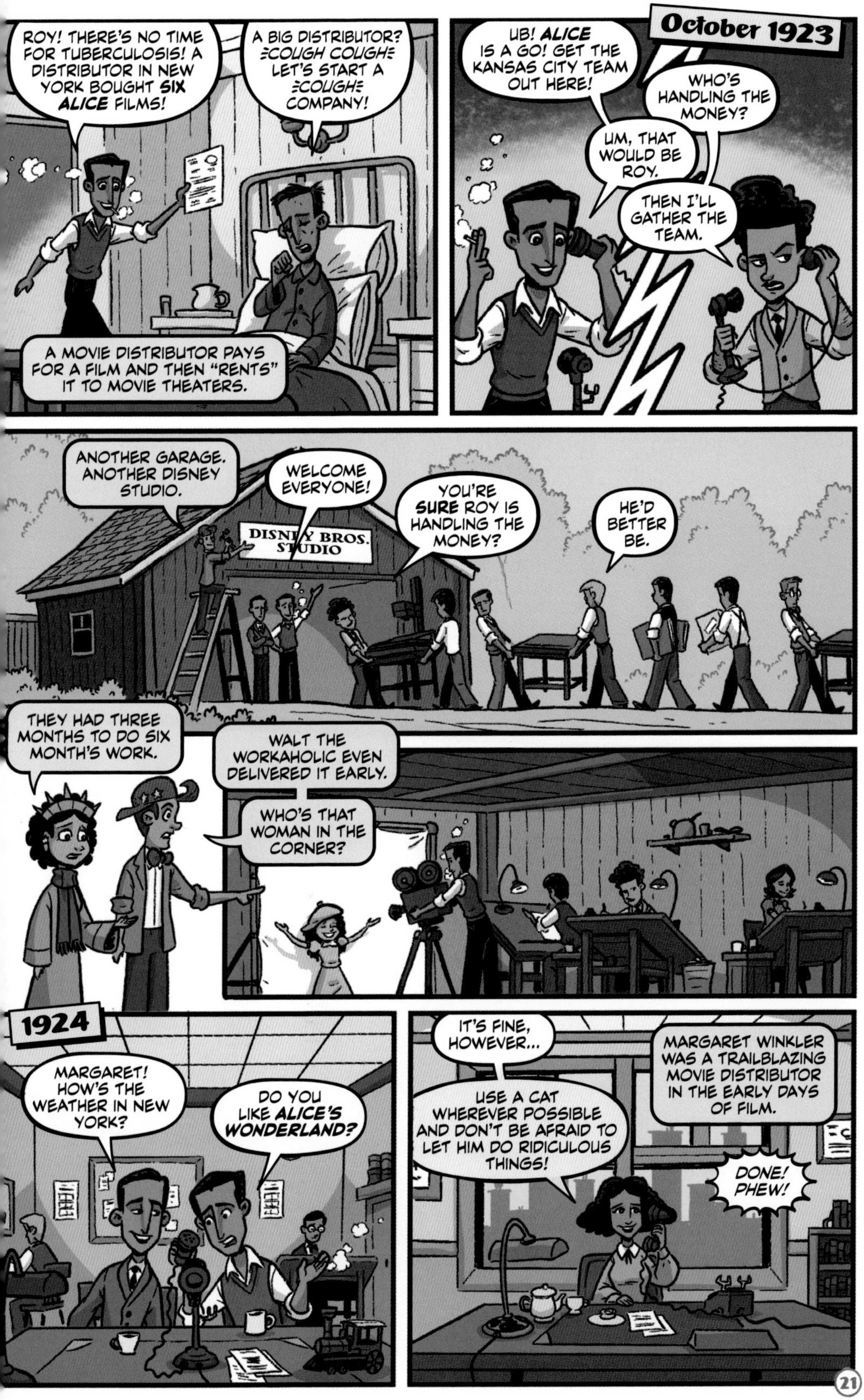
ROY! THERE'S NO TIME FOR TUBERCULOSIS! A DISTRIBUTOR IN NEW YORK BOUGHT SIX ALICE FILMS!
A BIG DISTRIBUTOR? =COUGH COUGH= LET'S START A =COUGH= COMPANY!
A MOVIE DISTRIBUTOR PAYS FOR A FILM AND THEN "RENTS" IT TO MOVIE THEATERS.
October 1923
UB! ALICE IS A GO! GET THE KANSAS CITY TEAM OUT HERE!
WHO'S HANDLING THE MONEY?
UM, THAT WOULD BE ROY.
THEN I'LL GATHER THE TEAM.
ANOTHER GARAGE. ANOTHER DISNEY STUDIO.
WELCOME EVERYONE!
DISNEY BROS. STUDIO
YOU'RE SURE ROY IS HANDLING THE MONEY?
HE'D BETTER BE.
THEY HAD THREE MONTHS TO DO SIX MONTH'S WORK.
WALT THE WORKAHOLIC EVEN DELIVERED IT EARLY.
WHO'S THAT WOMAN IN THE CORNER?
1924
MARGARET! HOW'S THE WEATHER IN NEW YORK?
DO YOU LIKE ALICE'S WONDERLAND?
IT'S FINE, HOWEVER...
USE A CAT WHEREVER POSSIBLE AND DON'T BE AFRAID TO LET HIM DO RIDICULOUS THINGS!
MARGARET WINKLER WAS A TRAILBLAZING MOVIE DISTRIBUTOR IN THE EARLY DAYS OF FILM.
DONE! PHEW!

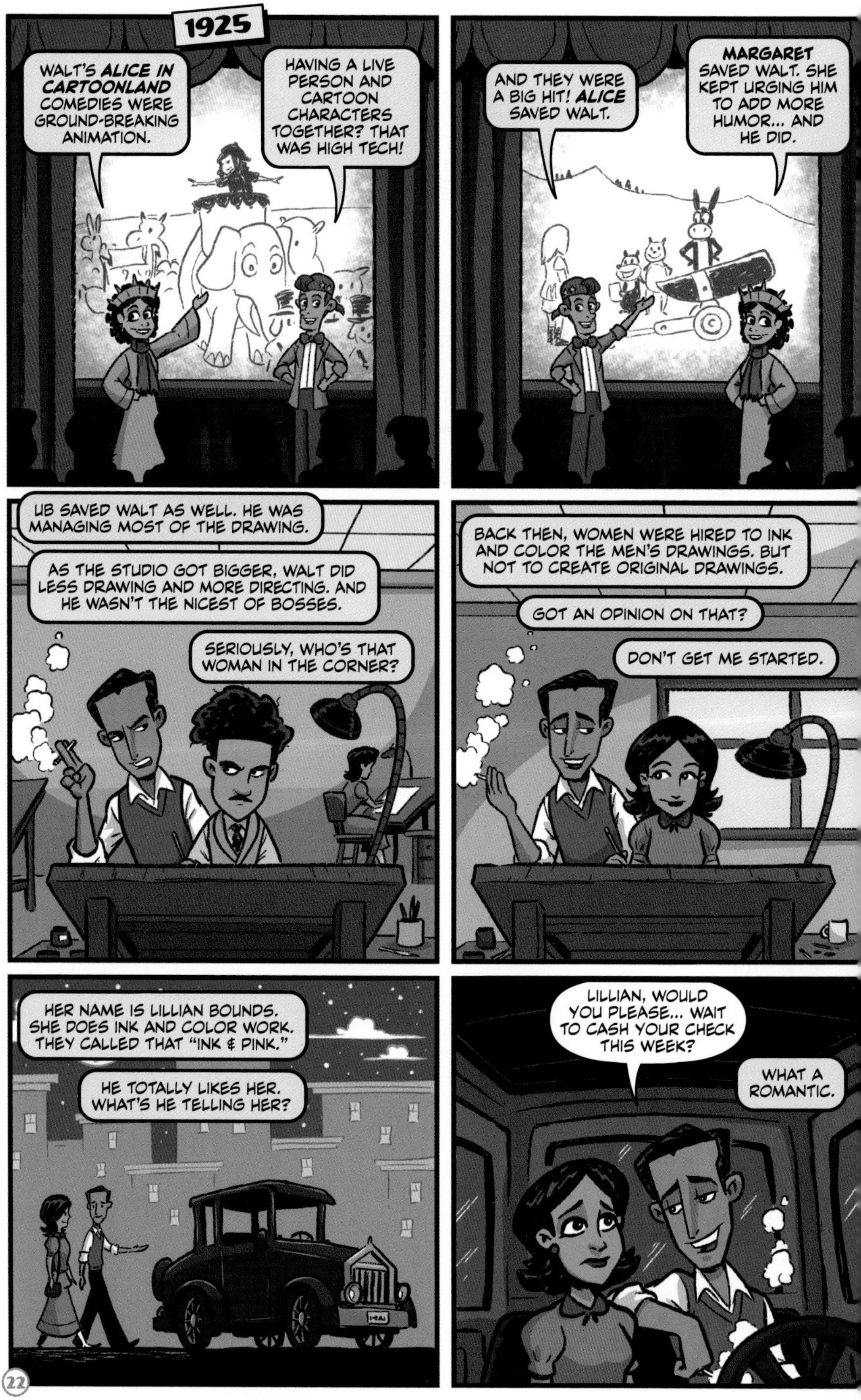
1925
WALT'S ALICE IN CARTOONLAND COMEDIES WERE GROUND-BREAKING ANIMATION.
HAVING A LIVE PERSON AND CARTOON CHARACTERS TOGETHER? THAT WAS HIGH TECH!
AND THEY WERE A BIG HIT! ALICE SAVED WALT.
MARGARET SAVED WALT. SHE KEPT URGING HIM TO ADD MORE HUMOR... AND HE DID.
UB SAVED WALT AS WELL. HE WAS MANAGING MOST OF THE DRAWING.
AS THE STUDIO GOT BIGGER, WALT DID LESS DRAWING AND MORE DIRECTING. AND HE WASN'T THE NICEST OF BOSSES.
SERIOUSLY, WHO'S THAT WOMAN IN THE CORNER?
BACK THEN, WOMEN WERE HIRED TO INK AND COLOR THE MEN'S DRAWINGS. BUT NOT TO CREATE ORIGINAL DRAWINGS.
GOT AN OPINION ON THAT?
DON'T GET ME STARTED.
HER NAME IS LILLIAN BOUNDS. SHE DOES INK AND COLOR WORK. THEY CALLED THAT "INK & PINK."
HE TOTALLY LIKES HER. WHAT'S HE TELLING HER?
LILLIAN, WOULD YOU PLEASE... WAIT TO CASH YOUR CHECK THIS WEEK?
WHAT A ROMANTIC.

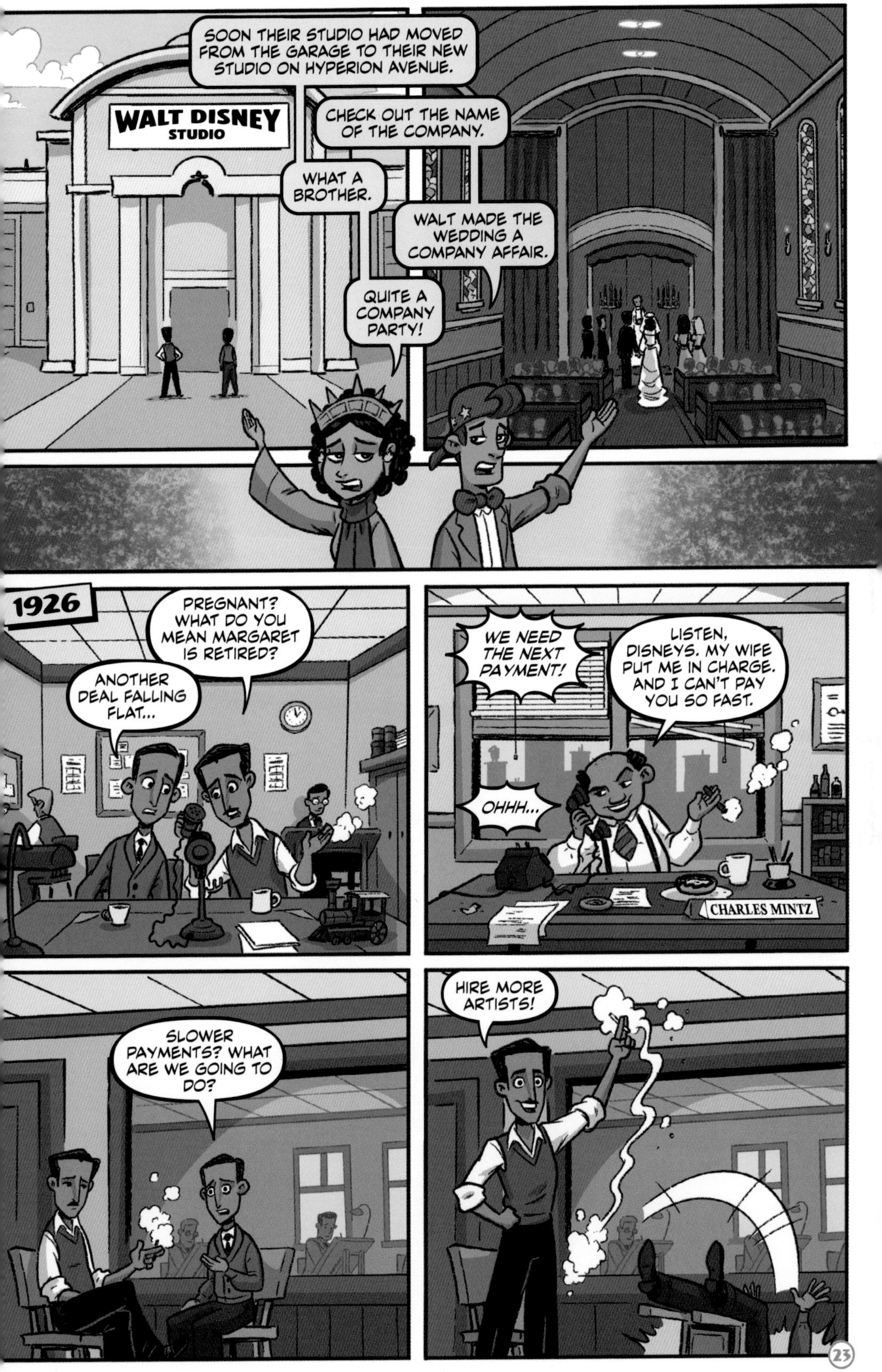
SOON THEIR STUDIO HAD MOVED FROM THE GARAGE TO THEIR NEW STUDIO ON HYPERION AVENUE.
WALT DISNEY STUDIO
CHECK OUT THE NAME OF THE COMPANY.
WHAT A BROTHER.
WALT MADE THE WEDDING A COMPANY AFFAIR.
QUITE A COMPANY PARTY!
1926
PREGNANT? WHAT DO YOU MEAN MARGARET IS RETIRED?
ANOTHER DEAL FALLING FLAT...
WE NEED THE NEXT PAYMENT!
LISTEN, DISNEYS. MY WIFE PUT ME IN CHARGE. AND I CAN'T PAY YOU SO FAST.
OHHH...
CHARLES MINTZ
SLOWER PAYMENTS? WHAT ARE WE GOING TO DO?
HIRE MORE ARTISTS!

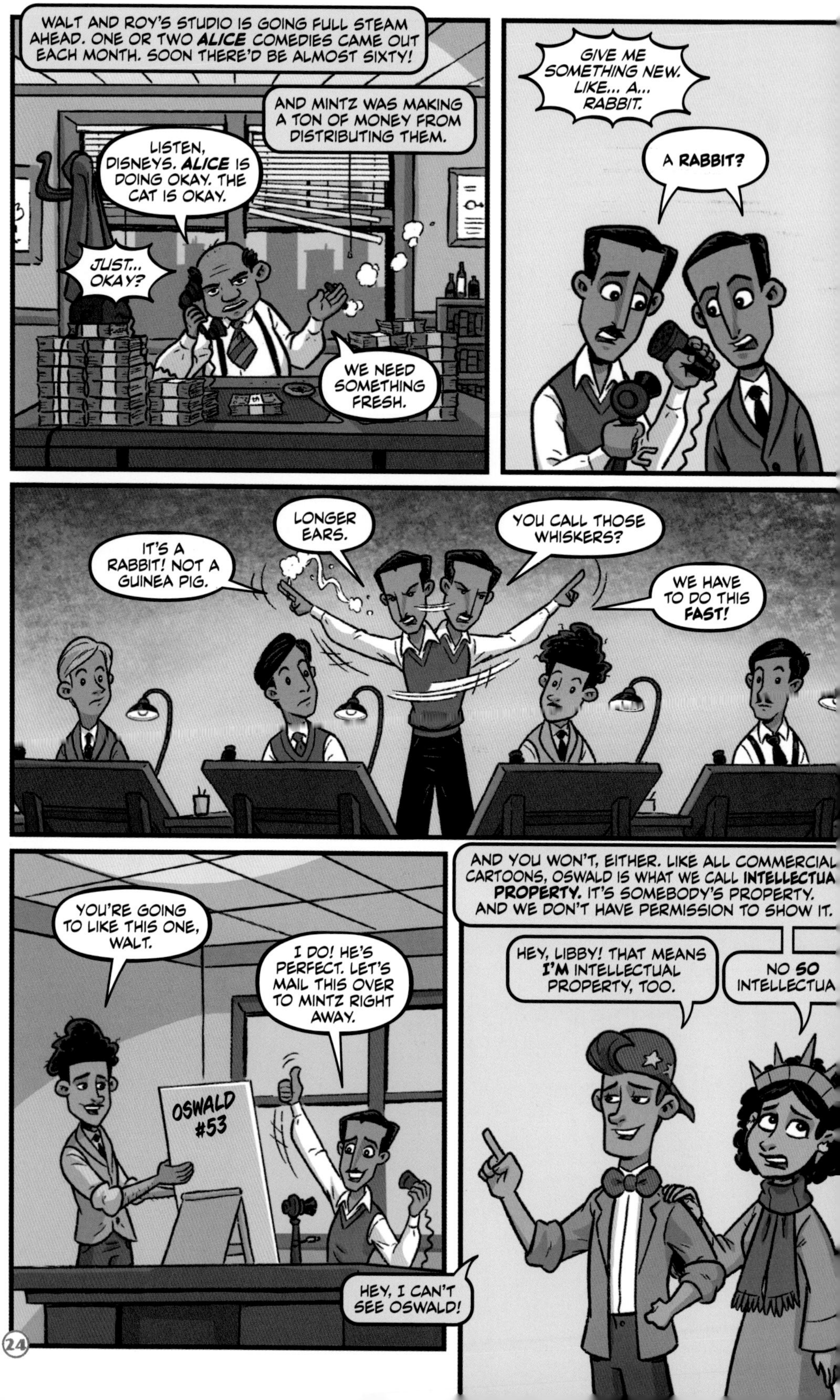
WALT AND ROY'S STUDIO IS GOING FULL STEAM AHEAD. ONE OR TWO ALICE COMEDIES CAME OUT EACH MONTH. SOON THERE'D BE ALMOST SIXTY!
AND MINTZ WAS MAKING A TON OF MONEY FROM DISTRIBUTING THEM.
LISTEN, DISNEYS. ALICE IS DOING OKAY. THE CAT IS OKAY.
JUST... OKAY?
WE NEED SOMETHING FRESH.
GIVE ME SOMETHING NEW. LIKE... A... RABBIT.
A RABBIT?
IT'S A RABBIT! NOT A GUINEA PIG.
LONGER EARS.
YOU CALL THOSE WHISKERS?
WE HAVE TO DO THIS FAST!
YOU'RE GOING TO LIKE THIS ONE, WALT.
OSWALD #53
I DO! HE'S PERFECT. LET'S MAIL THIS OVER TO MINTZ RIGHT AWAY.
HEY, I CAN'T SEE OSWALD!
AND YOU WON'T, EITHER. LIKE ALL COMMERCIAL CARTOONS, OSWALD IS WHAT WE CALL INTELLECTUA PROPERTY. IT'S SOMEBODY'S PROPERTY. AND WE DON'T HAVE PERMISSION TO SHOW IT.
HEY, LIBBY! THAT MEANS I'M INTELLECTUAL PROPERTY, TOO.
NO SO INTELLECTUA

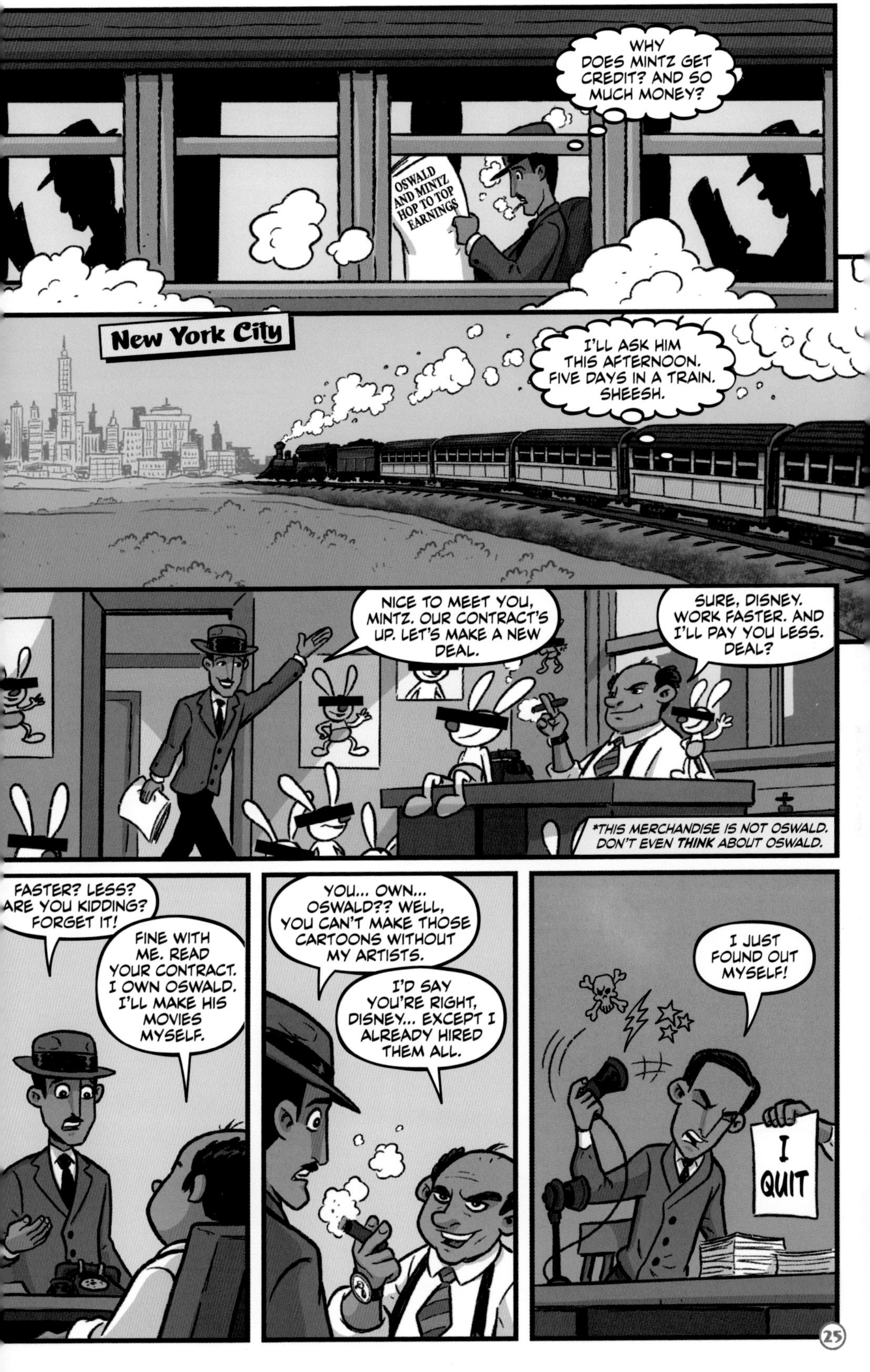
WHY DOES MINTZ GET CREDIT? AND SO MUCH MONEY?
OSWALD AND MINTZ HOP TO TOP EARNINGS
New York City
I'LL ASK HIM THIS AFTERNOON. FIVE DAYS IN A TRAIN. SHEESH.
NICE TO MEET YOU, MINTZ. OUR CONTRACT'S UP. LET'S MAKE A NEW DEAL.
SURE, DISNEY. WORK FASTER. AND I'LL PAY YOU LESS. DEAL?
*THIS MERCHANDISE IS NOT OSWALD. DON'T EVEN THINK ABOUT OSWALD.
FASTER? LESS? ARE YOU KIDDING? FORGET IT!
FINE WITH ME. READ YOUR CONTRACT. I OWN OSWALD. I'LL MAKE HIS MOVIES MYSELF.
YOU... OWN... OSWALD?? WELL, YOU CAN'T MAKE THOSE CARTOONS WITHOUT MY ARTISTS.
I'D SAY YOU'RE RIGHT, DISNEY... EXCEPT I ALREADY HIRED THEM ALL.
I JUST FOUND OUT MYSELF!
I QUIT

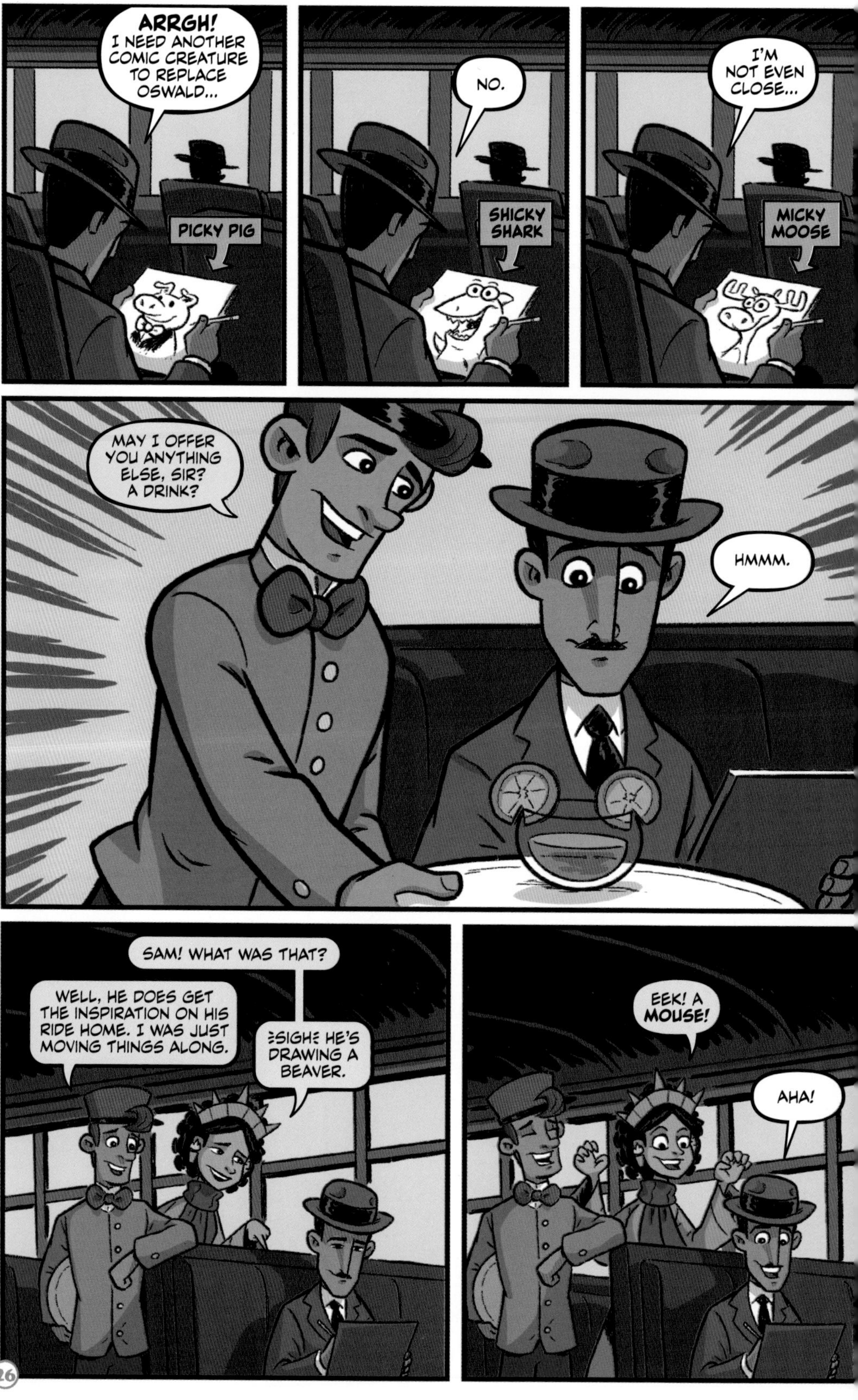

ARRGH! I NEED ANOTHER COMIC CREATURE TO REPLACE OSWALD...
PICKY PIG
NO.
SHICKY SHARK
I'M NOT EVEN CLOSE...
MICKY MOOSE
MAY I OFFER YOU ANYTHING ELSE, SIR? A DRINK?
HMMM.
SAM! WHAT WAS THAT?
WELL, HE DOES GET THE INSPIRATION ON HIS RIDE HOME. I WAS JUST MOVING THINGS ALONG.
SIGH HE'S DRAWING A BEAVER.
EEK! A MOUSE!
AHA!

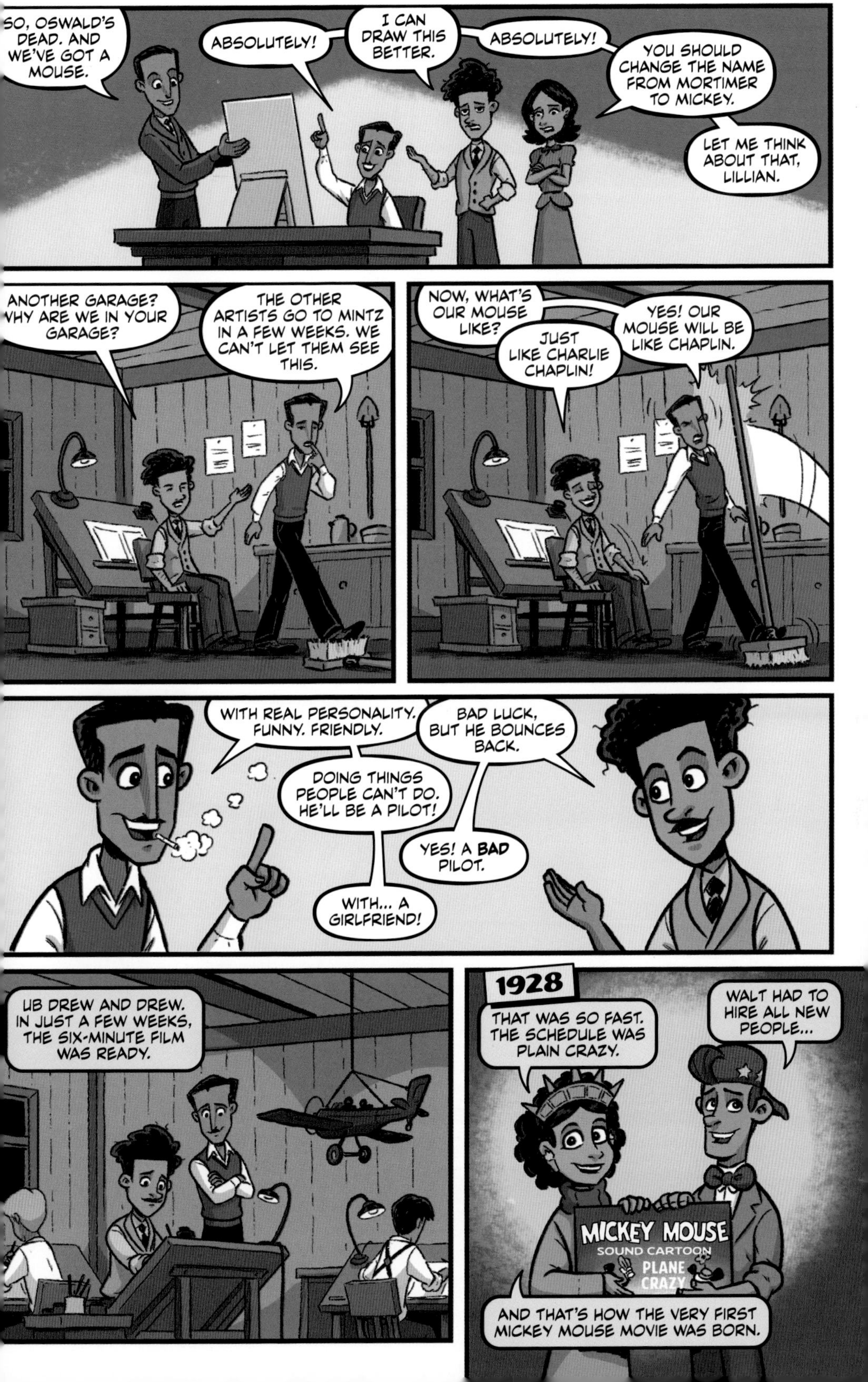
SO, OSWALD'S DEAD. AND WE'VE GOT A MOUSE.
ABSOLUTELY!
I CAN DRAW THIS BETTER.
ABSOLUTELY!
YOU SHOULD CHANGE THE NAME FROM MORTIMER TO MICKEY.
LET ME THINK ABOUT THAT, LILLIAN.
ANOTHER GARAGE? WHY ARE WE IN YOUR GARAGE?
THE OTHER ARTISTS GO TO MINTZ IN A FEW WEEKS. WE CAN'T LET THEM SEE THIS.
NOW, WHAT'S OUR MOUSE LIKE?
JUST LIKE CHARLIE CHAPLIN!
YES! OUR MOUSE WILL BE LIKE CHAPLIN.
WITH REAL PERSONALITY. FUNNY. FRIENDLY.
BAD LUCK, BUT HE BOUNCES BACK.
DOING THINGS PEOPLE CAN'T DO. HE'LL BE A PILOT!
YES! A **BAD** PILOT.
WITH... A GIRLFRIEND!
UB DREW AND DREW. IN JUST A FEW WEEKS, THE SIX-MINUTE FILM WAS READY.
1928
THAT WAS SO FAST. THE SCHEDULE WAS PLAIN CRAZY.
WALT HAD TO HIRE ALL NEW PEOPLE...
MICKEY MOUSE
SOUND CARTOON
PLANE CRAZY
AND THAT'S HOW THE VERY FIRST MICKEY MOUSE MOVIE WAS BORN.

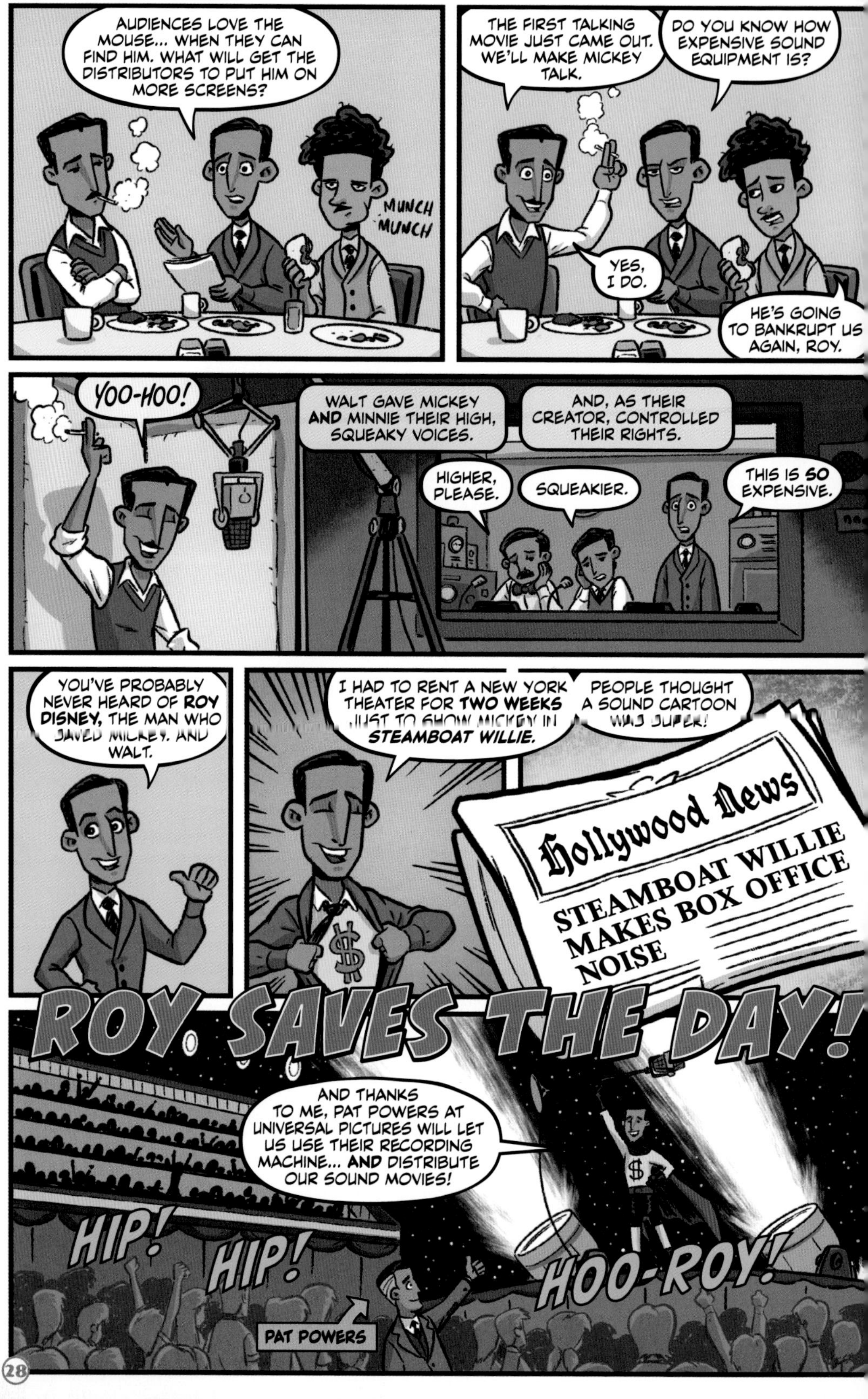
AUDIENCES LOVE THE MOUSE... WHEN THEY CAN FIND HIM. WHAT WILL GET THE DISTRIBUTORS TO PUT HIM ON MORE SCREENS?
MUNCH MUNCH
THE FIRST TALKING MOVIE JUST CAME OUT. WE'LL MAKE MICKEY TALK.
DO YOU KNOW HOW EXPENSIVE SOUND EQUIPMENT IS?
YES, I DO.
HE'S GOING TO BANKRUPT US AGAIN, ROY.
YOO-HOO!
WALT GAVE MICKEY **AND** MINNIE THEIR HIGH, SQUEAKY VOICES.
AND, AS THEIR CREATOR, CONTROLLED THEIR RIGHTS.
HIGHER, PLEASE.
SQUEAKIER.
THIS IS **SO** EXPENSIVE.
YOU'VE PROBABLY NEVER HEARD OF **ROY DISNEY,** THE MAN WHO SAVED MICKEY. AND WALT.
I HAD TO RENT A NEW YORK THEATER FOR **TWO WEEKS** JUST TO SHOW MICKEY IN ***STEAMBOAT WILLIE.***
PEOPLE THOUGHT A SOUND CARTOON WAS SUPER!
Hollywood News
STEAMBOAT WILLIE MAKES BOX OFFICE NOISE
ROY SAVES THE DAY!
AND THANKS TO ME, PAT POWERS AT UNIVERSAL PICTURES WILL LET US USE THEIR RECORDING MACHINE... **AND** DISTRIBUTE OUR SOUND MOVIES!
HIP! HIP! HOO-ROY!
PAT POWERS

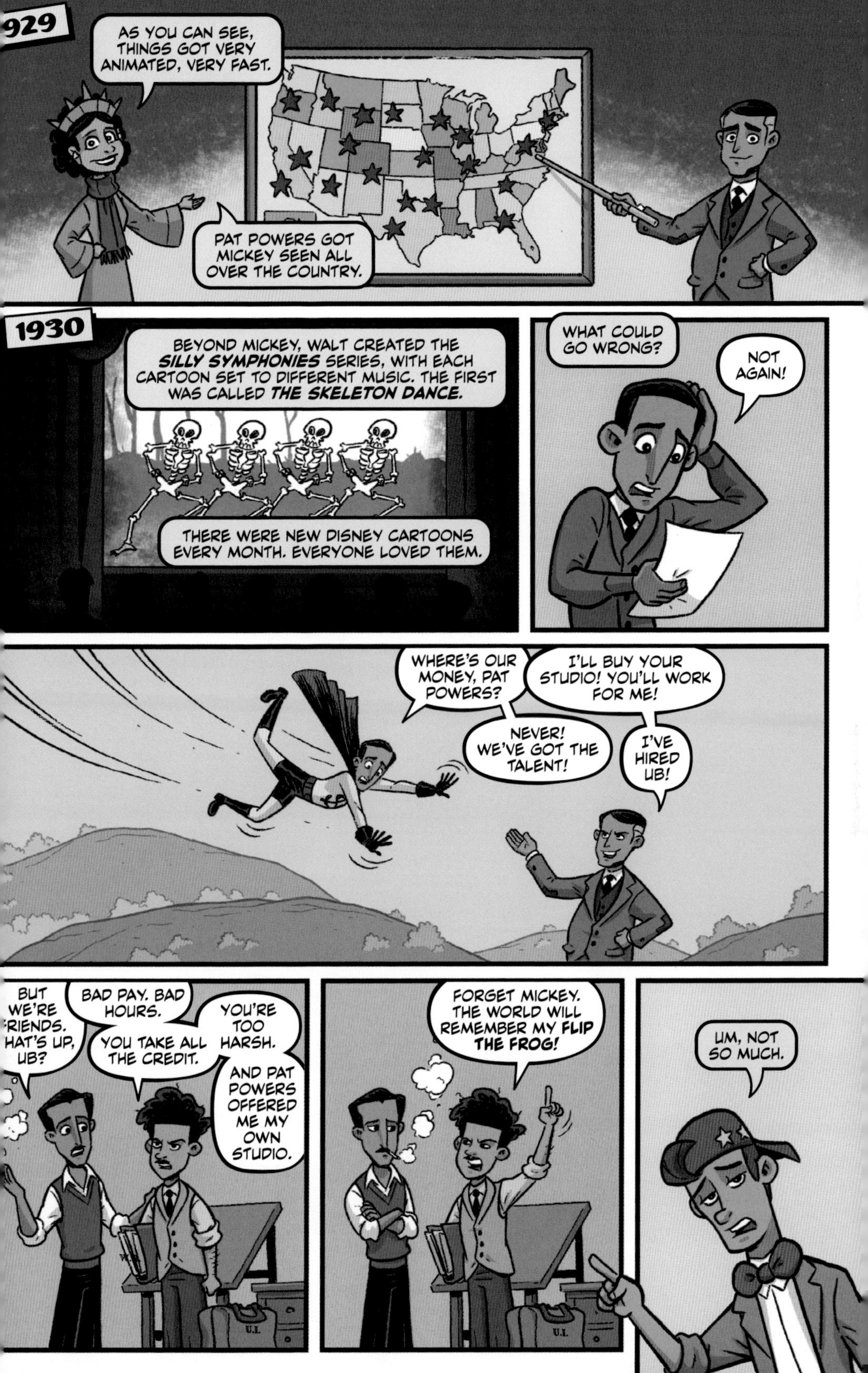
929
AS YOU CAN SEE, THINGS GOT VERY ANIMATED, VERY FAST.
PAT POWERS GOT MICKEY SEEN ALL OVER THE COUNTRY.
1930
BEYOND MICKEY, WALT CREATED THE SILLY SYMPHONIES SERIES, WITH EACH CARTOON SET TO DIFFERENT MUSIC. THE FIRST WAS CALLED THE SKELETON DANCE.
THERE WERE NEW DISNEY CARTOONS EVERY MONTH. EVERYONE LOVED THEM.
WHAT COULD GO WRONG?
NOT AGAIN!
WHERE'S OUR MONEY, PAT POWERS?
I'LL BUY YOUR STUDIO! YOU'LL WORK FOR ME!
NEVER! WE'VE GOT THE TALENT!
I'VE HIRED UB!
BUT WE'RE FRIENDS. HAT'S UP, UB?
BAD PAY. BAD HOURS.
YOU TAKE ALL THE CREDIT.
YOU'RE TOO HARSH.
AND PAT POWERS OFFERED ME MY OWN STUDIO.
FORGET MICKEY. THE WORLD WILL REMEMBER MY FLIP THE FROG!
UM, NOT SO MUCH.

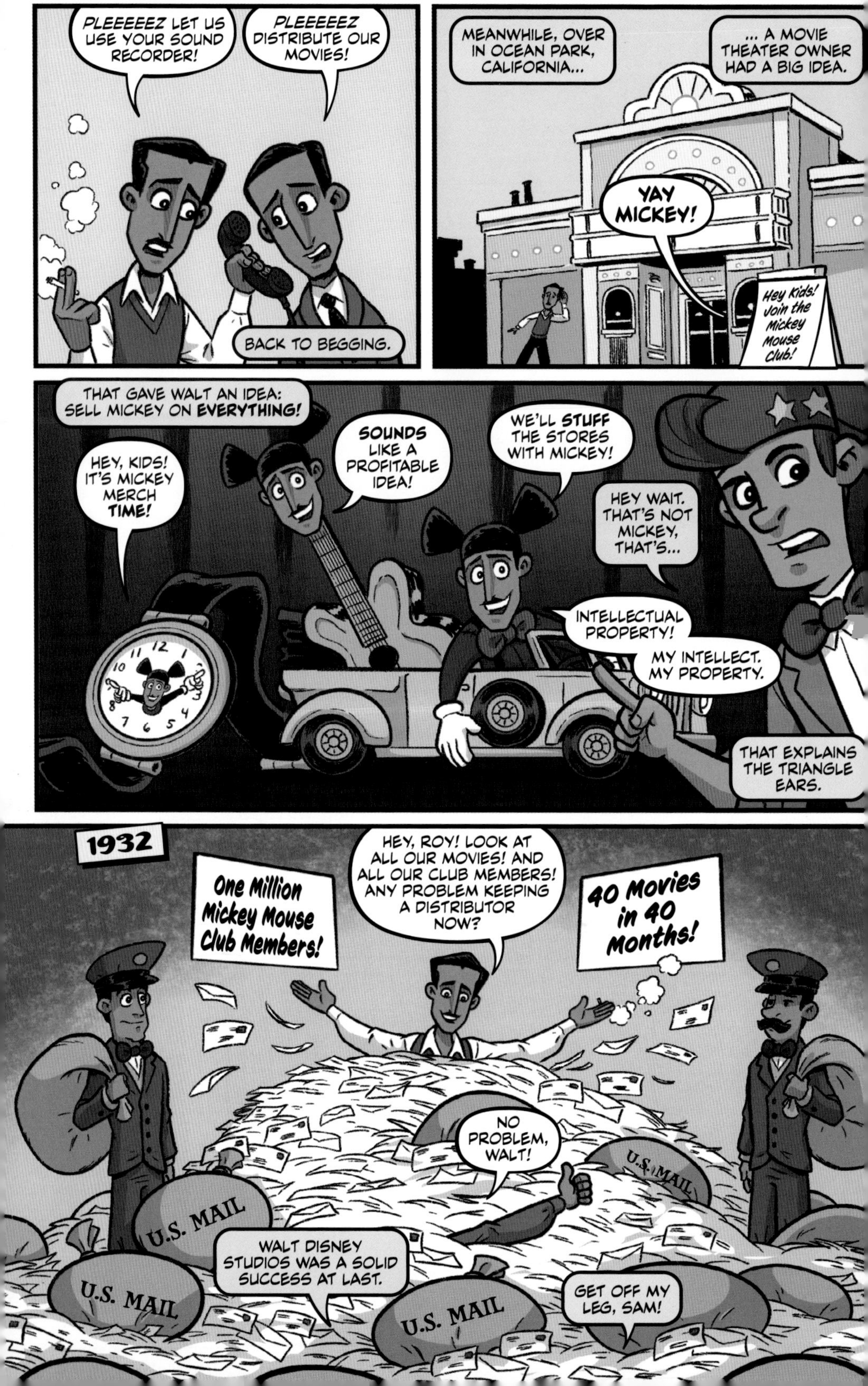
PLEEEEEZ LET US USE YOUR SOUND RECORDER!
PLEEEEEZ DISTRIBUTE OUR MOVIES!
BACK TO BEGGING.
MEANWHILE, OVER IN OCEAN PARK, CALIFORNIA...
... A MOVIE THEATER OWNER HAD A BIG IDEA.
YAY MICKEY!
Hey Kids! Join the Mickey Mouse Club!
THAT GAVE WALT AN IDEA: SELL MICKEY ON EVERYTHING!
HEY, KIDS! IT'S MICKEY MERCH TIME!
SOUNDS LIKE A PROFITABLE IDEA!
WE'LL STUFF THE STORES WITH MICKEY!
HEY WAIT. THAT'S NOT MICKEY, THAT'S...
INTELLECTUAL PROPERTY!
MY INTELLECT. MY PROPERTY.
THAT EXPLAINS THE TRIANGLE EARS.
1932
One Million Mickey Mouse Club Members!
HEY, ROY! LOOK AT ALL OUR MOVIES! AND ALL OUR CLUB MEMBERS! ANY PROBLEM KEEPING A DISTRIBUTOR NOW?
40 Movies in 40 Months!
NO PROBLEM, WALT!
U.S. MAIL
U.S. MAIL
U.S. MAIL
U.S. MAIL
WALT DISNEY STUDIOS WAS A SOLID SUCCESS AT LAST.
GET OFF MY LEG, SAM!

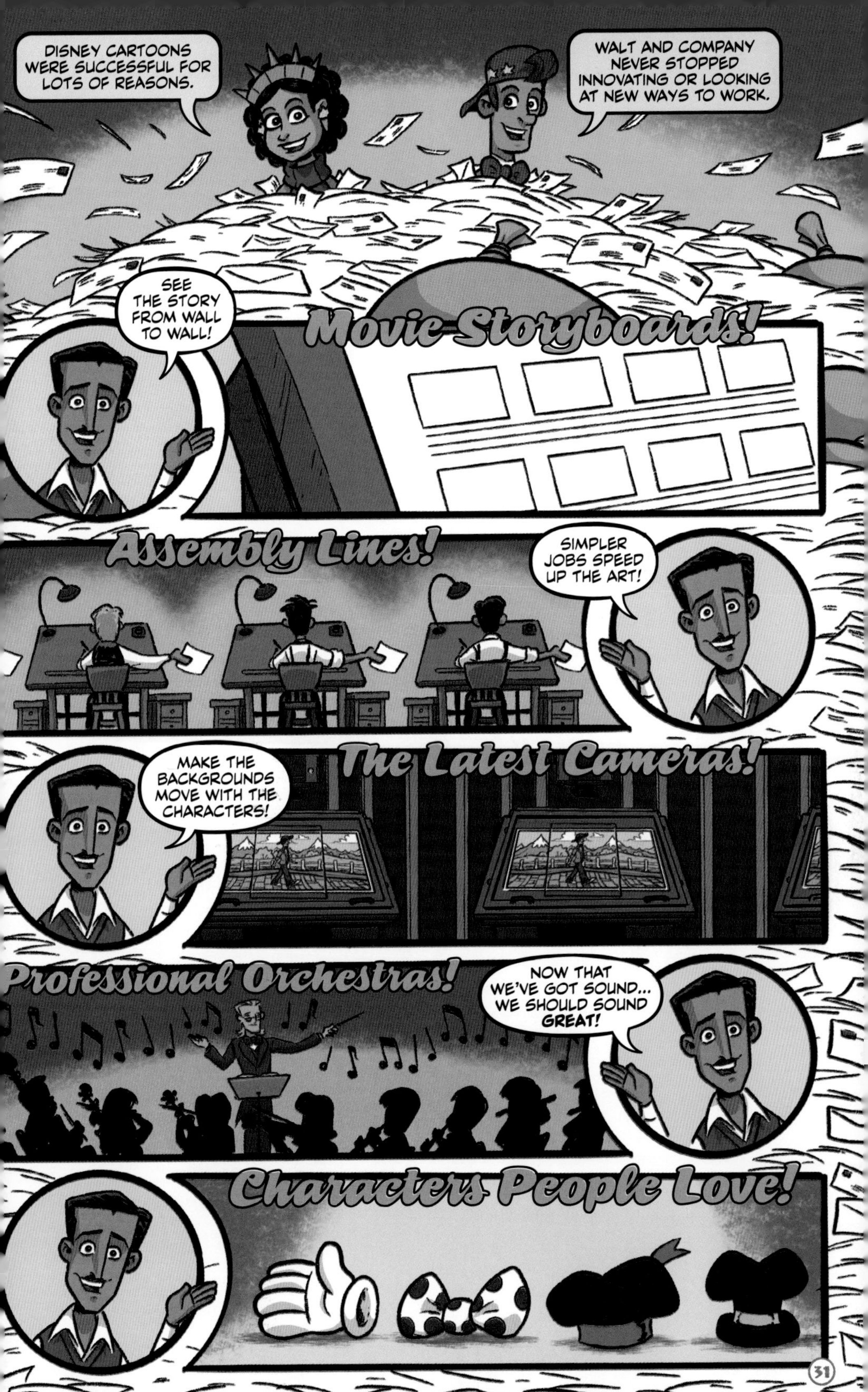
DISNEY CARTOONS WERE SUCCESSFUL FOR LOTS OF REASONS.
WALT AND COMPANY NEVER STOPPED INNOVATING OR LOOKING AT NEW WAYS TO WORK.
SEE THE STORY FROM WALL TO WALL!
Movie Storyboards!
Assembly Lines!
SIMPLER JOBS SPEED UP THE ART!
MAKE THE BACKGROUNDS MOVE WITH THE CHARACTERS!
The Latest Cameras!
Professional Orchestras!
NOW THAT WE'VE GOT SOUND... WE SHOULD SOUND GREAT!
Characters People Love!

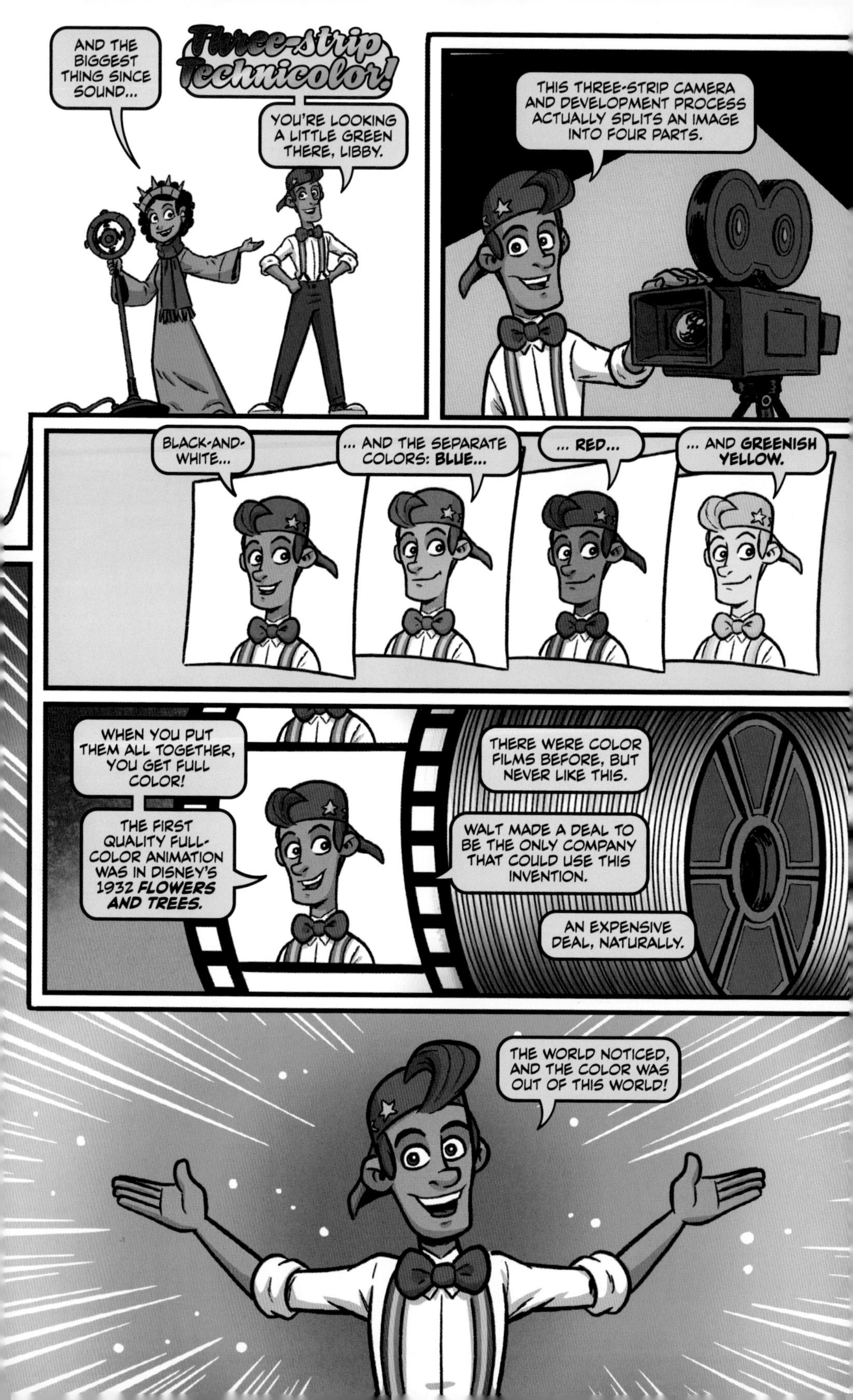
AND THE BIGGEST THING SINCE SOUND...
Three-strip Technicolor!
YOU'RE LOOKING A LITTLE GREEN THERE, LIBBY.
THIS THREE-STRIP CAMERA AND DEVELOPMENT PROCESS ACTUALLY SPLITS AN IMAGE INTO FOUR PARTS.
BLACK-AND-WHITE...
... AND THE SEPARATE COLORS: BLUE...
... RED...
... AND GREENISH YELLOW.
WHEN YOU PUT THEM ALL TOGETHER, YOU GET FULL COLOR!
THE FIRST QUALITY FULL-COLOR ANIMATION WAS IN DISNEY'S 1932 FLOWERS AND TREES.
THERE WERE COLOR FILMS BEFORE, BUT NEVER LIKE THIS.
WALT MADE A DEAL TO BE THE ONLY COMPANY THAT COULD USE THIS INVENTION.
AN EXPENSIVE DEAL, NATURALLY.
THE WORLD NOTICED, AND THE COLOR WAS OUT OF THIS WORLD!

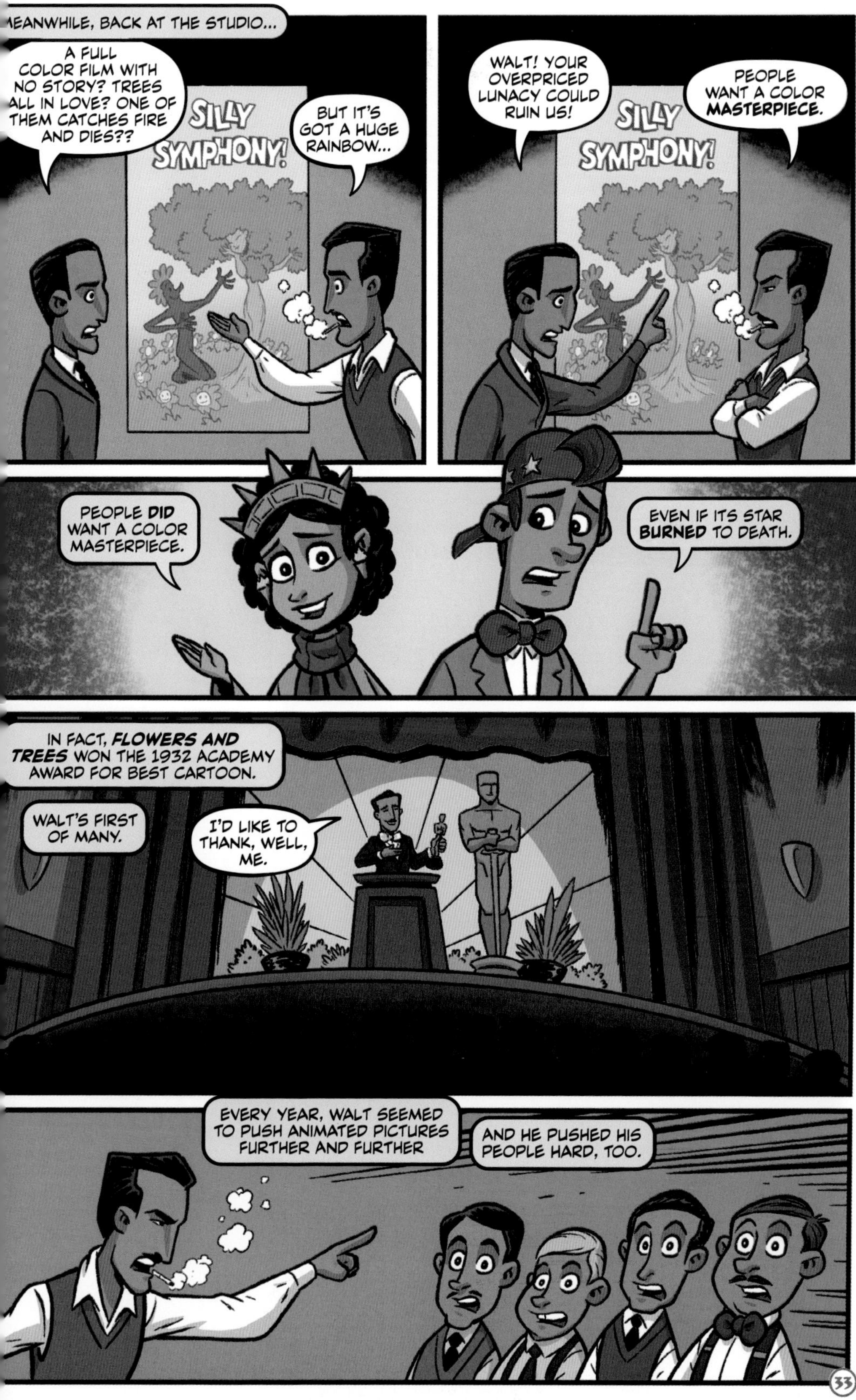

MEANWHILE, BACK AT THE STUDIO...
A FULL COLOR FILM WITH NO STORY? TREES ALL IN LOVE? ONE OF THEM CATCHES FIRE AND DIES??
SILLY SYMPHONY!
BUT IT'S GOT A HUGE RAINBOW...
WALT! YOUR OVERPRICED LUNACY COULD RUIN US!
SILLY SYMPHONY!
PEOPLE WANT A COLOR **MASTERPIECE.**
PEOPLE **DID** WANT A COLOR MASTERPIECE.
EVEN IF ITS STAR **BURNED** TO DEATH.
IN FACT, ***FLOWERS AND TREES*** WON THE 1932 ACADEMY AWARD FOR BEST CARTOON.
WALT'S FIRST OF MANY.
I'D LIKE TO THANK, WELL, ME.
EVERY YEAR, WALT SEEMED TO PUSH ANIMATED PICTURES FURTHER AND FURTHER
AND HE PUSHED HIS PEOPLE HARD, TOO.

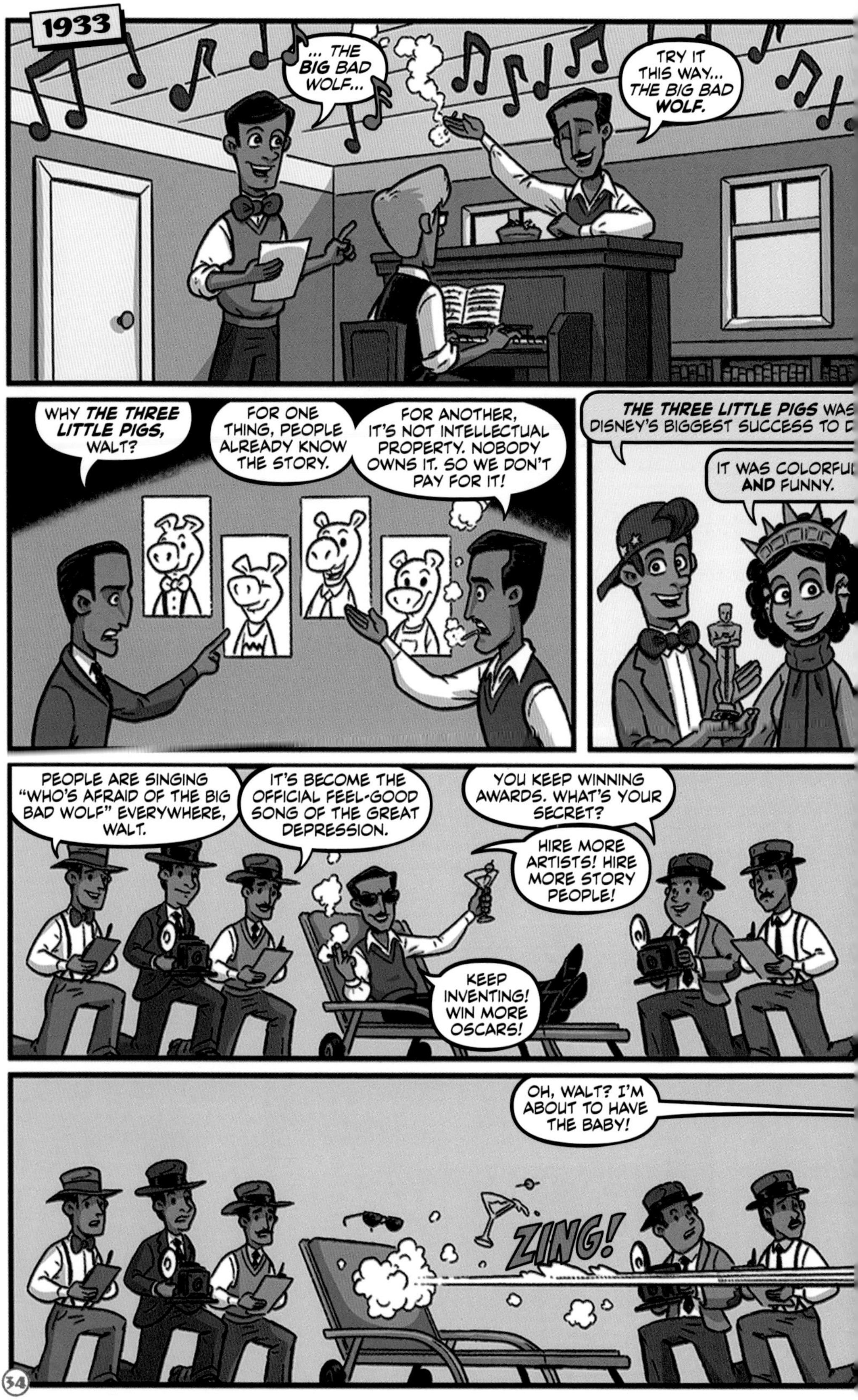
1933
... THE BIG BAD WOLF...
TRY IT THIS WAY... THE BIG BAD WOLF.
WHY THE THREE LITTLE PIGS, WALT?
FOR ONE THING, PEOPLE ALREADY KNOW THE STORY.
FOR ANOTHER, IT'S NOT INTELLECTUAL PROPERTY. NOBODY OWNS IT. SO WE DON'T PAY FOR IT!
THE THREE LITTLE PIGS WAS
DISNEY'S BIGGEST SUCCESS TO D
IT WAS COLORFU
AND FUNNY.
PEOPLE ARE SINGING "WHO'S AFRAID OF THE BIG BAD WOLF" EVERYWHERE, WALT.
IT'S BECOME THE OFFICIAL FEEL-GOOD SONG OF THE GREAT DEPRESSION.
YOU KEEP WINNING AWARDS. WHAT'S YOUR SECRET?
HIRE MORE ARTISTS! HIRE MORE STORY PEOPLE!
KEEP INVENTING! WIN MORE OSCARS!
OH, WALT? I'M ABOUT TO HAVE THE BABY!
ZING!

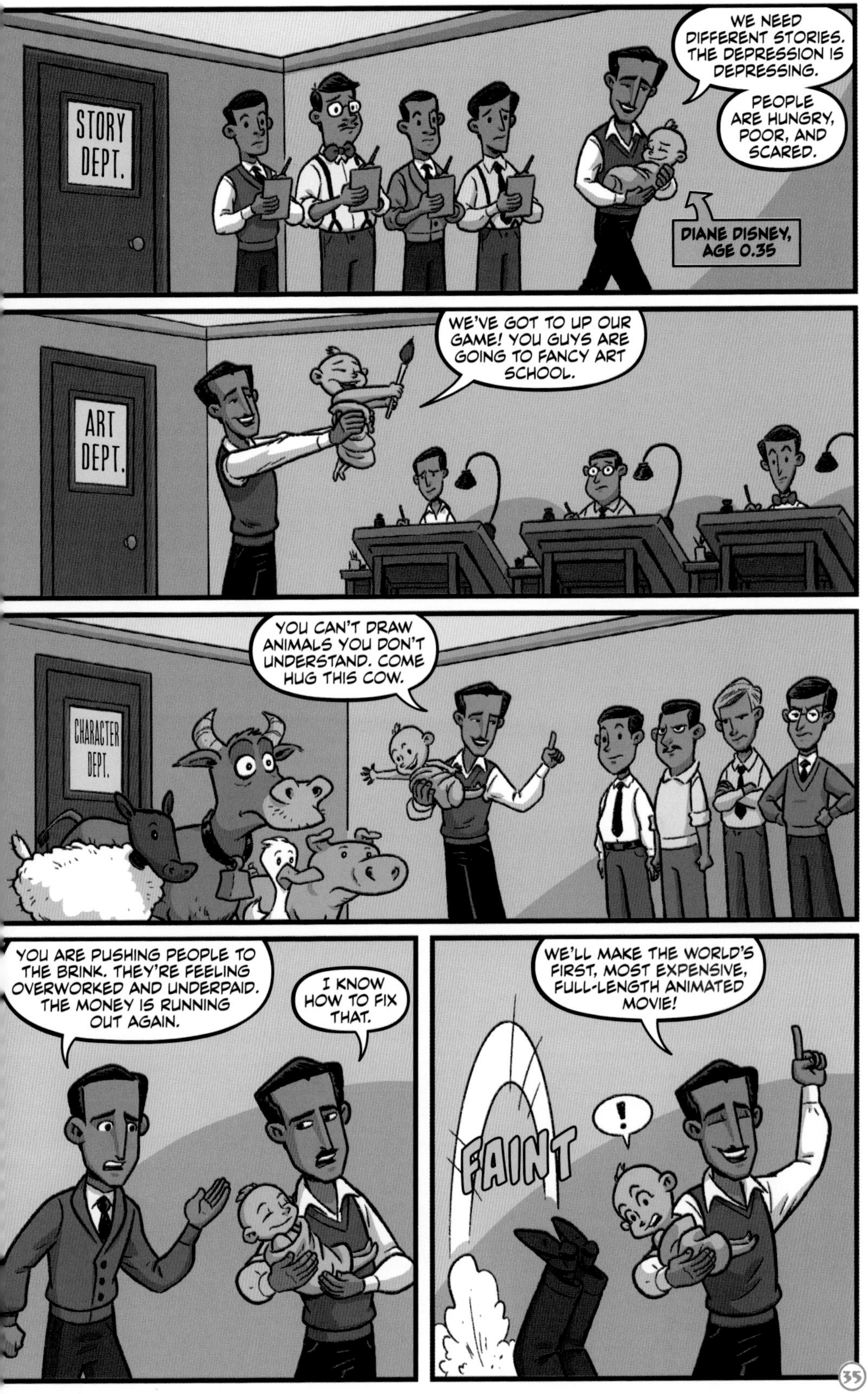
STORY DEPT.
WE NEED DIFFERENT STORIES. THE DEPRESSION IS DEPRESSING.
PEOPLE ARE HUNGRY, POOR, AND SCARED.
DIANE DISNEY, AGE 0.35
ART DEPT.
WE'VE GOT TO UP OUR GAME! YOU GUYS ARE GOING TO FANCY ART SCHOOL.
CHARACTER DEPT.
YOU CAN'T DRAW ANIMALS YOU DON'T UNDERSTAND. COME HUG THIS COW.
YOU ARE PUSHING PEOPLE TO THE BRINK. THEY'RE FEELING OVERWORKED AND UNDERPAID. THE MONEY IS RUNNING OUT AGAIN.
I KNOW HOW TO FIX THAT.
WE'LL MAKE THE WORLD'S FIRST, MOST EXPENSIVE, FULL-LENGTH ANIMATED MOVIE!
!
FAINT

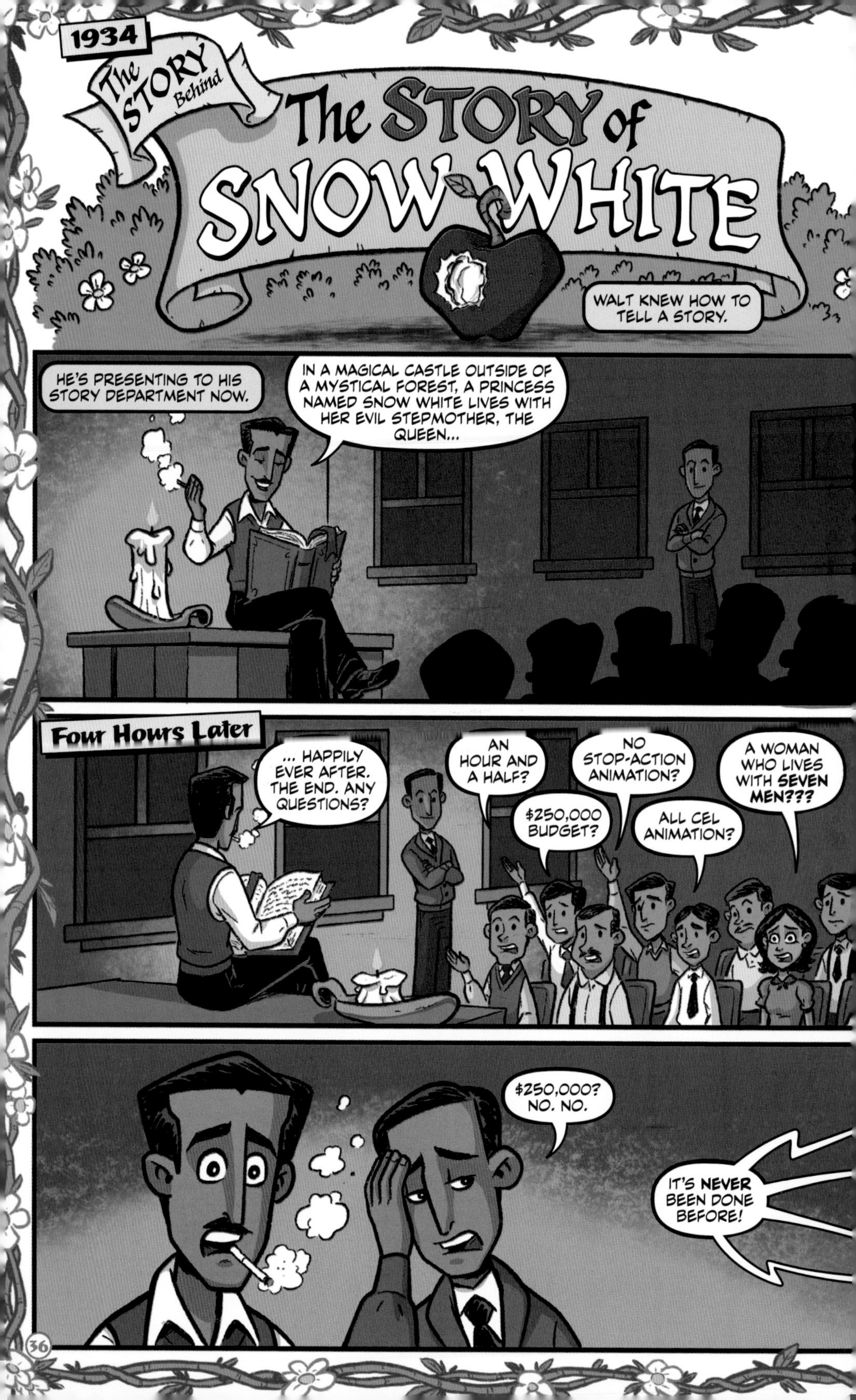
1934
The STORY Behind
The STORY of SNOW WHITE
WALT KNEW HOW TO TELL A STORY.
HE'S PRESENTING TO HIS STORY DEPARTMENT NOW.
IN A MAGICAL CASTLE OUTSIDE OF A MYSTICAL FOREST, A PRINCESS NAMED SNOW WHITE LIVES WITH HER EVIL STEPMOTHER, THE QUEEN...
Four Hours Later
... HAPPILY EVER AFTER. THE END. ANY QUESTIONS?
AN HOUR AND A HALF?
$250,000 BUDGET?
NO STOP-ACTION ANIMATION?
ALL CEL ANIMATION?
A WOMAN WHO LIVES WITH **SEVEN MEN???**
$250,000? NO. NO.
IT'S **NEVER** BEEN DONE BEFORE!

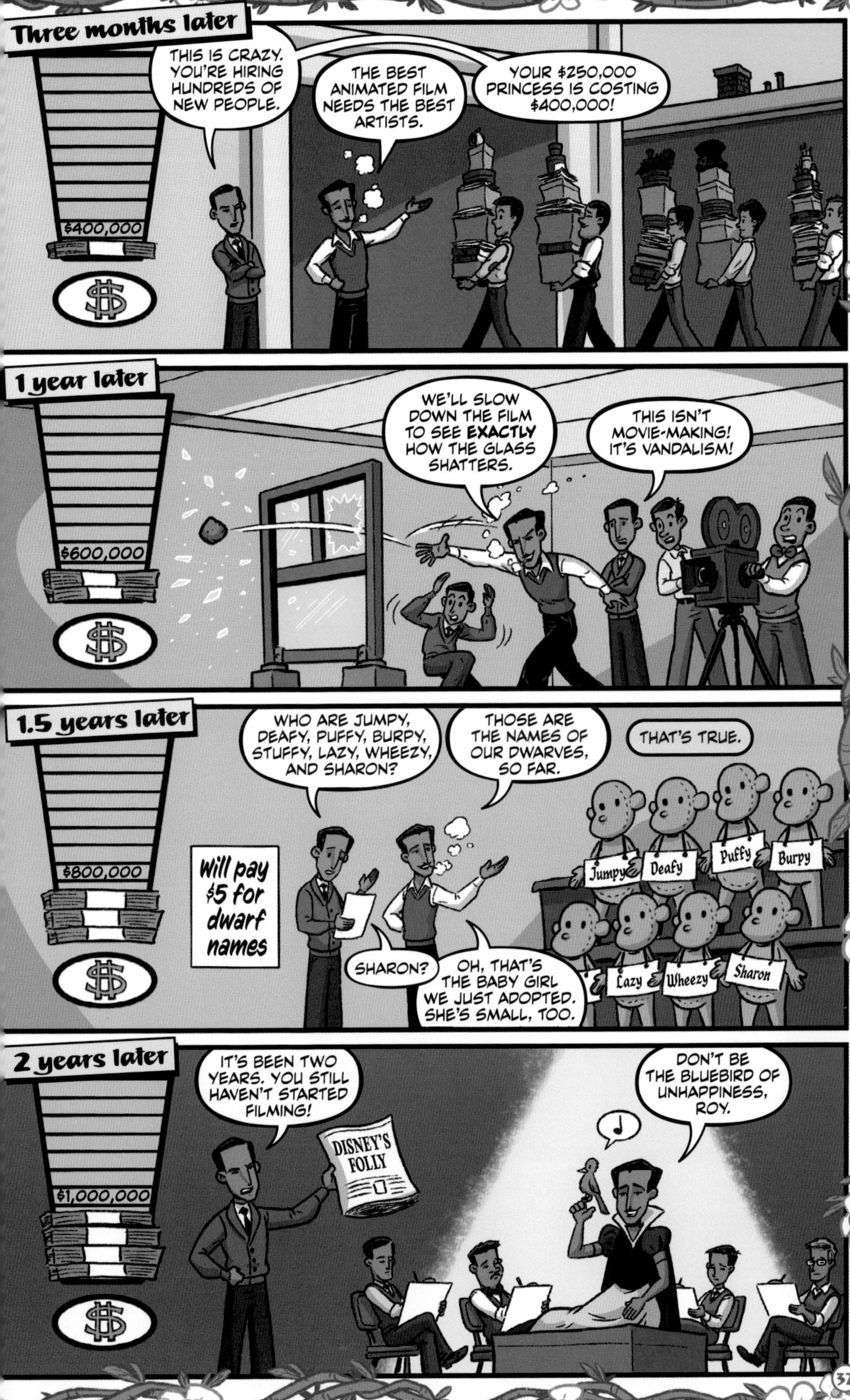
Three months later
$400,000
THIS IS CRAZY. YOU'RE HIRING HUNDREDS OF NEW PEOPLE.
THE BEST ANIMATED FILM NEEDS THE BEST ARTISTS.
YOUR $250,000 PRINCESS IS COSTING $400,000!
1 year later
$600,000
WE'LL SLOW DOWN THE FILM TO SEE EXACTLY HOW THE GLASS SHATTERS.
THIS ISN'T MOVIE-MAKING! IT'S VANDALISM!
1.5 years later
$800,000
WHO ARE JUMPY, DEAFY, PUFFY, BURPY, STUFFY, LAZY, WHEEZY, AND SHARON?
THOSE ARE THE NAMES OF OUR DWARVES, SO FAR.
THAT'S TRUE.
Will pay $5 for dwarf names
Jumpy
Deafy
Puffy
Burpy
Lazy
Wheezy
Sharon
SHARON?
OH, THAT'S THE BABY GIRL WE JUST ADOPTED. SHE'S SMALL, TOO.
2 years later
$1,000,000
IT'S BEEN TWO YEARS. YOU STILL HAVEN'T STARTED FILMING!
DISNEY'S FOLLY
DON'T BE THE BLUEBIRD OF UNHAPPINESS, ROY.

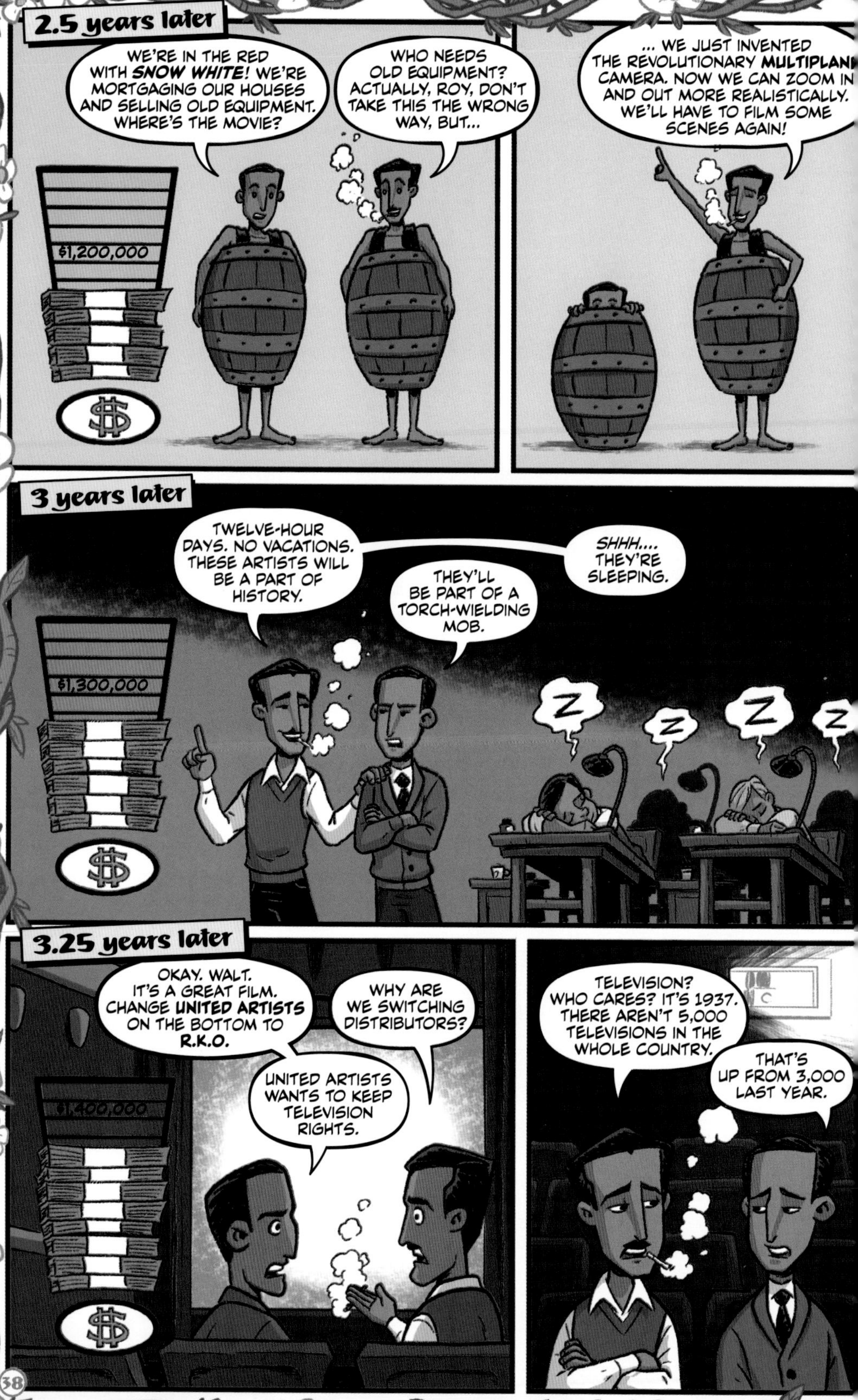
2.5 years later
WE'RE IN THE RED WITH SNOW WHITE! WE'RE MORTGAGING OUR HOUSES AND SELLING OLD EQUIPMENT. WHERE'S THE MOVIE?
$1,200,000
WHO NEEDS OLD EQUIPMENT? ACTUALLY, ROY, DON'T TAKE THIS THE WRONG WAY, BUT...
... WE JUST INVENTED THE REVOLUTIONARY MULTIPLANE CAMERA. NOW WE CAN ZOOM IN AND OUT MORE REALISTICALLY. WE'LL HAVE TO FILM SOME SCENES AGAIN!
3 years later
TWELVE-HOUR DAYS. NO VACATIONS. THESE ARTISTS WILL BE A PART OF HISTORY.
SHHH.... THEY'RE SLEEPING.
THEY'LL BE PART OF A TORCH-WIELDING MOB.
$1,300,000
Z
Z
Z
Z
3.25 years later
OKAY. WALT. IT'S A GREAT FILM. CHANGE UNITED ARTISTS ON THE BOTTOM TO R.K.O.
WHY ARE WE SWITCHING DISTRIBUTORS?
UNITED ARTISTS WANTS TO KEEP TELEVISION RIGHTS.
$1,400,000
TELEVISION? WHO CARES? IT'S 1937. THERE AREN'T 5,000 TELEVISIONS IN THE WHOLE COUNTRY.
THAT'S UP FROM 3,000 LAST YEAR.

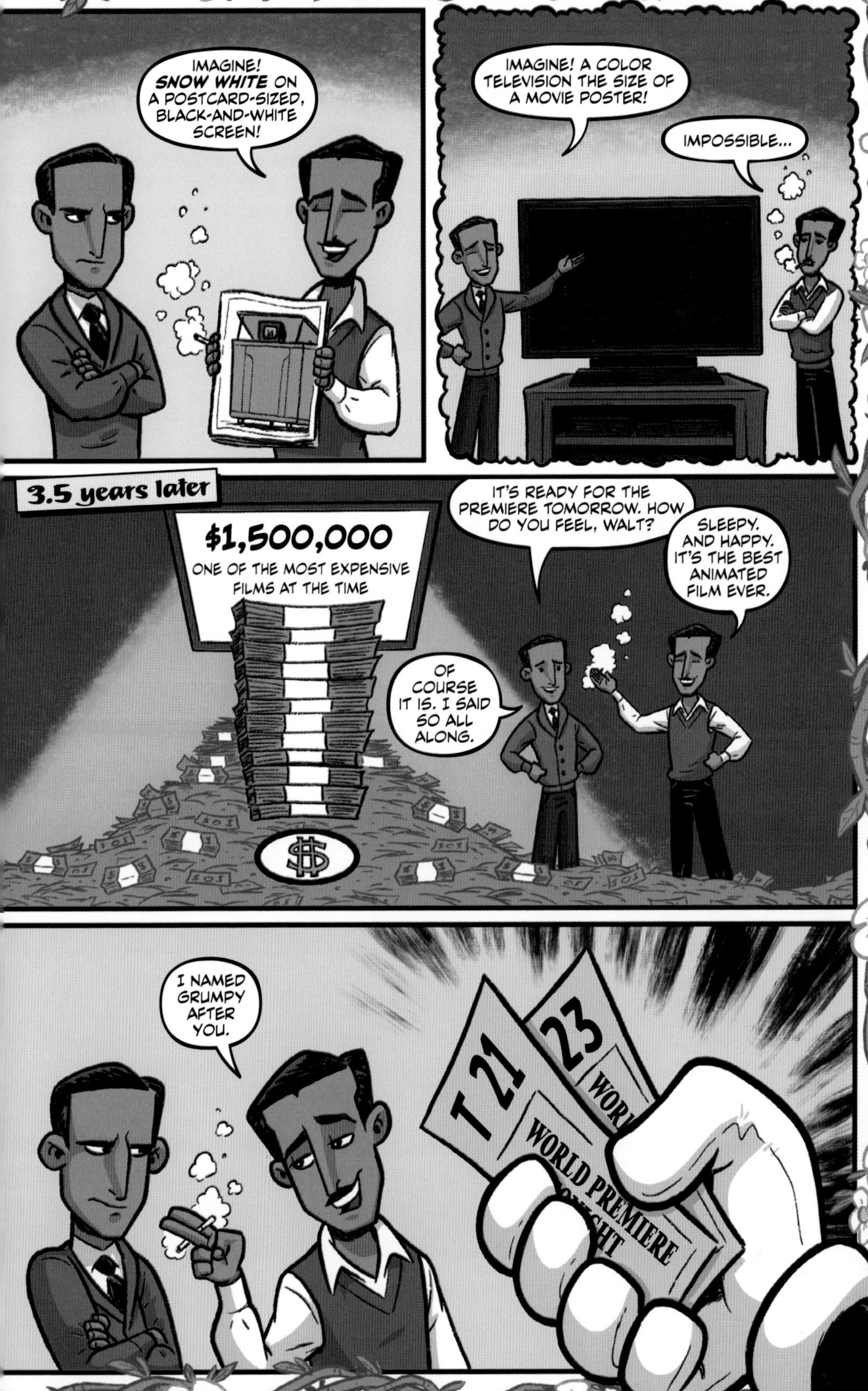
IMAGINE! SNOW WHITE ON A POSTCARD-SIZED, BLACK-AND-WHITE SCREEN!
IMAGINE! A COLOR TELEVISION THE SIZE OF A MOVIE POSTER!
IMPOSSIBLE...
3.5 years later
$1,500,000
ONE OF THE MOST EXPENSIVE FILMS AT THE TIME
IT'S READY FOR THE PREMIERE TOMORROW. HOW DO YOU FEEL, WALT?
SLEEPY. AND HAPPY. IT'S THE BEST ANIMATED FILM EVER.
OF COURSE IT IS. I SAID SO ALL ALONG.
I NAMED GRUMPY AFTER YOU.
T 21
23
WORLD PREMIERE

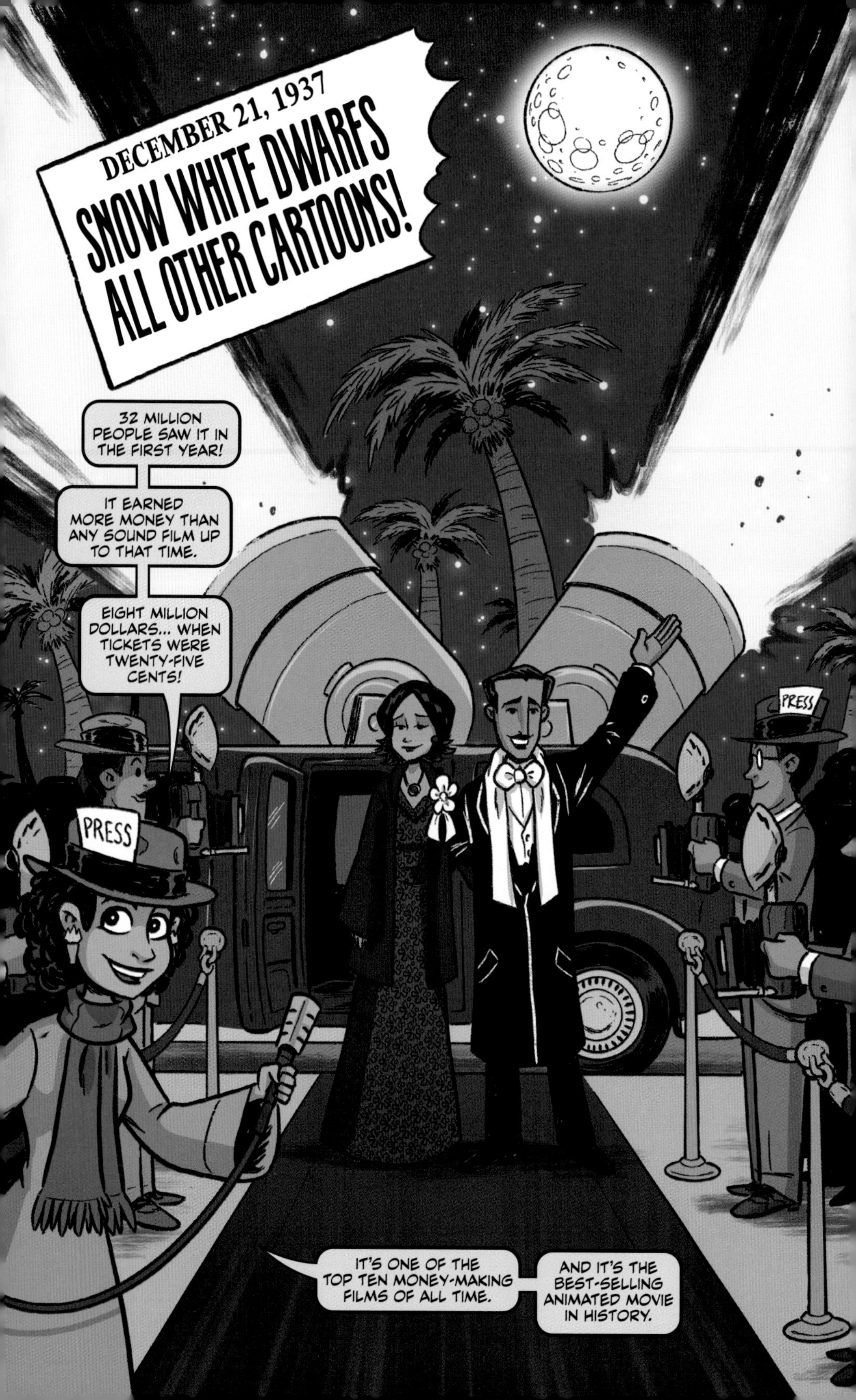
DECEMBER 21, 1937
SNOW WHITE DWARFS ALL OTHER CARTOONS!
32 MILLION PEOPLE SAW IT IN THE FIRST YEAR!
IT EARNED MORE MONEY THAN ANY SOUND FILM UP TO THAT TIME.
EIGHT MILLION DOLLARS... WHEN TICKETS WERE TWENTY-FIVE CENTS!
PRESS
PRESS
IT'S ONE OF THE TOP TEN MONEY-MAKING FILMS OF ALL TIME.
AND IT'S THE BEST-SELLING ANIMATED MOVIE IN HISTORY.

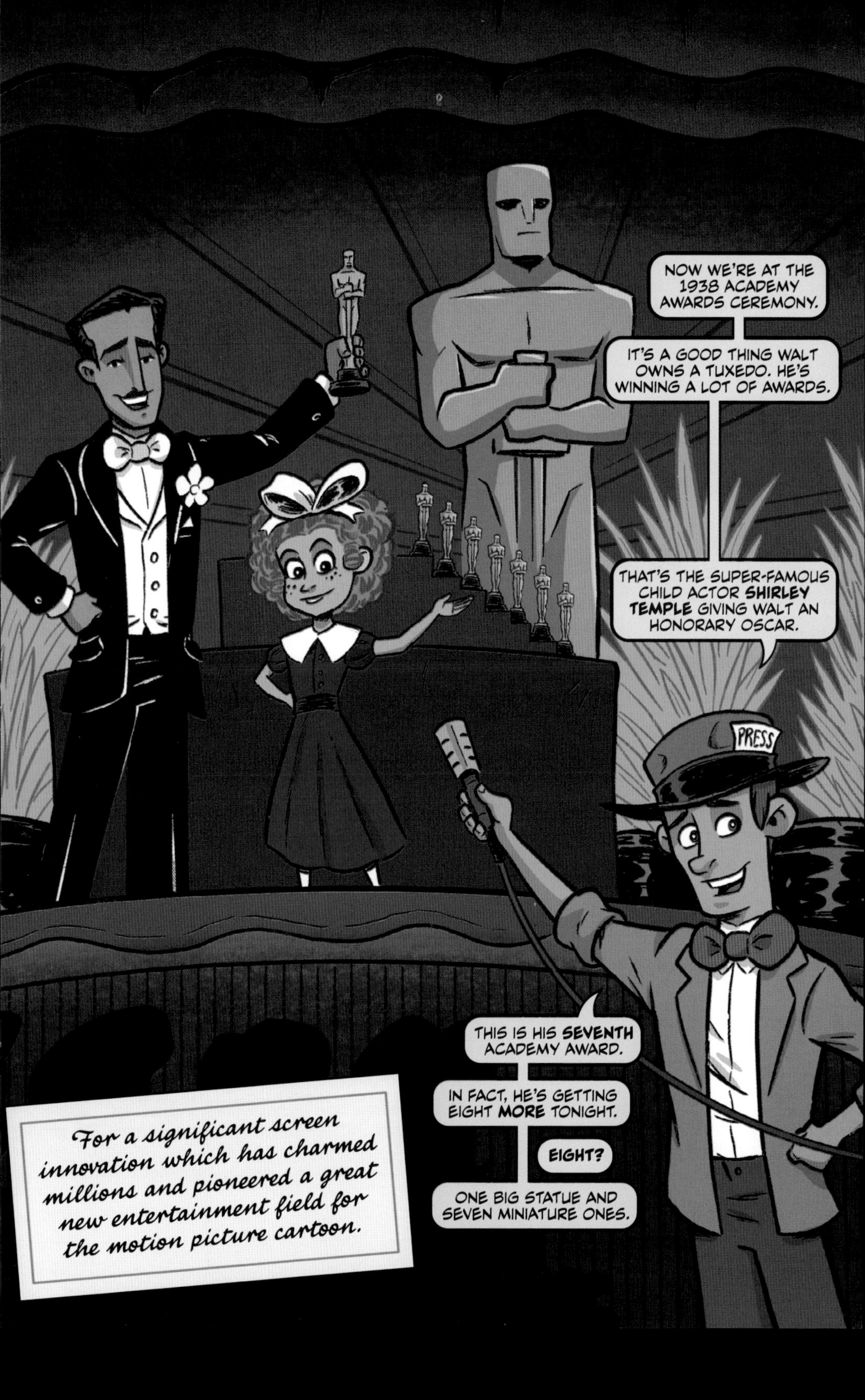

NOW WE'RE AT THE 1938 ACADEMY AWARDS CEREMONY.
IT'S A GOOD THING WALT OWNS A TUXEDO. HE'S WINNING A LOT OF AWARDS.
THAT'S THE SUPER-FAMOUS CHILD ACTOR **SHIRLEY TEMPLE** GIVING WALT AN HONORARY OSCAR.
PRESS
THIS IS HIS **SEVENTH** ACADEMY AWARD.
IN FACT, HE'S GETTING EIGHT **MORE** TONIGHT.
EIGHT?
ONE BIG STATUE AND SEVEN MINIATURE ONES.
For a significant screen innovation which has charmed millions and pioneered a great new entertainment field for the motion picture cartoon.

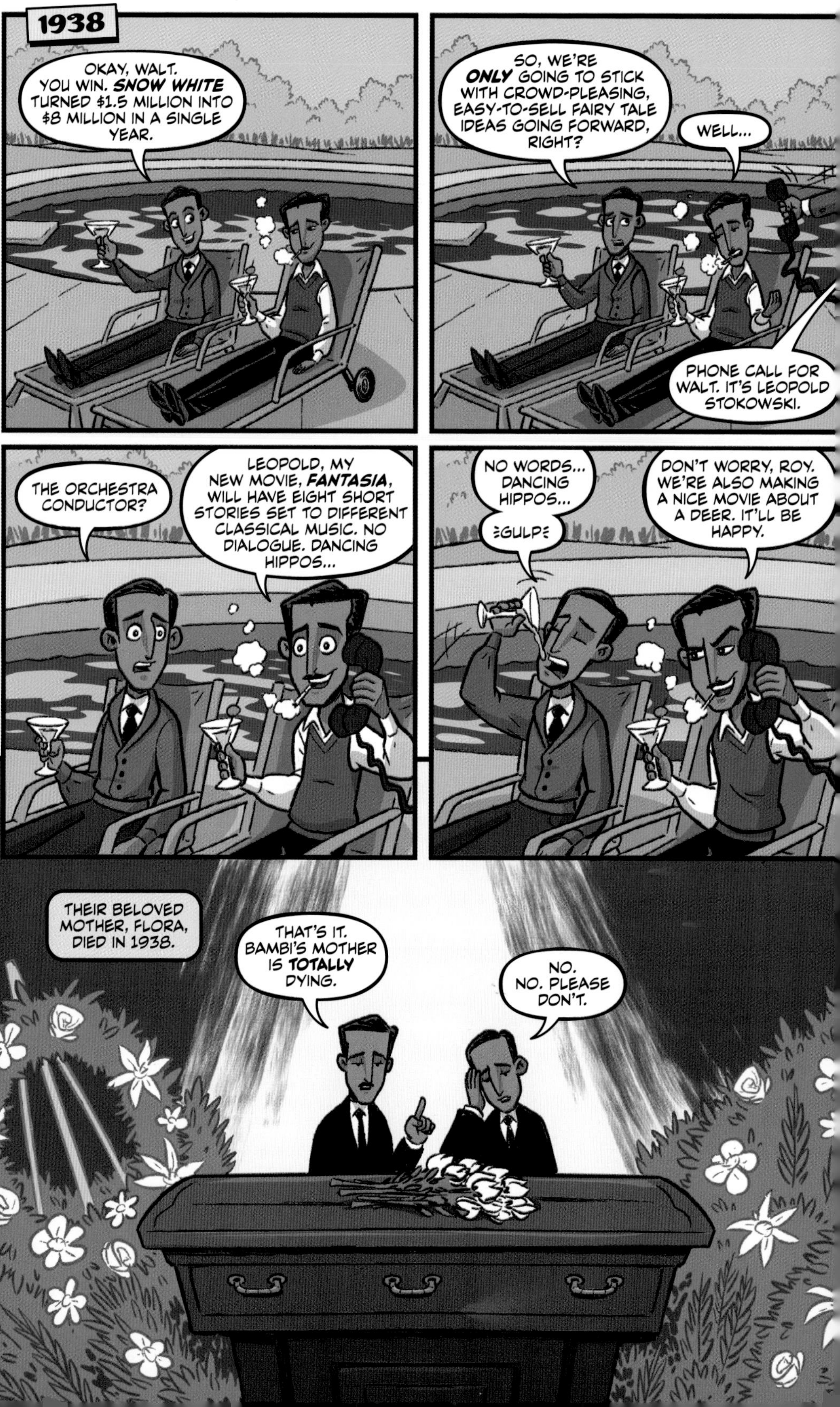
1938
OKAY, WALT. YOU WIN. SNOW WHITE TURNED $1.5 MILLION INTO $8 MILLION IN A SINGLE YEAR.
SO, WE'RE ONLY GOING TO STICK WITH CROWD-PLEASING, EASY-TO-SELL FAIRY TALE IDEAS GOING FORWARD, RIGHT?
WELL...
PHONE CALL FOR WALT. IT'S LEOPOLD STOKOWSKI.
THE ORCHESTRA CONDUCTOR?
LEOPOLD, MY NEW MOVIE, FANTASIA, WILL HAVE EIGHT SHORT STORIES SET TO DIFFERENT CLASSICAL MUSIC. NO DIALOGUE. DANCING HIPPOS...
NO WORDS... DANCING HIPPOS...
GULP
DON'T WORRY, ROY. WE'RE ALSO MAKING A NICE MOVIE ABOUT A DEER. IT'LL BE HAPPY.
THEIR BELOVED MOTHER, FLORA, DIED IN 1938.
THAT'S IT. BAMBI'S MOTHER IS TOTALLY DYING.
NO. NO. PLEASE DON'T.

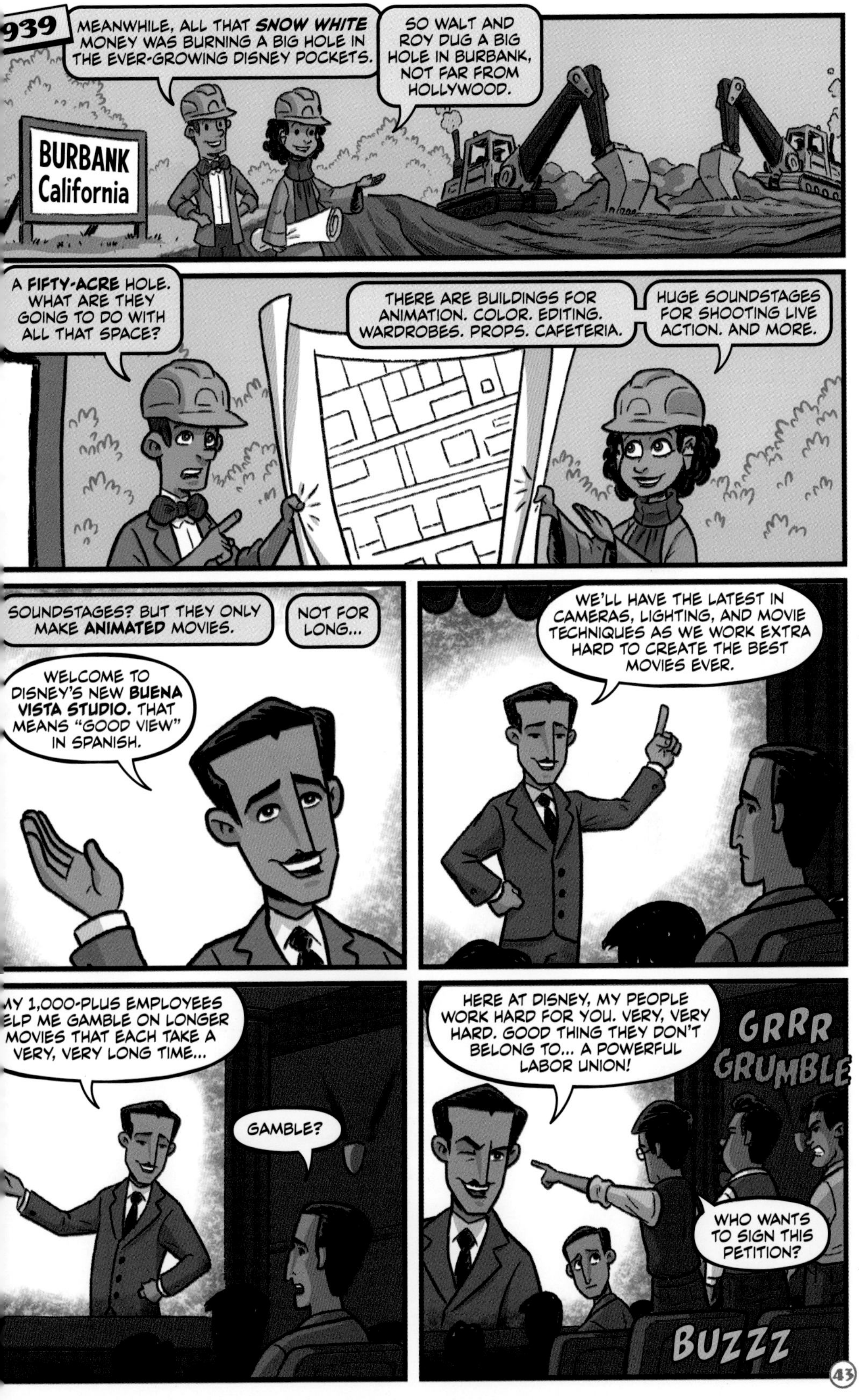
939
MEANWHILE, ALL THAT SNOW WHITE MONEY WAS BURNING A BIG HOLE IN THE EVER-GROWING DISNEY POCKETS.
SO WALT AND ROY DUG A BIG HOLE IN BURBANK, NOT FAR FROM HOLLYWOOD.
BURBANK California
A FIFTY-ACRE HOLE. WHAT ARE THEY GOING TO DO WITH ALL THAT SPACE?
THERE ARE BUILDINGS FOR ANIMATION. COLOR. EDITING. WARDROBES. PROPS. CAFETERIA.
HUGE SOUNDSTAGES FOR SHOOTING LIVE ACTION. AND MORE.
SOUNDSTAGES? BUT THEY ONLY MAKE ANIMATED MOVIES.
NOT FOR LONG...
WELCOME TO DISNEY'S NEW BUENA VISTA STUDIO. THAT MEANS "GOOD VIEW" IN SPANISH.
WE'LL HAVE THE LATEST IN CAMERAS, LIGHTING, AND MOVIE TECHNIQUES AS WE WORK EXTRA HARD TO CREATE THE BEST MOVIES EVER.
MY 1,000-PLUS EMPLOYEES ELP ME GAMBLE ON LONGER MOVIES THAT EACH TAKE A VERY, VERY LONG TIME...
GAMBLE?
HERE AT DISNEY, MY PEOPLE WORK HARD FOR YOU. VERY, VERY HARD. GOOD THING THEY DON'T BELONG TO... A POWERFUL LABOR UNION!
GRRR GRUMBLE
WHO WANTS TO SIGN THIS PETITION?
BUZZZ

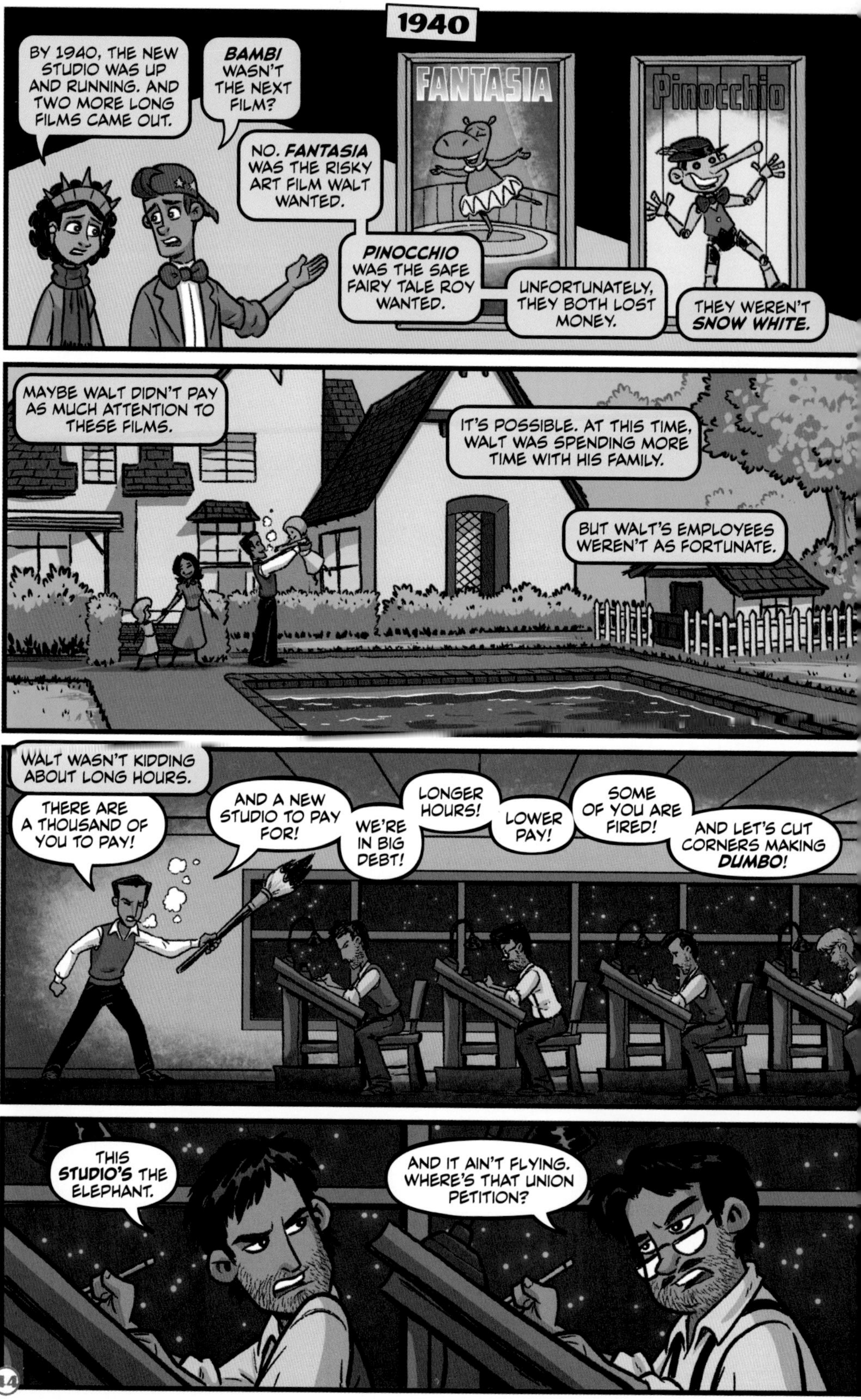
1940
BY 1940, THE NEW STUDIO WAS UP AND RUNNING. AND TWO MORE LONG FILMS CAME OUT.
BAMBI WASN'T THE NEXT FILM?
NO. FANTASIA WAS THE RISKY ART FILM WALT WANTED.
FANTASIA
Pinocchio
PINOCCHIO WAS THE SAFE FAIRY TALE ROY WANTED.
UNFORTUNATELY, THEY BOTH LOST MONEY.
THEY WEREN'T SNOW WHITE.
MAYBE WALT DIDN'T PAY AS MUCH ATTENTION TO THESE FILMS.
IT'S POSSIBLE. AT THIS TIME, WALT WAS SPENDING MORE TIME WITH HIS FAMILY.
BUT WALT'S EMPLOYEES WEREN'T AS FORTUNATE.
WALT WASN'T KIDDING ABOUT LONG HOURS.
THERE ARE A THOUSAND OF YOU TO PAY!
AND A NEW STUDIO TO PAY FOR!
WE'RE IN BIG DEBT!
LONGER HOURS!
LOWER PAY!
SOME OF YOU ARE FIRED!
AND LET'S CUT CORNERS MAKING DUMBO!
THIS STUDIO'S THE ELEPHANT.
AND IT AIN'T FLYING. WHERE'S THAT UNION PETITION?

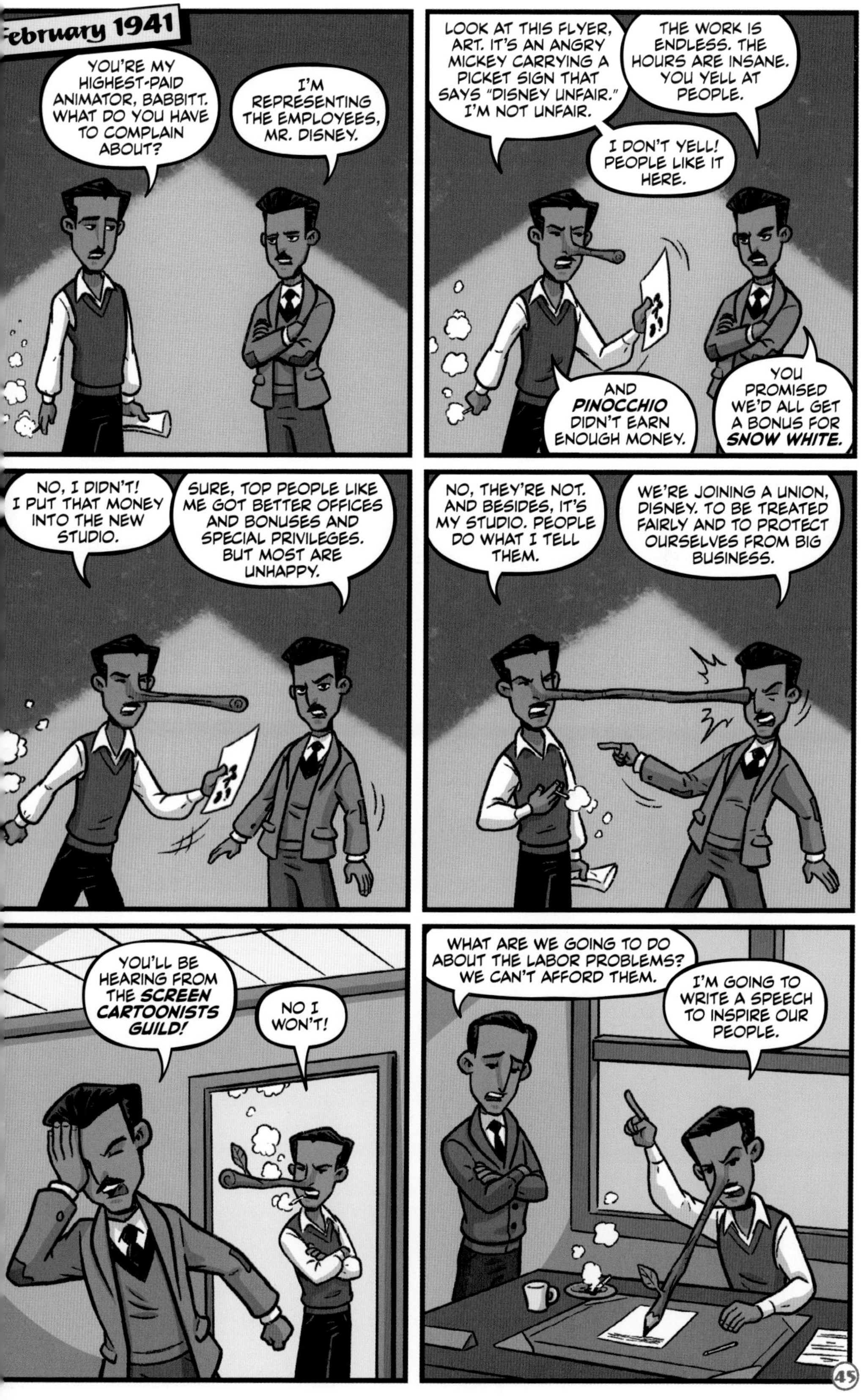
February 1941
YOU'RE MY HIGHEST-PAID ANIMATOR, BABBITT. WHAT DO YOU HAVE TO COMPLAIN ABOUT?
I'M REPRESENTING THE EMPLOYEES, MR. DISNEY.
LOOK AT THIS FLYER, ART. IT'S AN ANGRY MICKEY CARRYING A PICKET SIGN THAT SAYS "DISNEY UNFAIR." I'M NOT UNFAIR.
THE WORK IS ENDLESS. THE HOURS ARE INSANE. YOU YELL AT PEOPLE.
I DON'T YELL! PEOPLE LIKE IT HERE.
AND *PINOCCHIO* DIDN'T EARN ENOUGH MONEY.
YOU PROMISED WE'D ALL GET A BONUS FOR *SNOW WHITE.*
NO, I DIDN'T! I PUT THAT MONEY INTO THE NEW STUDIO.
SURE, TOP PEOPLE LIKE ME GOT BETTER OFFICES AND BONUSES AND SPECIAL PRIVILEGES. BUT MOST ARE UNHAPPY.
NO, THEY'RE NOT. AND BESIDES, IT'S MY STUDIO. PEOPLE DO WHAT I TELL THEM.
WE'RE JOINING A UNION, DISNEY. TO BE TREATED FAIRLY AND TO PROTECT OURSELVES FROM BIG BUSINESS.
YOU'LL BE HEARING FROM THE *SCREEN CARTOONISTS GUILD!*
NO I WON'T!
WHAT ARE WE GOING TO DO ABOUT THE LABOR PROBLEMS? WE CAN'T AFFORD THEM.
I'M GOING TO WRITE A SPEECH TO INSPIRE OUR PEOPLE.

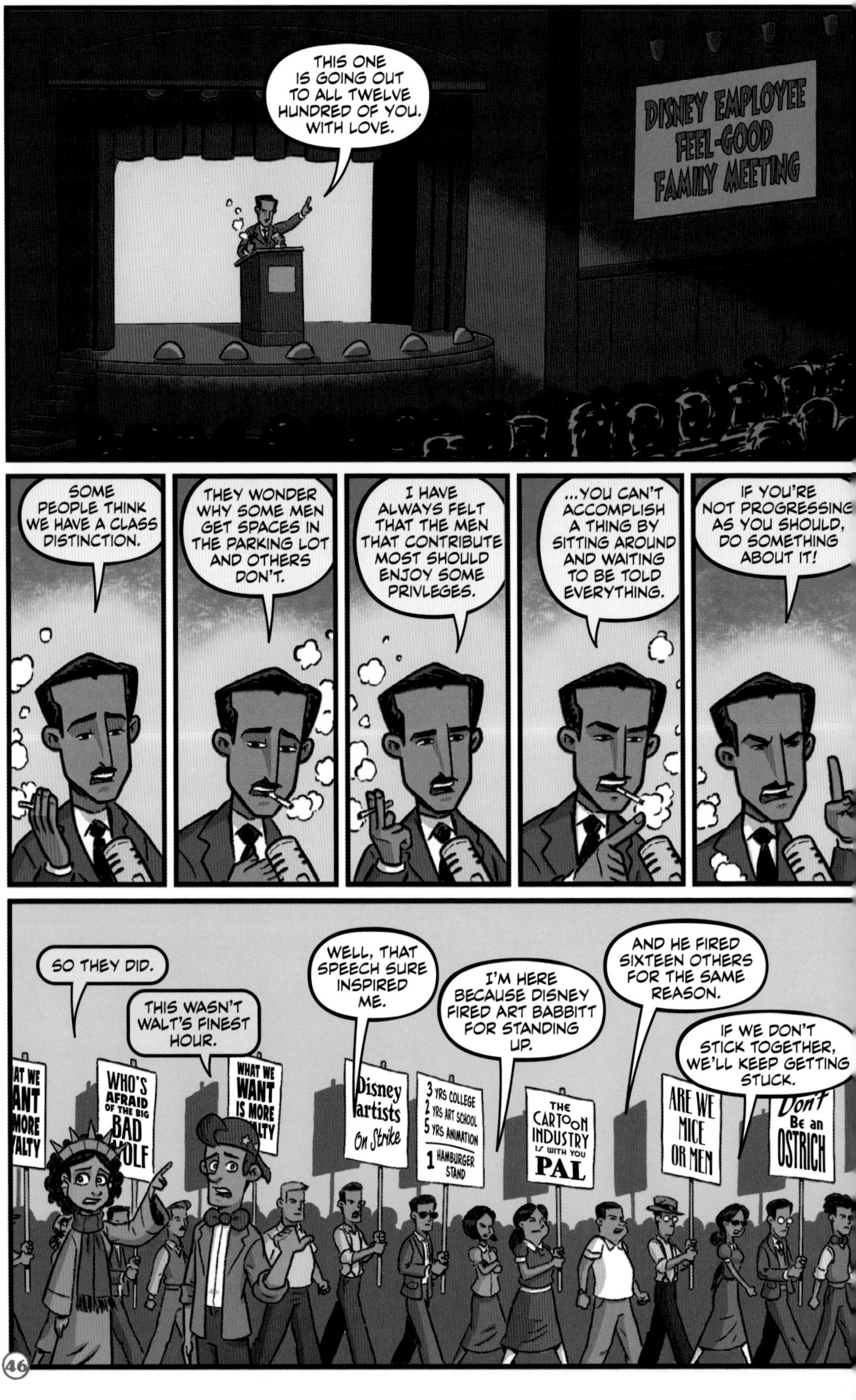
THIS ONE IS GOING OUT TO ALL TWELVE HUNDRED OF YOU. WITH LOVE.
DISNEY EMPLOYEE FEEL-GOOD FAMILY MEETING
SOME PEOPLE THINK WE HAVE A CLASS DISTINCTION.
THEY WONDER WHY SOME MEN GET SPACES IN THE PARKING LOT AND OTHERS DON'T.
I HAVE ALWAYS FELT THAT THE MEN THAT CONTRIBUTE MOST SHOULD ENJOY SOME PRIVLEGES.
...YOU CAN'T ACCOMPLISH A THING BY SITTING AROUND AND WAITING TO BE TOLD EVERYTHING.
IF YOU'RE NOT PROGRESSING AS YOU SHOULD, DO SOMETHING ABOUT IT!
SO THEY DID.
THIS WASN'T WALT'S FINEST HOUR.
WELL, THAT SPEECH SURE INSPIRED ME.
I'M HERE BECAUSE DISNEY FIRED ART BABBITT FOR STANDING UP.
AND HE FIRED SIXTEEN OTHERS FOR THE SAME REASON.
IF WE DON'T STICK TOGETHER, WE'LL KEEP GETTING STUCK.
3 YRS COLLEGE 2 YRS ART SCHOOL 5 YRS ANIMATION 1 HAMBURGER STAND
THE CARTOON INDUSTRY IS WITH YOU PAL
ARE WE MICE OR MEN

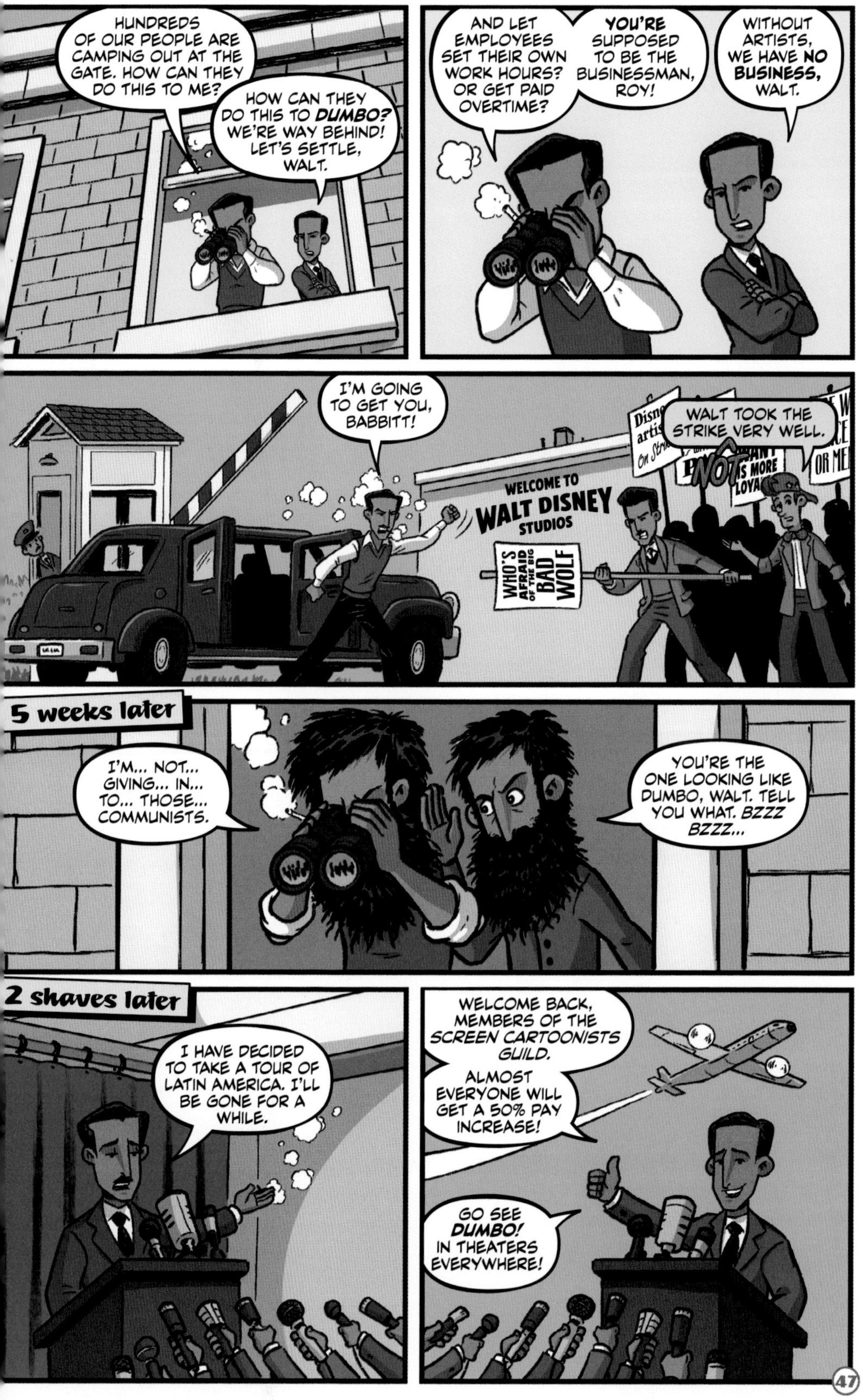
HUNDREDS OF OUR PEOPLE ARE CAMPING OUT AT THE GATE. HOW CAN THEY DO THIS TO ME?
HOW CAN THEY DO THIS TO *DUMBO?* WE'RE WAY BEHIND! LET'S SETTLE, WALT.
AND LET EMPLOYEES SET THEIR OWN WORK HOURS? OR GET PAID OVERTIME?
YOU'RE SUPPOSED TO BE THE BUSINESSMAN, ROY!
WITHOUT ARTISTS, WE HAVE **NO BUSINESS,** WALT.
I'M GOING TO GET YOU, BABBITT!
WELCOME TO WALT DISNEY STUDIOS
WHO'S AFRAID OF THE BIG BAD WOLF
WALT TOOK THE STRIKE VERY WELL.
NOT
5 weeks later
I'M... NOT... GIVING... IN... TO... THOSE... COMMUNISTS.
YOU'RE THE ONE LOOKING LIKE DUMBO, WALT. TELL YOU WHAT. *BZZZ BZZZ...*
2 shaves later
I HAVE DECIDED TO TAKE A TOUR OF LATIN AMERICA. I'LL BE GONE FOR A WHILE.
WELCOME BACK, MEMBERS OF THE *SCREEN CARTOONISTS GUILD.*
ALMOST EVERYONE WILL GET A 50% PAY INCREASE!
GO SEE ***DUMBO!*** IN THEATERS EVERYWHERE!

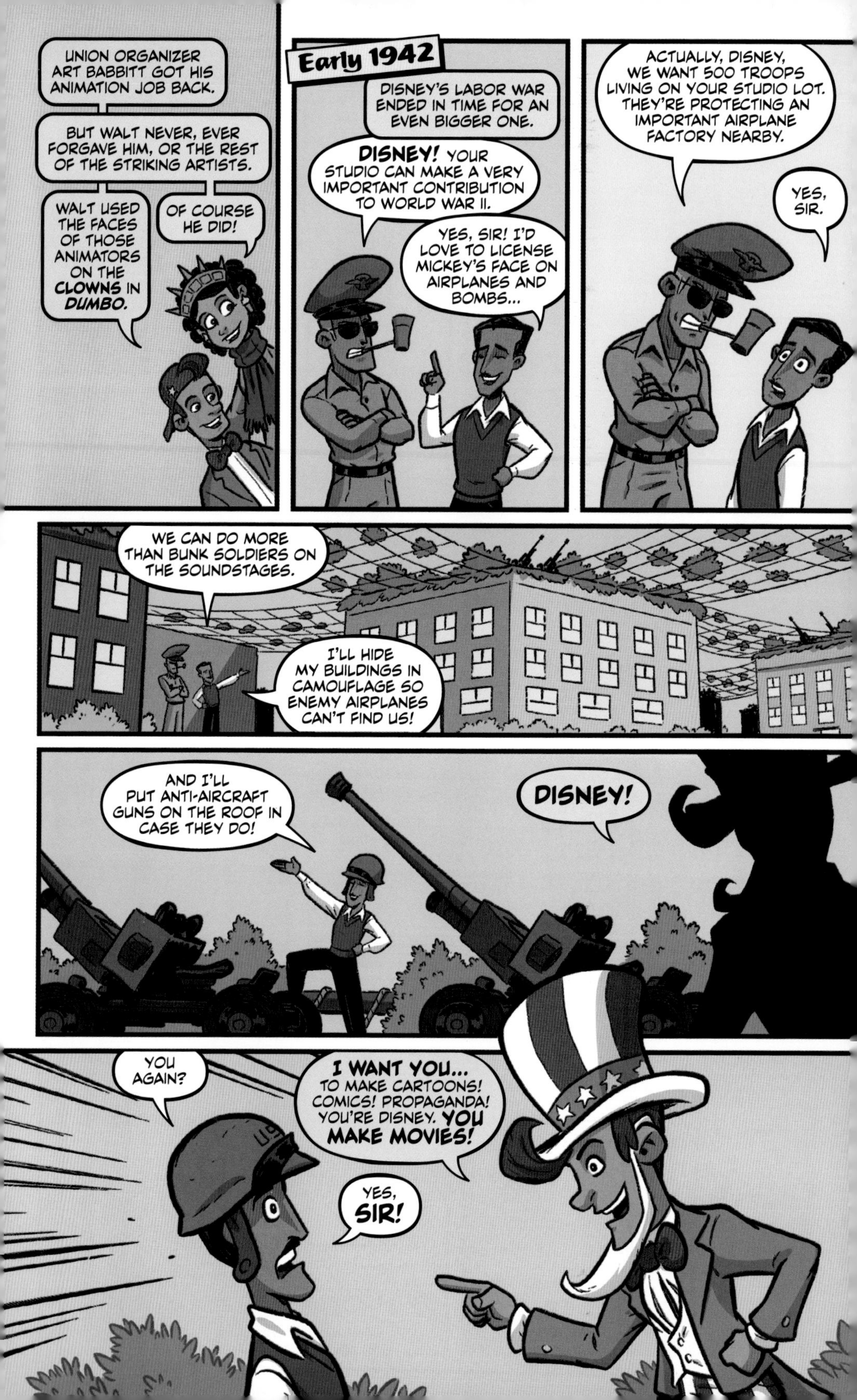
UNION ORGANIZER ART BABBITT GOT HIS ANIMATION JOB BACK.
BUT WALT NEVER, EVER FORGAVE HIM, OR THE REST OF THE STRIKING ARTISTS.
WALT USED THE FACES OF THOSE ANIMATORS ON THE CLOWNS IN DUMBO.
OF COURSE HE DID!
Early 1942
DISNEY'S LABOR WAR ENDED IN TIME FOR AN EVEN BIGGER ONE.
DISNEY! YOUR STUDIO CAN MAKE A VERY IMPORTANT CONTRIBUTION TO WORLD WAR II.
YES, SIR! I'D LOVE TO LICENSE MICKEY'S FACE ON AIRPLANES AND BOMBS...
ACTUALLY, DISNEY, WE WANT 500 TROOPS LIVING ON YOUR STUDIO LOT. THEY'RE PROTECTING AN IMPORTANT AIRPLANE FACTORY NEARBY.
YES, SIR.
WE CAN DO MORE THAN BUNK SOLDIERS ON THE SOUNDSTAGES.
I'LL HIDE MY BUILDINGS IN CAMOUFLAGE SO ENEMY AIRPLANES CAN'T FIND US!
AND I'LL PUT ANTI-AIRCRAFT GUNS ON THE ROOF IN CASE THEY DO!
DISNEY!
YOU AGAIN?
I WANT YOU... TO MAKE CARTOONS! COMICS! PROPAGANDA! YOU'RE DISNEY. YOU MAKE MOVIES!
YES, SIR!

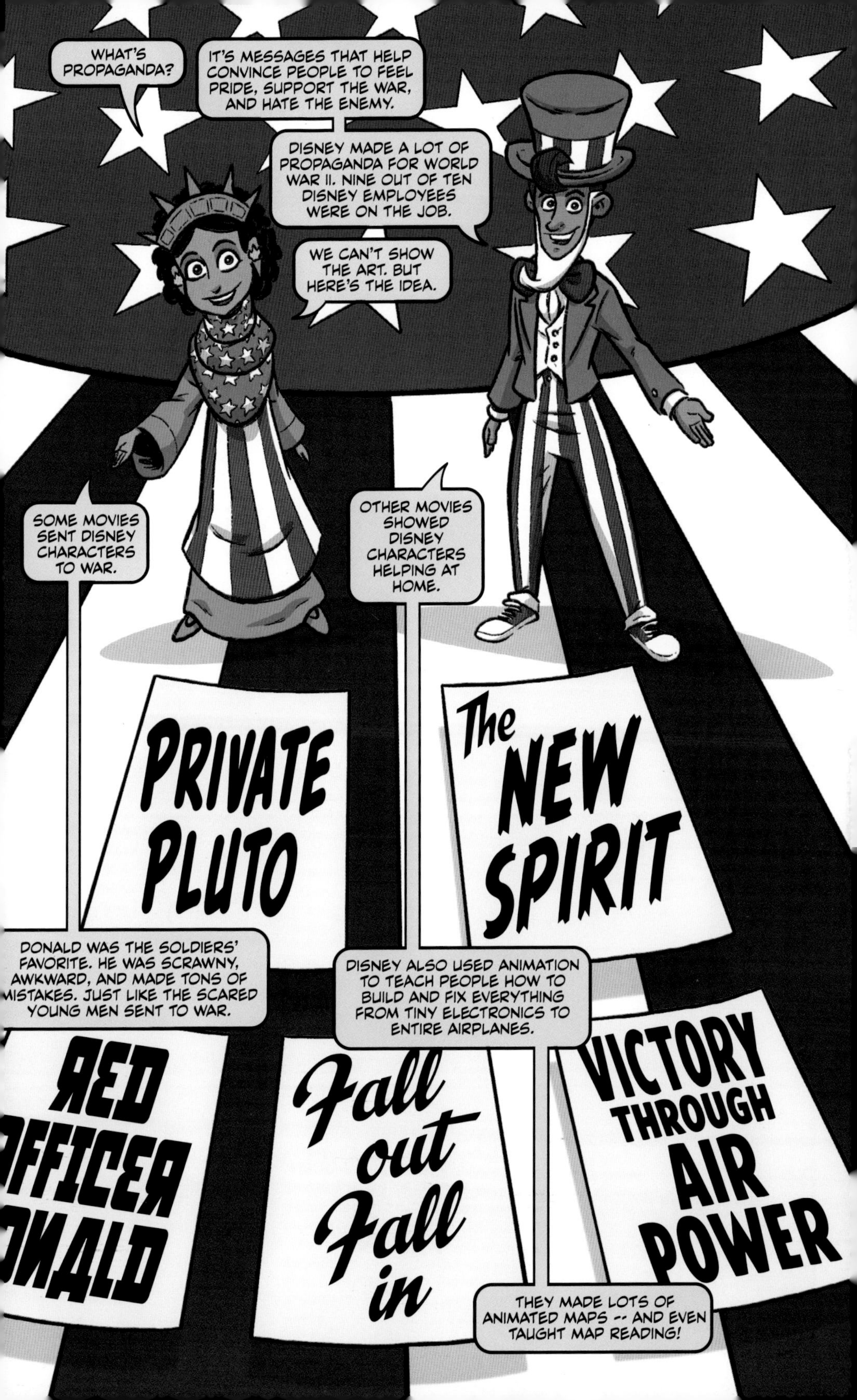

WHAT'S PROPAGANDA?
IT'S MESSAGES THAT HELP CONVINCE PEOPLE TO FEEL PRIDE, SUPPORT THE WAR, AND HATE THE ENEMY.
DISNEY MADE A LOT OF PROPAGANDA FOR WORLD WAR II. NINE OUT OF TEN DISNEY EMPLOYEES WERE ON THE JOB.
WE CAN'T SHOW THE ART. BUT HERE'S THE IDEA.
SOME MOVIES SENT DISNEY CHARACTERS TO WAR.
OTHER MOVIES SHOWED DISNEY CHARACTERS HELPING AT HOME.
PRIVATE PLUTO
The NEW SPIRIT
DONALD WAS THE SOLDIERS' FAVORITE. HE WAS SCRAWNY, AWKWARD, AND MADE TONS OF MISTAKES. JUST LIKE THE SCARED YOUNG MEN SENT TO WAR.
DISNEY ALSO USED ANIMATION TO TEACH PEOPLE HOW TO BUILD AND FIX EVERYTHING FROM TINY ELECTRONICS TO ENTIRE AIRPLANES.
Fall out Fall in
VICTORY THROUGH AIR POWER
THEY MADE LOTS OF ANIMATED MAPS -- AND EVEN TAUGHT MAP READING!

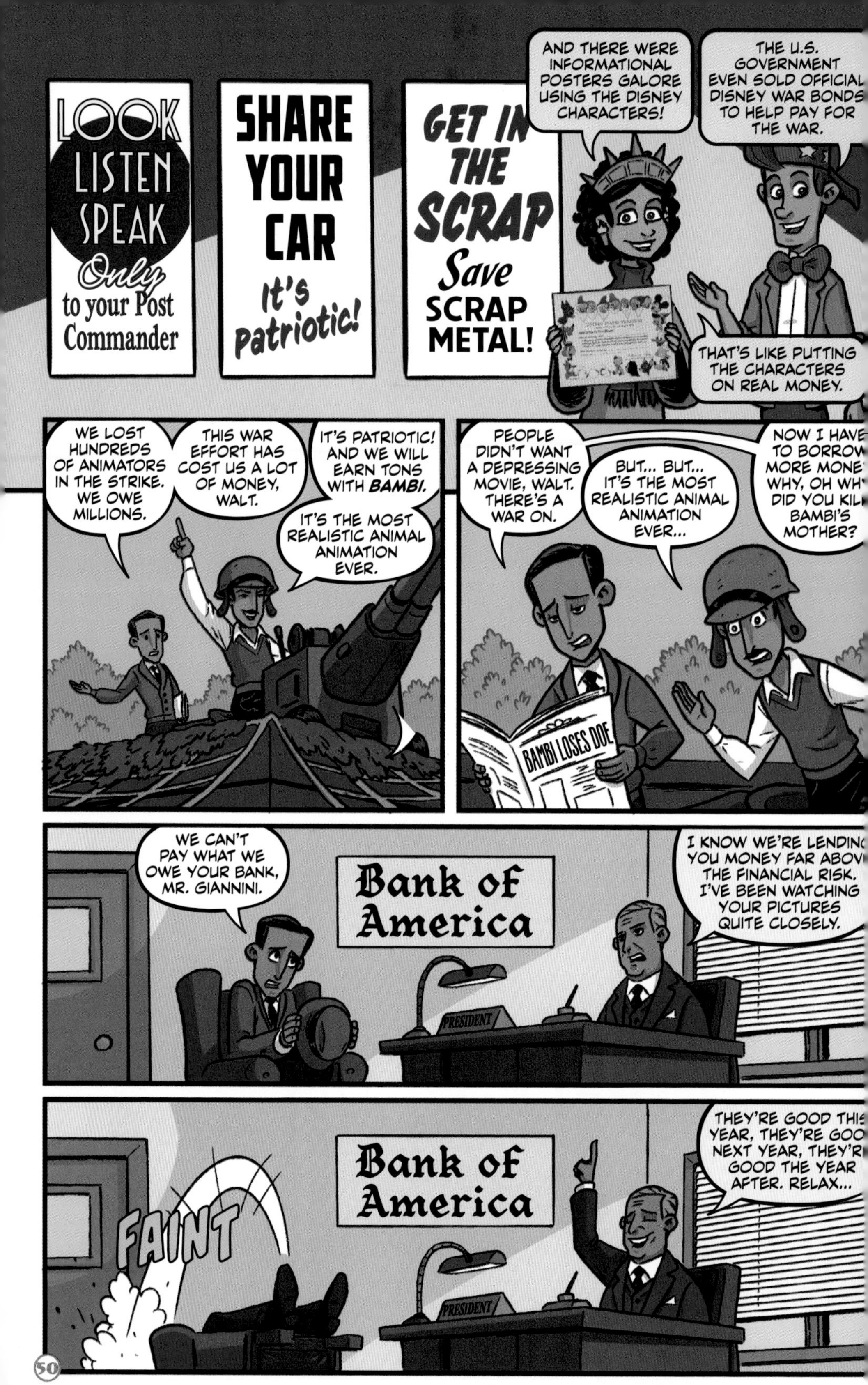
LOOK LISTEN SPEAK Only to your Post Commander
SHARE YOUR CAR It's patriotic!
GET IN THE SCRAP Save SCRAP METAL!
AND THERE WERE INFORMATIONAL POSTERS GALORE USING THE DISNEY CHARACTERS!
THE U.S. GOVERNMENT EVEN SOLD OFFICIAL DISNEY WAR BONDS TO HELP PAY FOR THE WAR.
THAT'S LIKE PUTTING THE CHARACTERS ON REAL MONEY.
WE LOST HUNDREDS OF ANIMATORS IN THE STRIKE. WE OWE MILLIONS.
THIS WAR EFFORT HAS COST US A LOT OF MONEY, WALT.
IT'S PATRIOTIC! AND WE WILL EARN TONS WITH BAMBI.
IT'S THE MOST REALISTIC ANIMAL ANIMATION EVER.
PEOPLE DIDN'T WANT A DEPRESSING MOVIE, WALT. THERE'S A WAR ON.
BUT... BUT... IT'S THE MOST REALISTIC ANIMAL ANIMATION EVER...
NOW I HAVE TO BORROW MORE MONE WHY, OH WH DID YOU KIL BAMBI'S MOTHER?
BAMBI LOSES DOE
WE CAN'T PAY WHAT WE OWE YOUR BANK, MR. GIANNINI.
Bank of America
I KNOW WE'RE LENDIN YOU MONEY FAR ABOV THE FINANCIAL RISK. I'VE BEEN WATCHING YOUR PICTURES QUITE CLOSELY.
PRESIDENT
FAINT
Bank of America
THEY'RE GOOD THIS YEAR, THEY'RE GOO NEXT YEAR, THEY'R GOOD THE YEAR AFTER. RELAX...
PRESIDENT

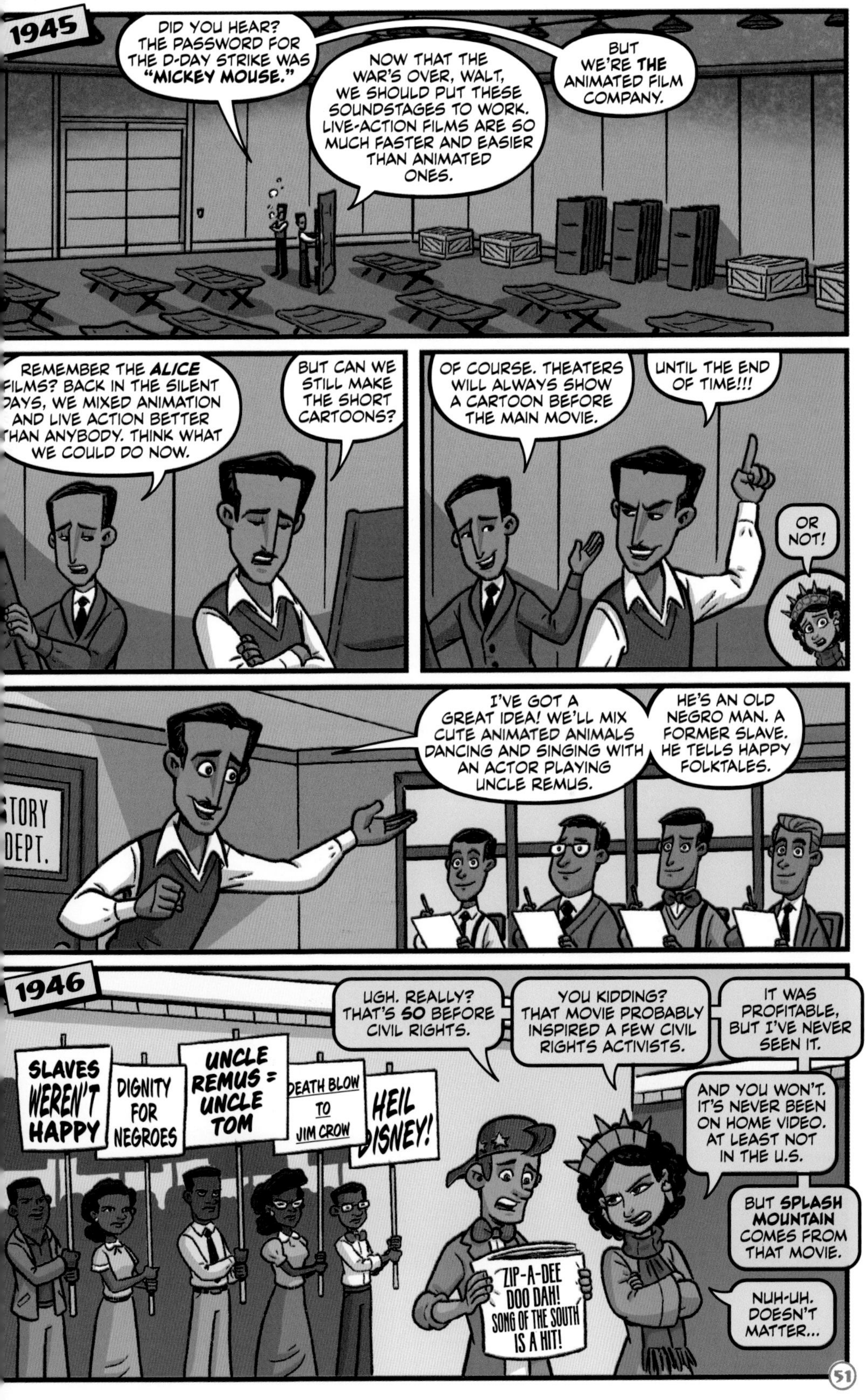
1945
DID YOU HEAR? THE PASSWORD FOR THE D-DAY STRIKE WAS "MICKEY MOUSE."
BUT WE'RE THE ANIMATED FILM COMPANY.
NOW THAT THE WAR'S OVER, WALT, WE SHOULD PUT THESE SOUNDSTAGES TO WORK. LIVE-ACTION FILMS ARE SO MUCH FASTER AND EASIER THAN ANIMATED ONES.
REMEMBER THE ALICE FILMS? BACK IN THE SILENT DAYS, WE MIXED ANIMATION AND LIVE ACTION BETTER THAN ANYBODY. THINK WHAT WE COULD DO NOW.
BUT CAN WE STILL MAKE THE SHORT CARTOONS?
OF COURSE. THEATERS WILL ALWAYS SHOW A CARTOON BEFORE THE MAIN MOVIE.
UNTIL THE END OF TIME!!!
OR NOT!
TORY DEPT.
I'VE GOT A GREAT IDEA! WE'LL MIX CUTE ANIMATED ANIMALS DANCING AND SINGING WITH AN ACTOR PLAYING UNCLE REMUS.
HE'S AN OLD NEGRO MAN. A FORMER SLAVE. HE TELLS HAPPY FOLKTALES.
1946
SLAVES WEREN'T HAPPY
DIGNITY FOR NEGROES
UNCLE REMUS = UNCLE TOM
DEATH BLOW TO JIM CROW
HEIL DISNEY!
UGH. REALLY? THAT'S SO BEFORE CIVIL RIGHTS.
YOU KIDDING? THAT MOVIE PROBABLY INSPIRED A FEW CIVIL RIGHTS ACTIVISTS.
IT WAS PROFITABLE, BUT I'VE NEVER SEEN IT.
AND YOU WON'T. IT'S NEVER BEEN ON HOME VIDEO. AT LEAST NOT IN THE U.S.
BUT SPLASH MOUNTAIN COMES FROM THAT MOVIE.
NUH-UH. DOESN'T MATTER...
ZIP-A-DEE DOO DAH! SONG OF THE SOUTH IS A HIT!

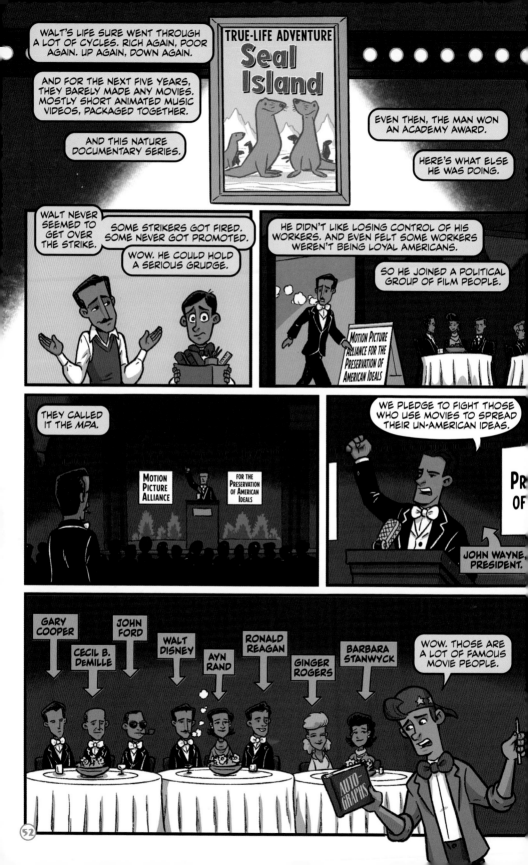

WALT'S LIFE SURE WENT THROUGH A LOT OF CYCLES. RICH AGAIN, POOR AGAIN. UP AGAIN, DOWN AGAIN.

AND FOR THE NEXT FIVE YEARS, THEY BARELY MADE ANY MOVIES. MOSTLY SHORT ANIMATED MUSIC VIDEOS, PACKAGED TOGETHER.

AND THIS NATURE DOCUMENTARY SERIES.

TRUE-LIFE ADVENTURE
Seal Island

EVEN THEN, THE MAN WON AN ACADEMY AWARD.

HERE'S WHAT ELSE HE WAS DOING.

WALT NEVER SEEMED TO GET OVER THE STRIKE.

SOME STRIKERS GOT FIRED. SOME NEVER GOT PROMOTED.

WOW. HE COULD HOLD A SERIOUS GRUDGE.

HE DIDN'T LIKE LOSING CONTROL OF HIS WORKERS. AND EVEN FELT SOME WORKERS WEREN'T BEING LOYAL AMERICANS.

SO HE JOINED A POLITICAL GROUP OF FILM PEOPLE.

MOTION PICTURE ALLIANCE FOR THE PRESERVATION OF AMERICAN IDEALS

THEY CALLED IT THE MPA.

MOTION PICTURE ALLIANCE   FOR THE PRESERVATION OF AMERICAN IDEALS

WE PLEDGE TO FIGHT THOSE WHO USE MOVIES TO SPREAD THEIR UN-AMERICAN IDEAS.

PR
OF

JOHN WAYNE, PRESIDENT.

GARY COOPER

JOHN FORD

CECIL B. DeMILLE

WALT DISNEY

AYN RAND

RONALD REAGAN

GINGER ROGERS

BARBARA STANWYCK

WOW. THOSE ARE A LOT OF FAMOUS MOVIE PEOPLE.

AUTO-GRAPHS

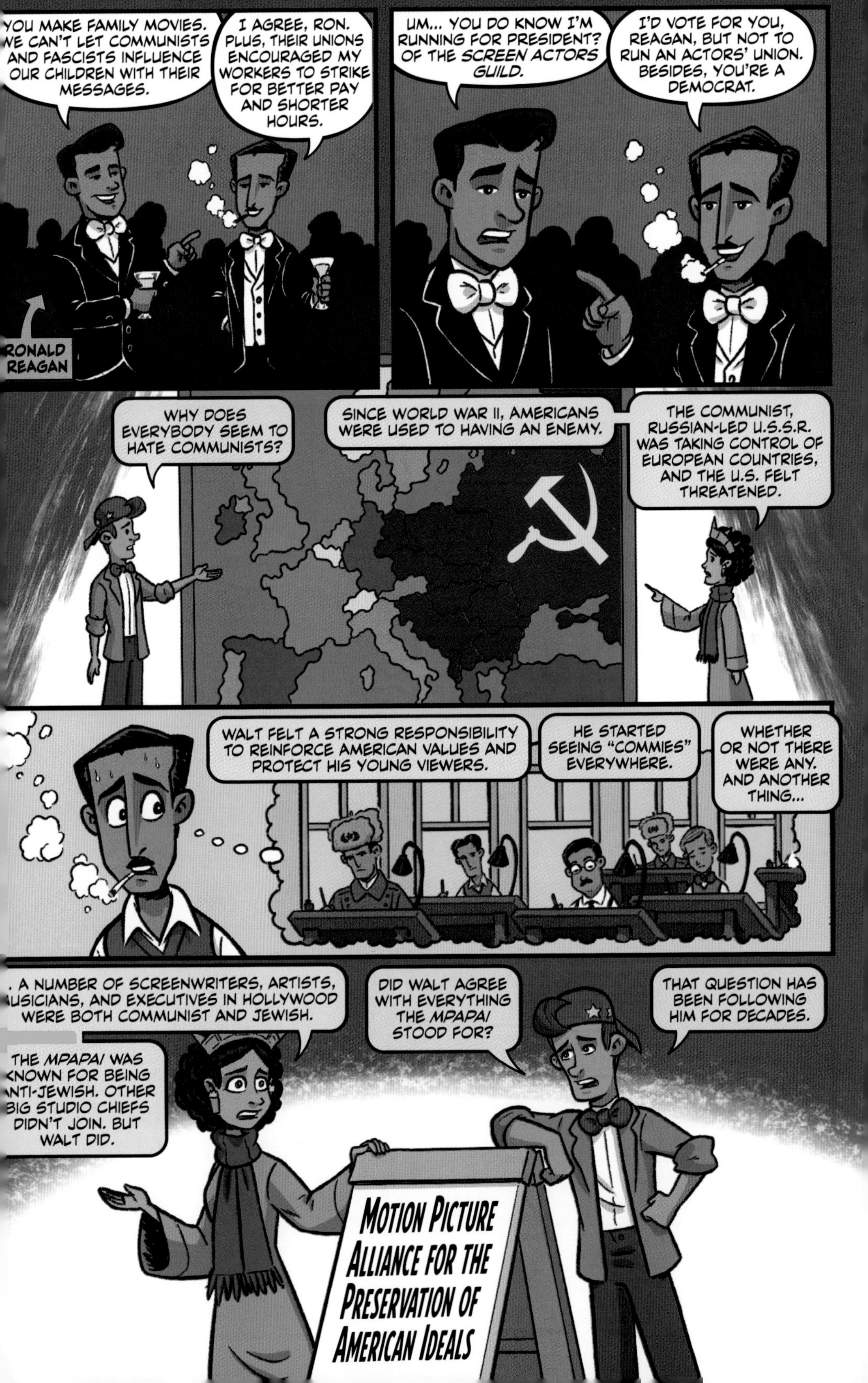
YOU MAKE FAMILY MOVIES. WE CAN'T LET COMMUNISTS AND FASCISTS INFLUENCE OUR CHILDREN WITH THEIR MESSAGES.
I AGREE, RON. PLUS, THEIR UNIONS ENCOURAGED MY WORKERS TO STRIKE FOR BETTER PAY AND SHORTER HOURS.
RONALD REAGAN
UM... YOU DO KNOW I'M RUNNING FOR PRESIDENT? OF THE *SCREEN ACTORS GUILD.*
I'D VOTE FOR YOU, REAGAN, BUT NOT TO RUN AN ACTORS' UNION. BESIDES, YOU'RE A DEMOCRAT.
WHY DOES EVERYBODY SEEM TO HATE COMMUNISTS?
SINCE WORLD WAR II, AMERICANS WERE USED TO HAVING AN ENEMY.
THE COMMUNIST, RUSSIAN-LED U.S.S.R. WAS TAKING CONTROL OF EUROPEAN COUNTRIES, AND THE U.S. FELT THREATENED.
WALT FELT A STRONG RESPONSIBILITY TO REINFORCE AMERICAN VALUES AND PROTECT HIS YOUNG VIEWERS.
HE STARTED SEEING "COMMIES" EVERYWHERE.
WHETHER OR NOT THERE WERE ANY. AND ANOTHER THING...
... A NUMBER OF SCREENWRITERS, ARTISTS, MUSICIANS, AND EXECUTIVES IN HOLLYWOOD WERE BOTH COMMUNIST AND JEWISH.
THE *MPAPAI* WAS KNOWN FOR BEING ANTI-JEWISH. OTHER BIG STUDIO CHIEFS DIDN'T JOIN. BUT WALT DID.
DID WALT AGREE WITH EVERYTHING THE *MPAPAI* STOOD FOR?
THAT QUESTION HAS BEEN FOLLOWING HIM FOR DECADES.
MOTION PICTURE ALLIANCE FOR THE PRESERVATION OF AMERICAN IDEALS

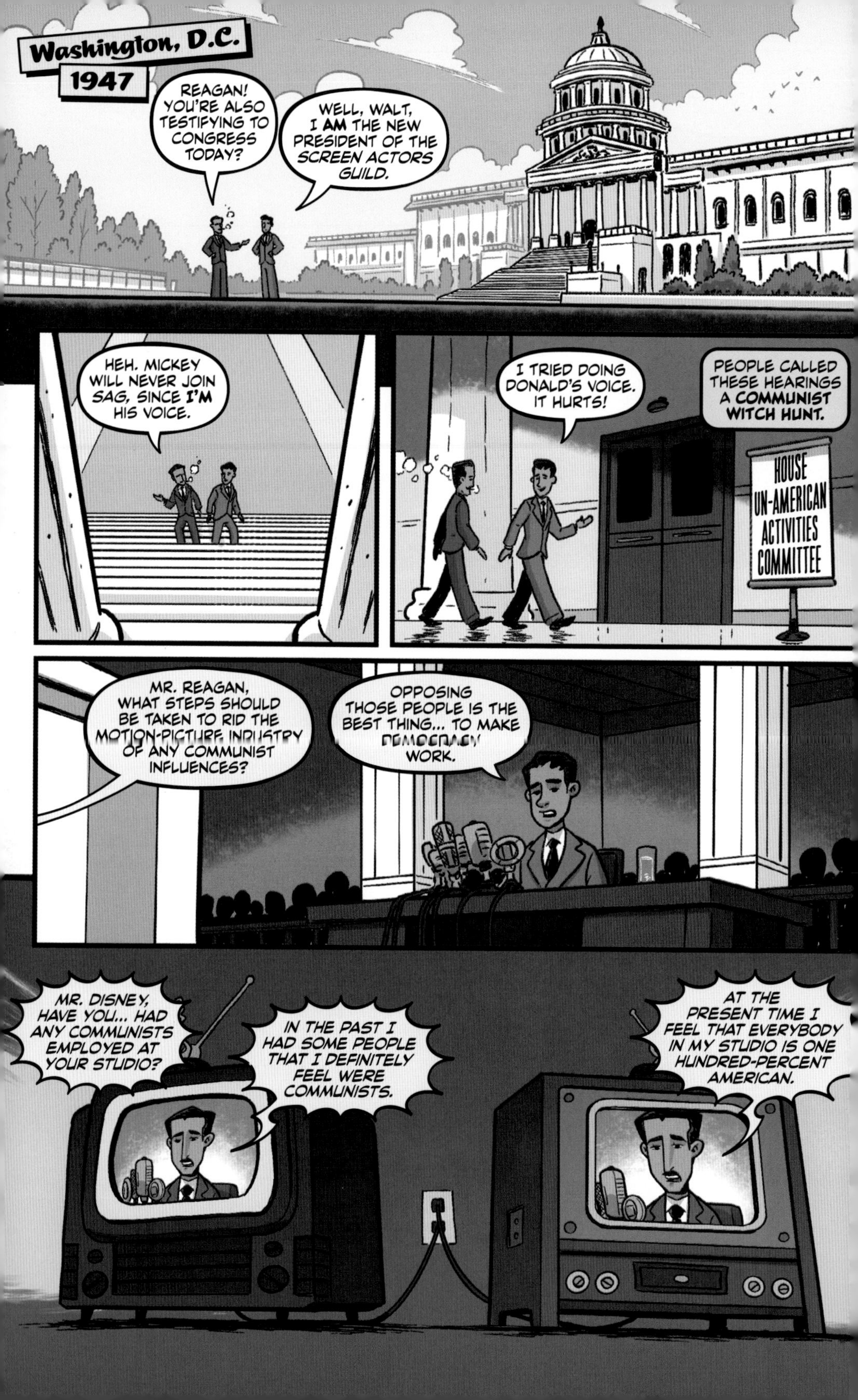
Washington, D.C.
1947
REAGAN! YOU'RE ALSO TESTIFYING TO CONGRESS TODAY?
WELL, WALT, I AM THE NEW PRESIDENT OF THE SCREEN ACTORS GUILD.
HEH. MICKEY WILL NEVER JOIN SAG, SINCE I'M HIS VOICE.
I TRIED DOING DONALD'S VOICE. IT HURTS!
PEOPLE CALLED THESE HEARINGS A COMMUNIST WITCH HUNT.
HOUSE UN-AMERICAN ACTIVITIES COMMITTEE
MR. REAGAN, WHAT STEPS SHOULD BE TAKEN TO RID THE MOTION-PICTURE INDUSTRY OF ANY COMMUNIST INFLUENCES?
OPPOSING THOSE PEOPLE IS THE BEST THING... TO MAKE DEMOCRACY WORK.
MR. DISNEY, HAVE YOU... HAD ANY COMMUNISTS EMPLOYED AT YOUR STUDIO?
IN THE PAST I HAD SOME PEOPLE THAT I DEFINITELY FEEL WERE COMMUNISTS.
AT THE PRESENT TIME I FEEL THAT EVERYBODY IN MY STUDIO IS ONE HUNDRED-PERCENT AMERICAN.

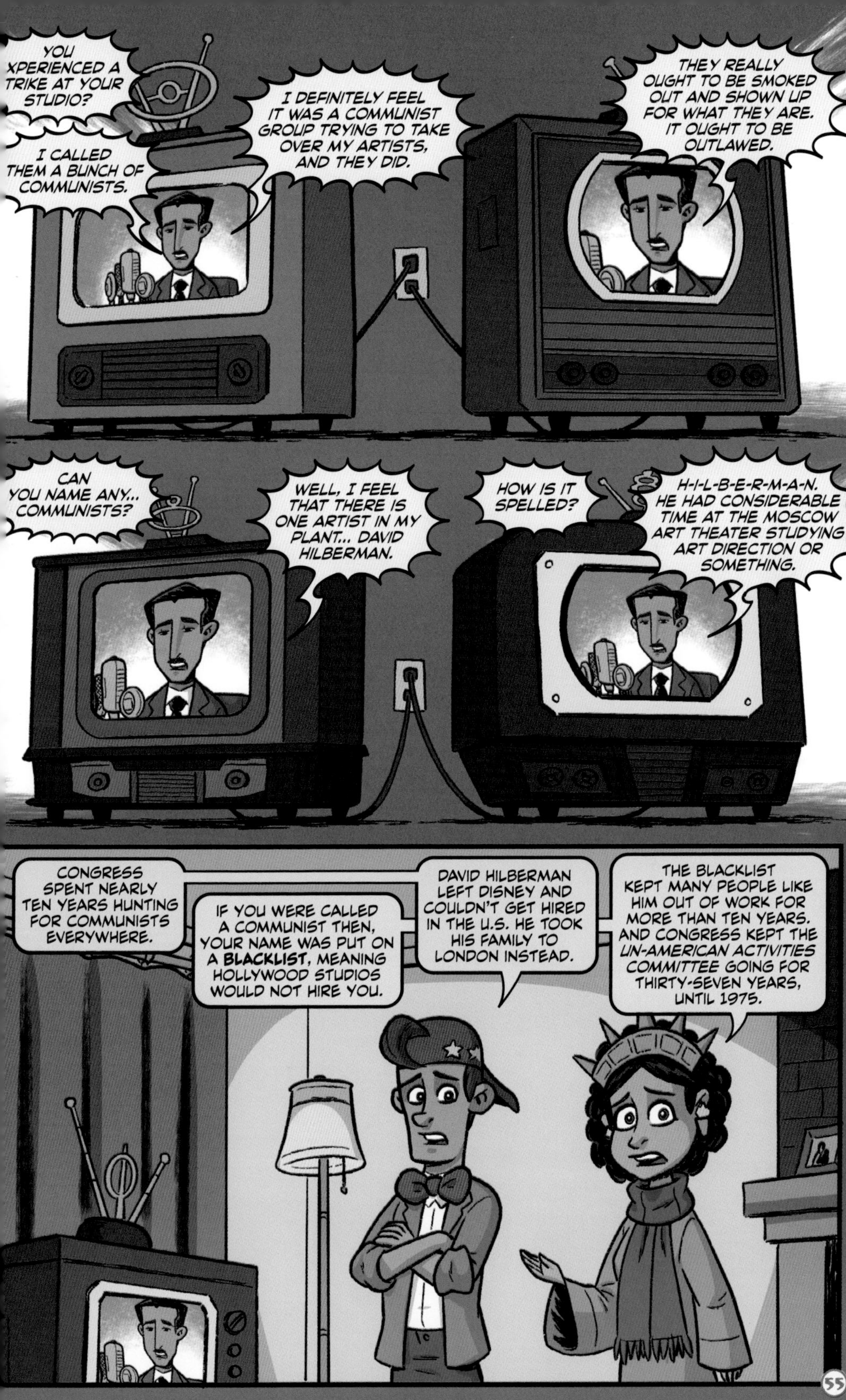
YOU XPERIENCED A TRIKE AT YOUR STUDIO?
I CALLED THEM A BUNCH OF COMMUNISTS.
I DEFINITELY FEEL IT WAS A COMMUNIST GROUP TRYING TO TAKE OVER MY ARTISTS, AND THEY DID.
THEY REALLY OUGHT TO BE SMOKED OUT AND SHOWN UP FOR WHAT THEY ARE. IT OUGHT TO BE OUTLAWED.
CAN YOU NAME ANY... COMMUNISTS?
WELL, I FEEL THAT THERE IS ONE ARTIST IN MY PLANT... DAVID HILBERMAN.
HOW IS IT SPELLED?
H-I-L-B-E-R-M-A-N. HE HAD CONSIDERABLE TIME AT THE MOSCOW ART THEATER STUDYING ART DIRECTION OR SOMETHING.
CONGRESS SPENT NEARLY TEN YEARS HUNTING FOR COMMUNISTS EVERYWHERE.
IF YOU WERE CALLED A COMMUNIST THEN, YOUR NAME WAS PUT ON A **BLACKLIST**, MEANING HOLLYWOOD STUDIOS WOULD NOT HIRE YOU.
DAVID HILBERMAN LEFT DISNEY AND COULDN'T GET HIRED IN THE U.S. HE TOOK HIS FAMILY TO LONDON INSTEAD.
THE BLACKLIST KEPT MANY PEOPLE LIKE HIM OUT OF WORK FOR MORE THAN TEN YEARS. AND CONGRESS KEPT THE *UN-AMERICAN ACTIVITIES COMMITTEE* GOING FOR THIRTY-SEVEN YEARS, UNTIL 1975.

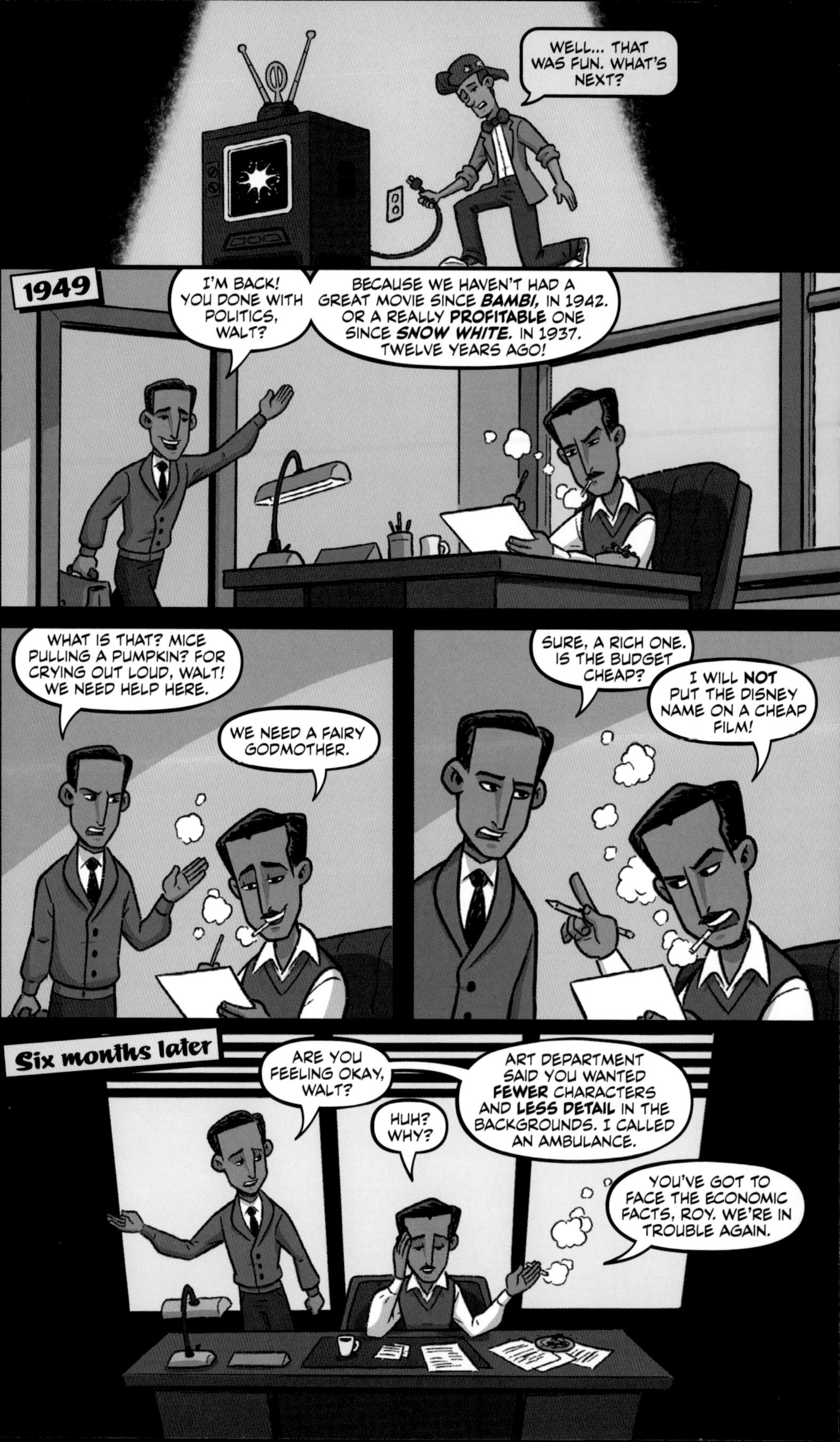
WELL... THAT WAS FUN. WHAT'S NEXT?
1949
I'M BACK! YOU DONE WITH POLITICS, WALT?
BECAUSE WE HAVEN'T HAD A GREAT MOVIE SINCE **BAMBI,** IN 1942. OR A REALLY **PROFITABLE** ONE SINCE **SNOW WHITE.** IN 1937. TWELVE YEARS AGO!
WHAT IS THAT? MICE PULLING A PUMPKIN? FOR CRYING OUT LOUD, WALT! WE NEED HELP HERE.
WE NEED A FAIRY GODMOTHER.
SURE, A RICH ONE. IS THE BUDGET CHEAP?
I WILL **NOT** PUT THE DISNEY NAME ON A CHEAP FILM!
Six months later
ARE YOU FEELING OKAY, WALT?
ART DEPARTMENT SAID YOU WANTED **FEWER** CHARACTERS AND **LESS DETAIL** IN THE BACKGROUNDS. I CALLED AN AMBULANCE.
HUH? WHY?
YOU'VE GOT TO FACE THE ECONOMIC FACTS, ROY. WE'RE IN TROUBLE AGAIN.

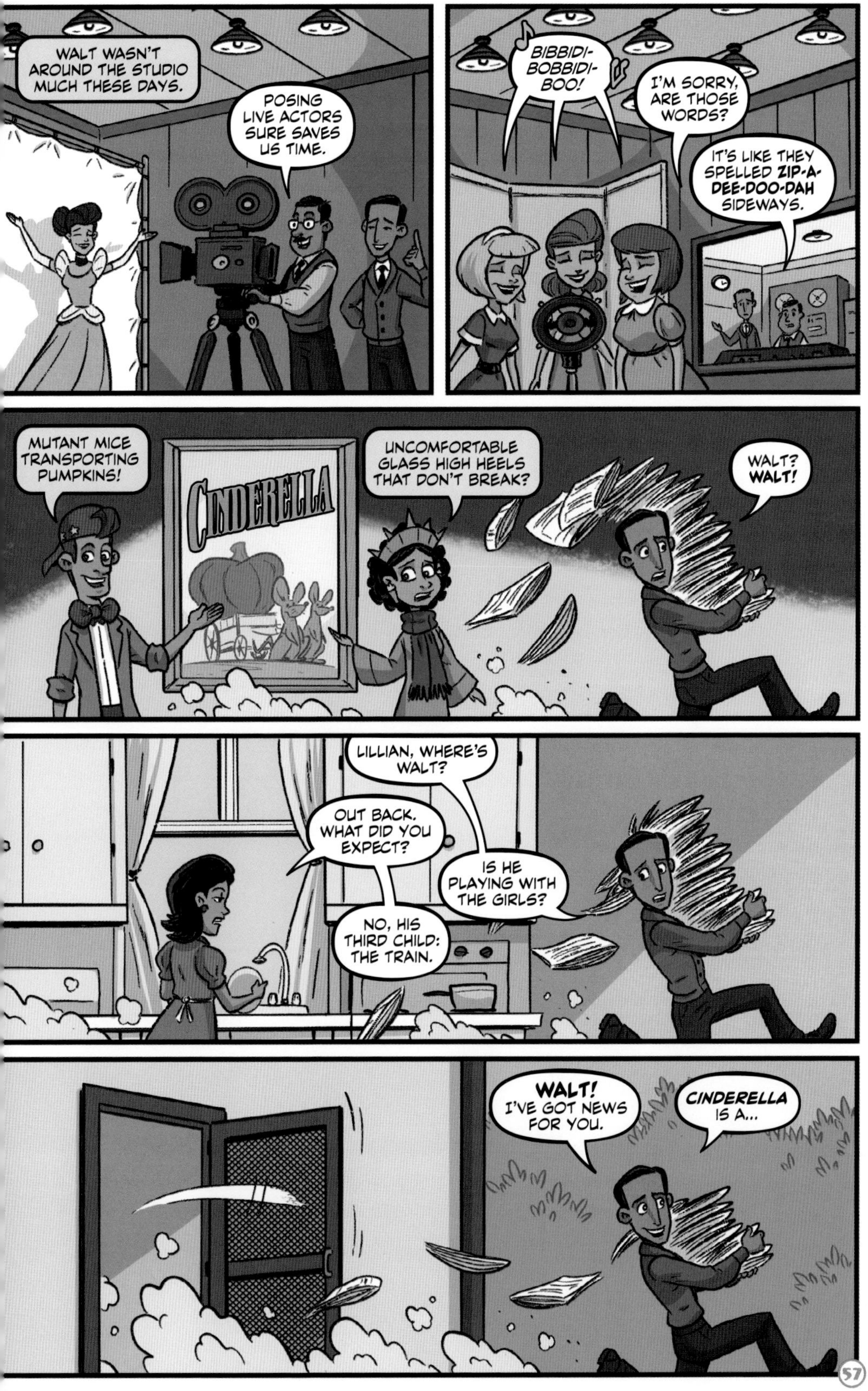
WALT WASN'T AROUND THE STUDIO MUCH THESE DAYS.
POSING LIVE ACTORS SURE SAVES US TIME.
BIBBIDI-BOBBIDI-BOO!
I'M SORRY, ARE THOSE WORDS?
IT'S LIKE THEY SPELLED ZIP-A-DEE-DOO-DAH SIDEWAYS.
MUTANT MICE TRANSPORTING PUMPKINS!
CINDERELLA
UNCOMFORTABLE GLASS HIGH HEELS THAT DON'T BREAK?
WALT? WALT!
LILLIAN, WHERE'S WALT?
OUT BACK. WHAT DID YOU EXPECT?
IS HE PLAYING WITH THE GIRLS?
NO, HIS THIRD CHILD: THE TRAIN.
WALT! I'VE GOT NEWS FOR YOU.
CINDERELLA IS A...

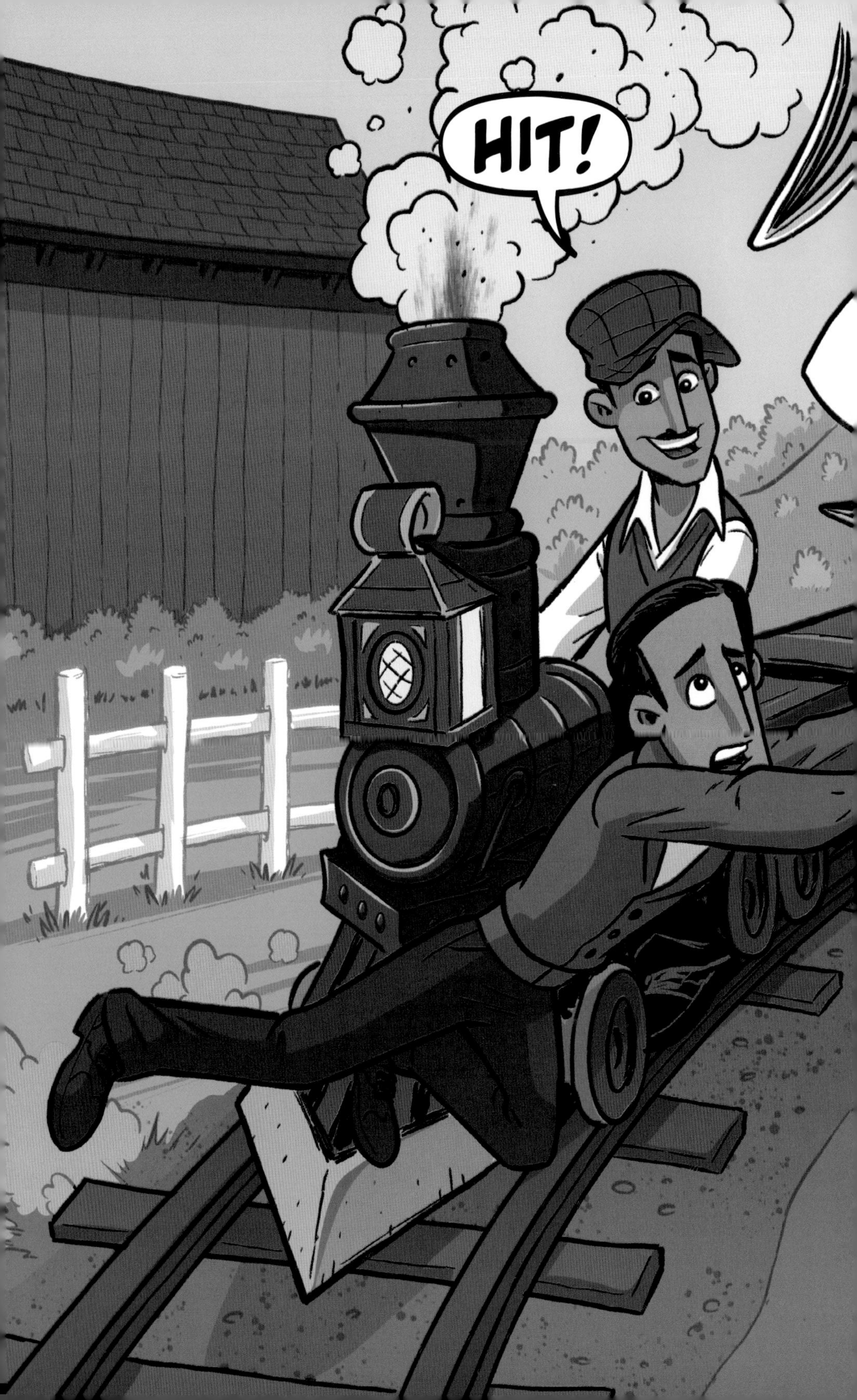
HIT!

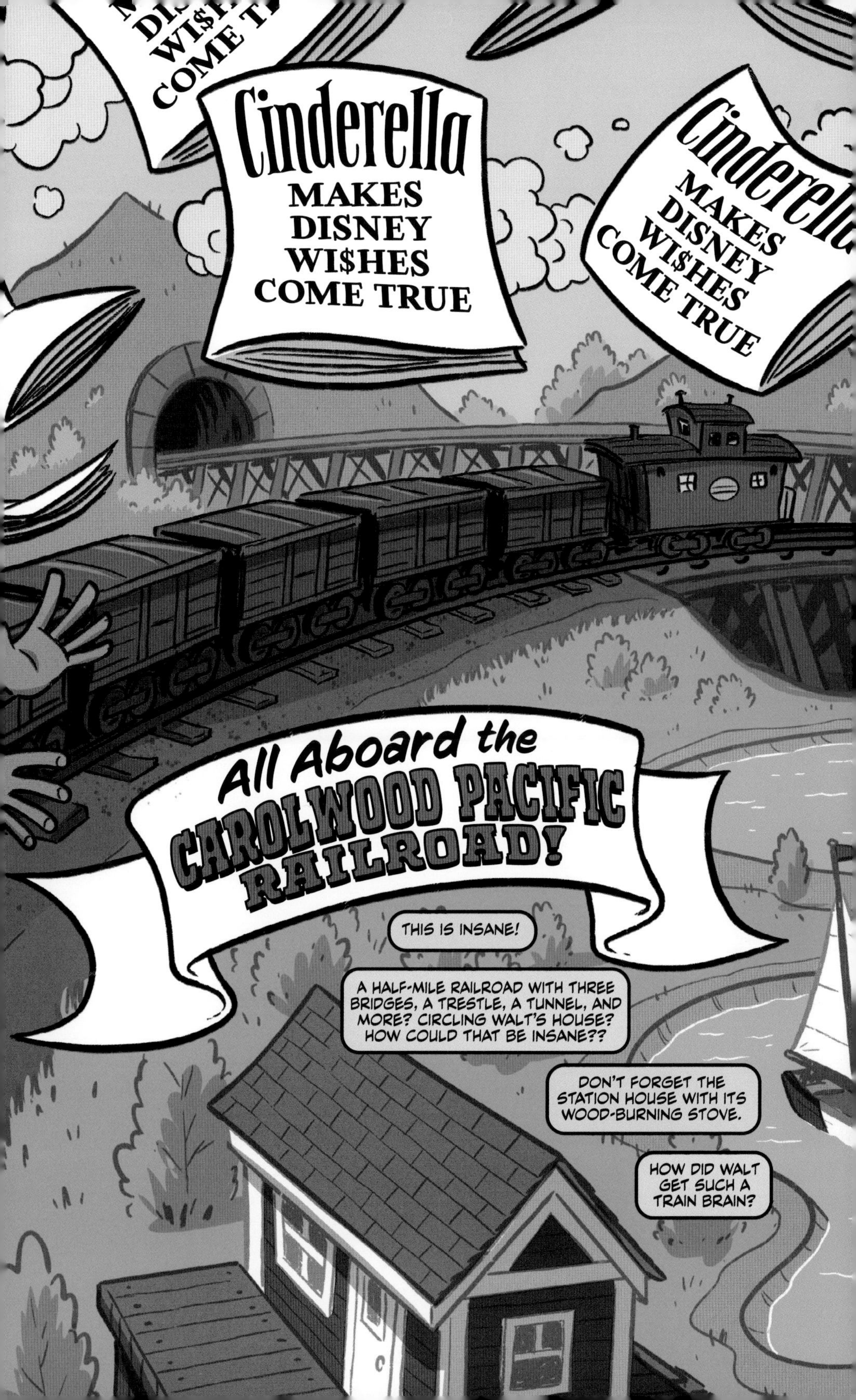
Cinderella
MAKES
DISNEY
WI$HES
COME TRUE
Cinderella
MAKES
DISNEY
WI$HES
COME TRUE
All Aboard the
CAROLWOOD PACIFIC
RAILROAD!
THIS IS INSANE!
A HALF-MILE RAILROAD WITH THREE BRIDGES, A TRESTLE, A TUNNEL, AND MORE? CIRCLING WALT'S HOUSE? HOW COULD THAT BE INSANE??
DON'T FORGET THE STATION HOUSE WITH ITS WOOD-BURNING STOVE.
HOW DID WALT GET SUCH A TRAIN BRAIN?

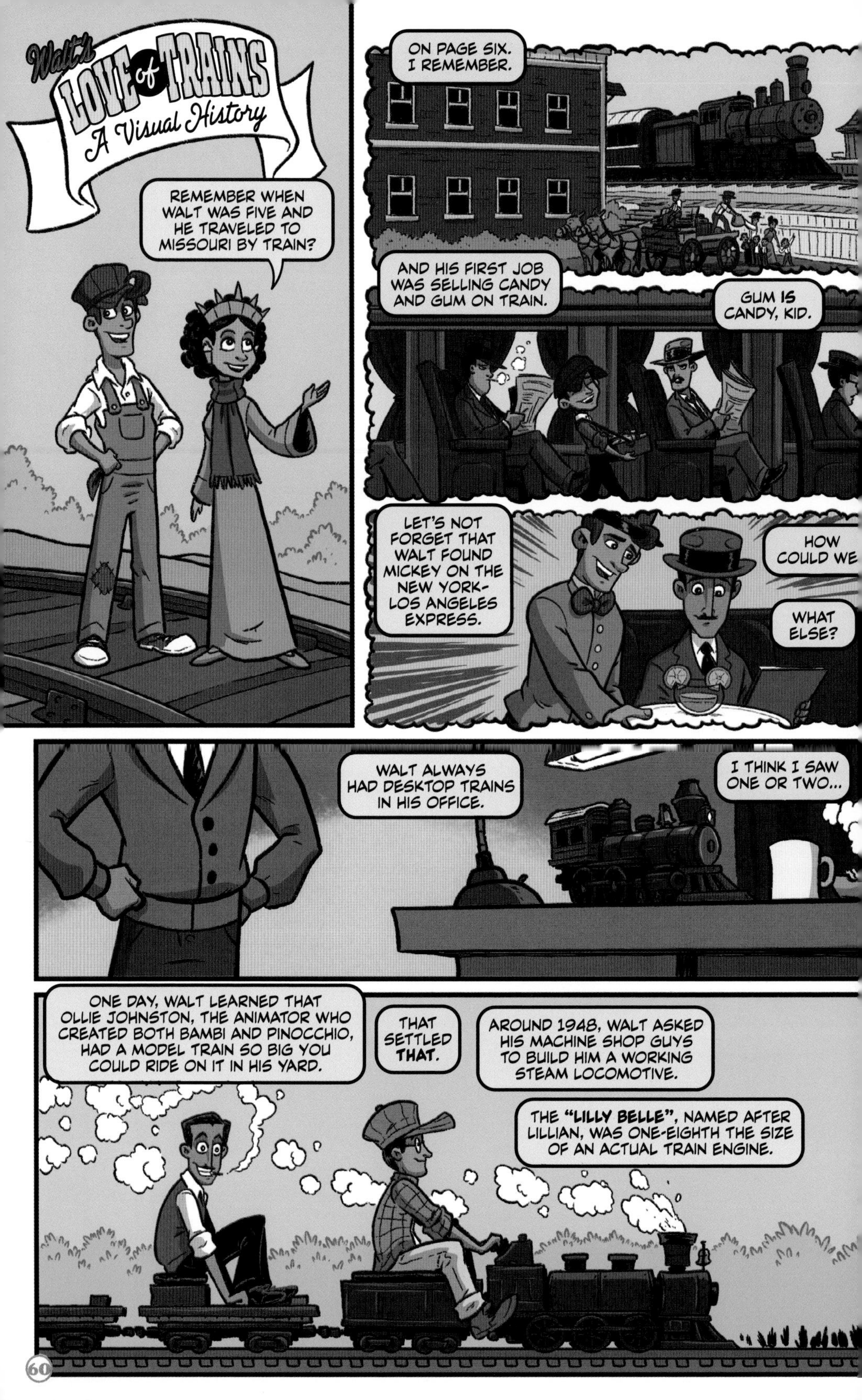
Walt's LOVE of TRAINS A Visual History
REMEMBER WHEN WALT WAS FIVE AND HE TRAVELED TO MISSOURI BY TRAIN?
ON PAGE SIX. I REMEMBER.
AND HIS FIRST JOB WAS SELLING CANDY AND GUM ON TRAIN.
GUM IS CANDY, KID.
LET'S NOT FORGET THAT WALT FOUND MICKEY ON THE NEW YORK-LOS ANGELES EXPRESS.
HOW COULD WE
WHAT ELSE?
WALT ALWAYS HAD DESKTOP TRAINS IN HIS OFFICE.
I THINK I SAW ONE OR TWO...
ONE DAY, WALT LEARNED THAT OLLIE JOHNSTON, THE ANIMATOR WHO CREATED BOTH BAMBI AND PINOCCHIO, HAD A MODEL TRAIN SO BIG YOU COULD RIDE ON IT IN HIS YARD.
THAT SETTLED THAT.
AROUND 1948, WALT ASKED HIS MACHINE SHOP GUYS TO BUILD HIM A WORKING STEAM LOCOMOTIVE.
THE "LILLY BELLE", NAMED AFTER LILLIAN, WAS ONE-EIGHTH THE SIZE OF AN ACTUAL TRAIN ENGINE.

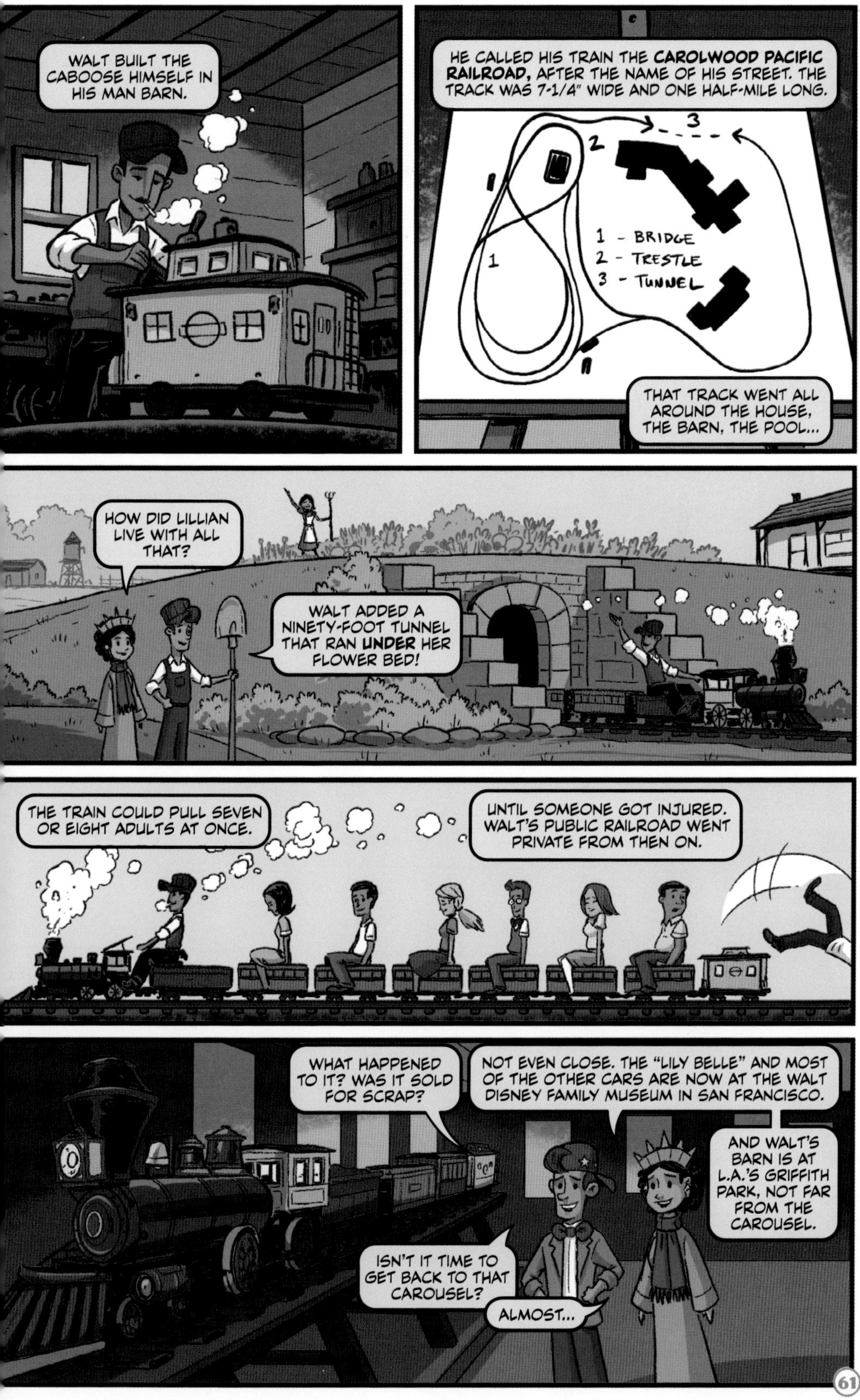
WALT BUILT THE CABOOSE HIMSELF IN HIS MAN BARN.
HE CALLED HIS TRAIN THE **CAROLWOOD PACIFIC RAILROAD,** AFTER THE NAME OF HIS STREET. THE TRACK WAS 7-1/4" WIDE AND ONE HALF-MILE LONG.
3
2
1
1
1 - BRIDGE
2 - TRESTLE
3 - TUNNEL
THAT TRACK WENT ALL AROUND THE HOUSE, THE BARN, THE POOL...
HOW DID LILLIAN LIVE WITH ALL THAT?
WALT ADDED A NINETY-FOOT TUNNEL THAT RAN **UNDER** HER FLOWER BED!
THE TRAIN COULD PULL SEVEN OR EIGHT ADULTS AT ONCE.
UNTIL SOMEONE GOT INJURED. WALT'S PUBLIC RAILROAD WENT PRIVATE FROM THEN ON.
WHAT HAPPENED TO IT? WAS IT SOLD FOR SCRAP?
NOT EVEN CLOSE. THE "LILY BELLE" AND MOST OF THE OTHER CARS ARE NOW AT THE WALT DISNEY FAMILY MUSEUM IN SAN FRANCISCO.
AND WALT'S BARN IS AT L.A.'S GRIFFITH PARK, NOT FAR FROM THE CAROUSEL.
ISN'T IT TIME TO GET BACK TO THAT CAROUSEL?
ALMOST...

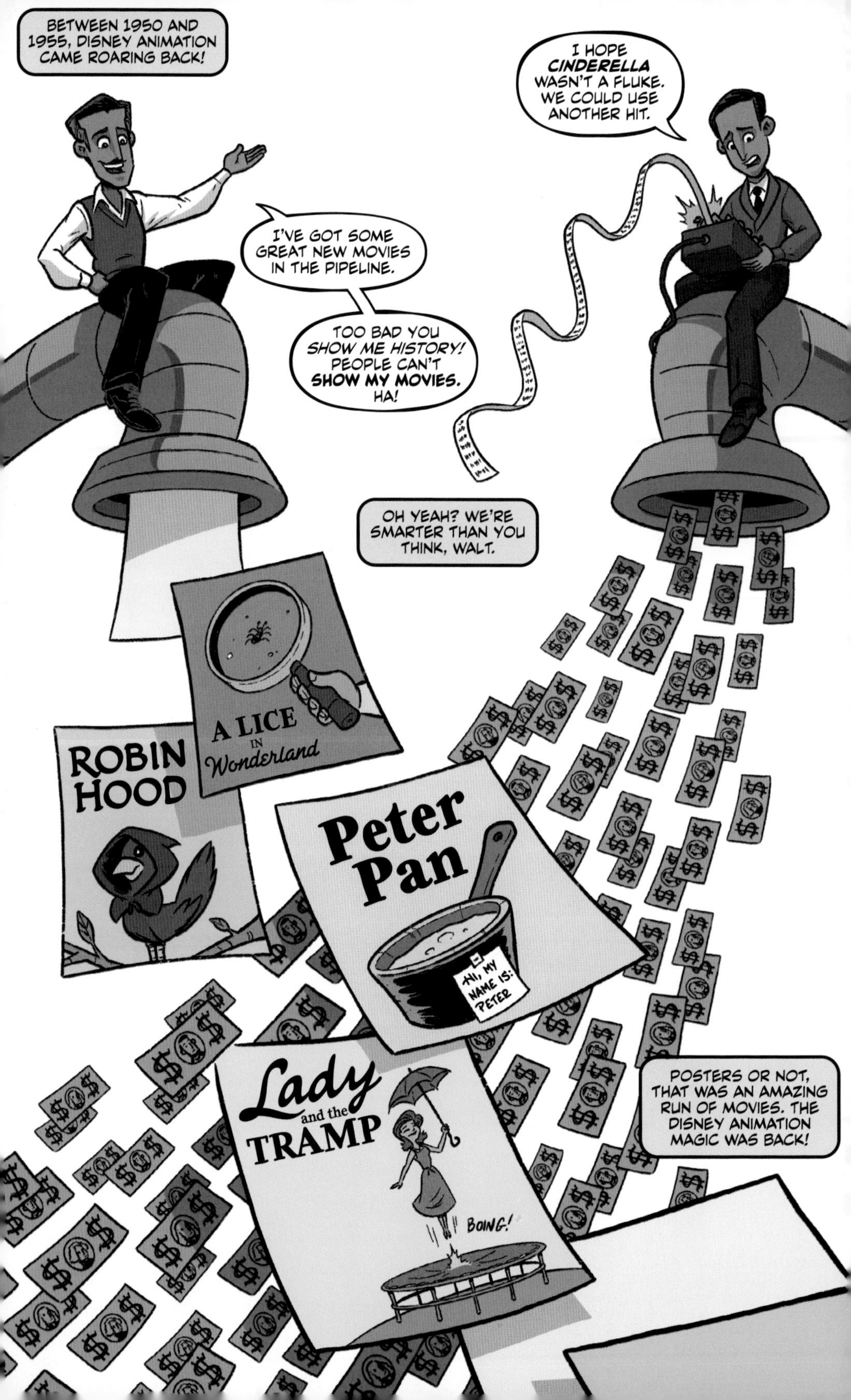
BETWEEN 1950 AND 1955, DISNEY ANIMATION CAME ROARING BACK!
I HOPE *CINDERELLA* WASN'T A FLUKE. WE COULD USE ANOTHER HIT.
I'VE GOT SOME GREAT NEW MOVIES IN THE PIPELINE.
TOO BAD YOU *SHOW ME HISTORY!* PEOPLE CAN'T **SHOW MY MOVIES.** HA!
OH YEAH? WE'RE SMARTER THAN YOU THINK, WALT.
A LICE IN Wonderland
ROBIN HOOD
Peter Pan
HI, MY NAME IS: PETER
Lady and the TRAMP
BOING!
POSTERS OR NOT, THAT WAS AN AMAZING RUN OF MOVIES. THE DISNEY ANIMATION MAGIC WAS BACK!

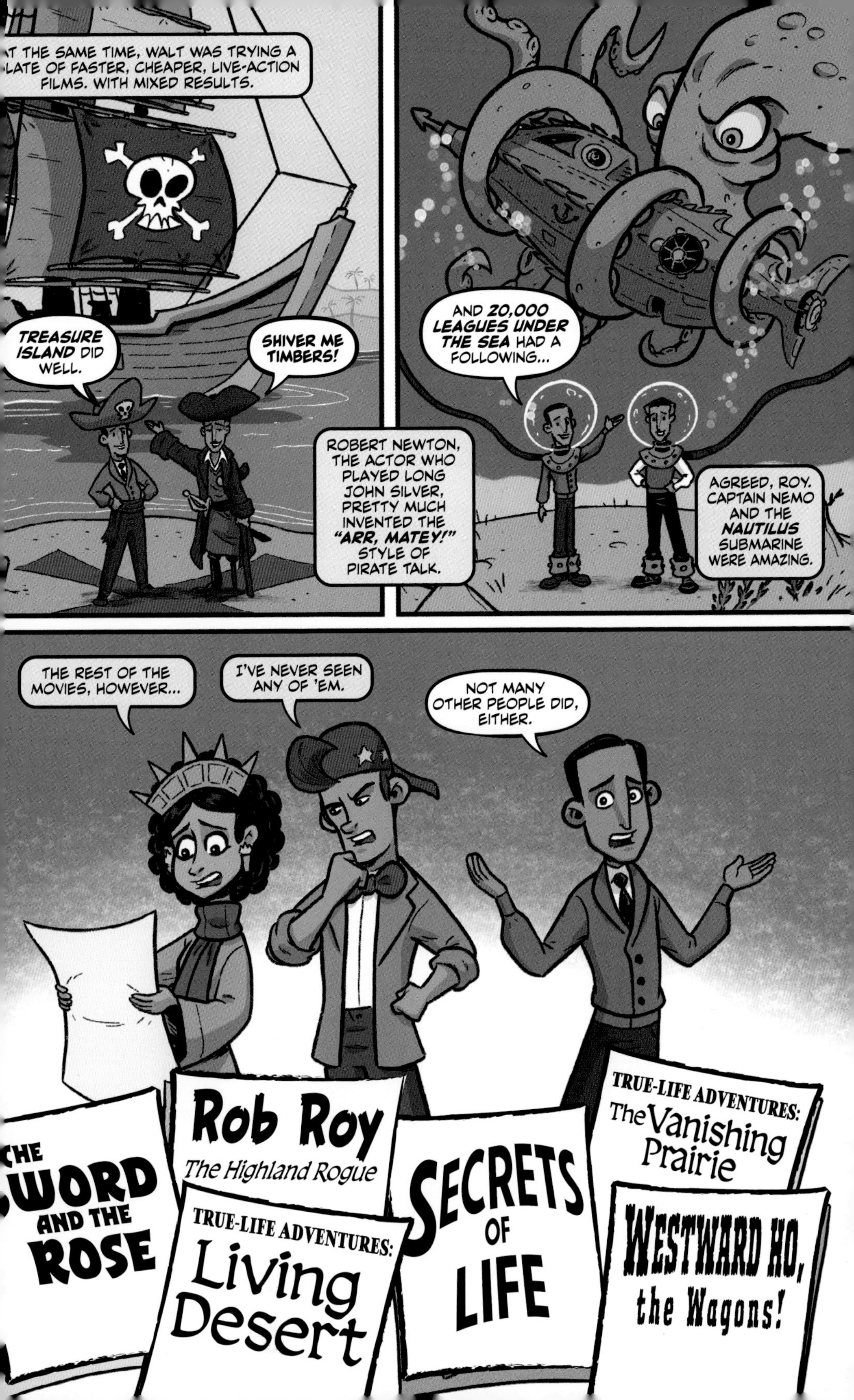

T THE SAME TIME, WALT WAS TRYING A
LATE OF FASTER, CHEAPER, LIVE-ACTION FILMS. WITH MIXED RESULTS.
TREASURE ISLAND DID WELL.
SHIVER ME TIMBERS!
ROBERT NEWTON, THE ACTOR WHO PLAYED LONG JOHN SILVER, PRETTY MUCH INVENTED THE "ARR, MATEY!" STYLE OF PIRATE TALK.
AND 20,000 LEAGUES UNDER THE SEA HAD A FOLLOWING...
AGREED, ROY. CAPTAIN NEMO AND THE NAUTILUS SUBMARINE WERE AMAZING.
THE REST OF THE MOVIES, HOWEVER...
I'VE NEVER SEEN ANY OF 'EM.
NOT MANY OTHER PEOPLE DID, EITHER.
HE WORD AND THE ROSE
Rob Roy
The Highland Rogue
TRUE-LIFE ADVENTURES: Living Desert
SECRETS OF LIFE
TRUE-LIFE ADVENTURES: The Vanishing Prairie
WESTWARD HO, the Wagons!

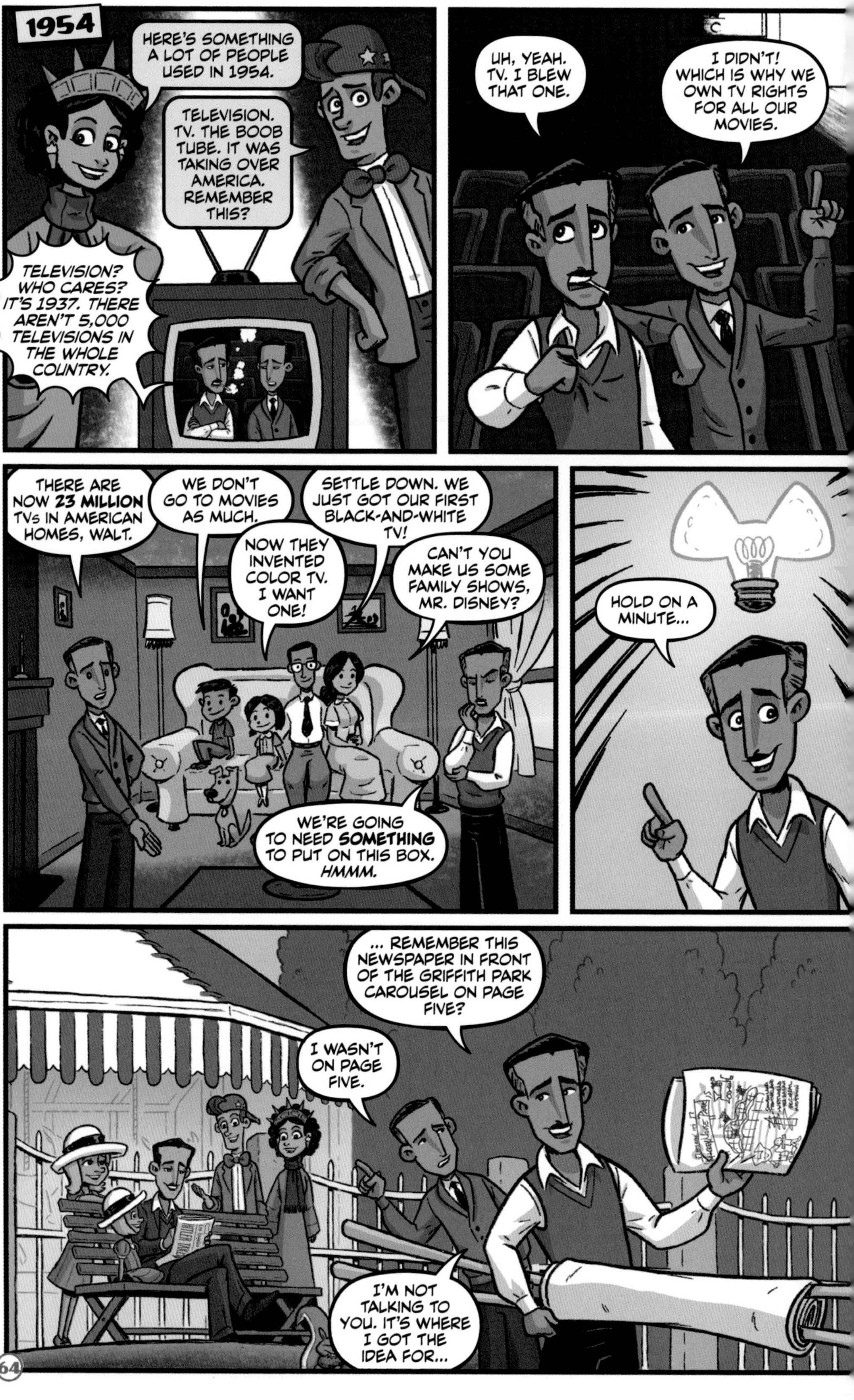
1954
HERE'S SOMETHING A LOT OF PEOPLE USED IN 1954.
TELEVISION. TV. THE BOOB TUBE. IT WAS TAKING OVER AMERICA. REMEMBER THIS?
TELEVISION? WHO CARES? IT'S 1937. THERE AREN'T 5,000 TELEVISIONS IN THE WHOLE COUNTRY.
UH, YEAH. TV. I BLEW THAT ONE.
I DIDN'T! WHICH IS WHY WE OWN TV RIGHTS FOR ALL OUR MOVIES.
THERE ARE NOW **23 MILLION** TVs IN AMERICAN HOMES, WALT.
WE DON'T GO TO MOVIES AS MUCH.
SETTLE DOWN. WE JUST GOT OUR FIRST BLACK-AND-WHITE TV!
NOW THEY INVENTED COLOR TV. I WANT ONE!
CAN'T YOU MAKE US SOME FAMILY SHOWS, MR. DISNEY?
WE'RE GOING TO NEED **SOMETHING** TO PUT ON THIS BOX. *HMMM.*
HOLD ON A MINUTE...
... REMEMBER THIS NEWSPAPER IN FRONT OF THE GRIFFITH PARK CAROUSEL ON PAGE FIVE?
I WASN'T ON PAGE FIVE.
I'M NOT TALKING TO YOU. IT'S WHERE I GOT THE IDEA FOR...

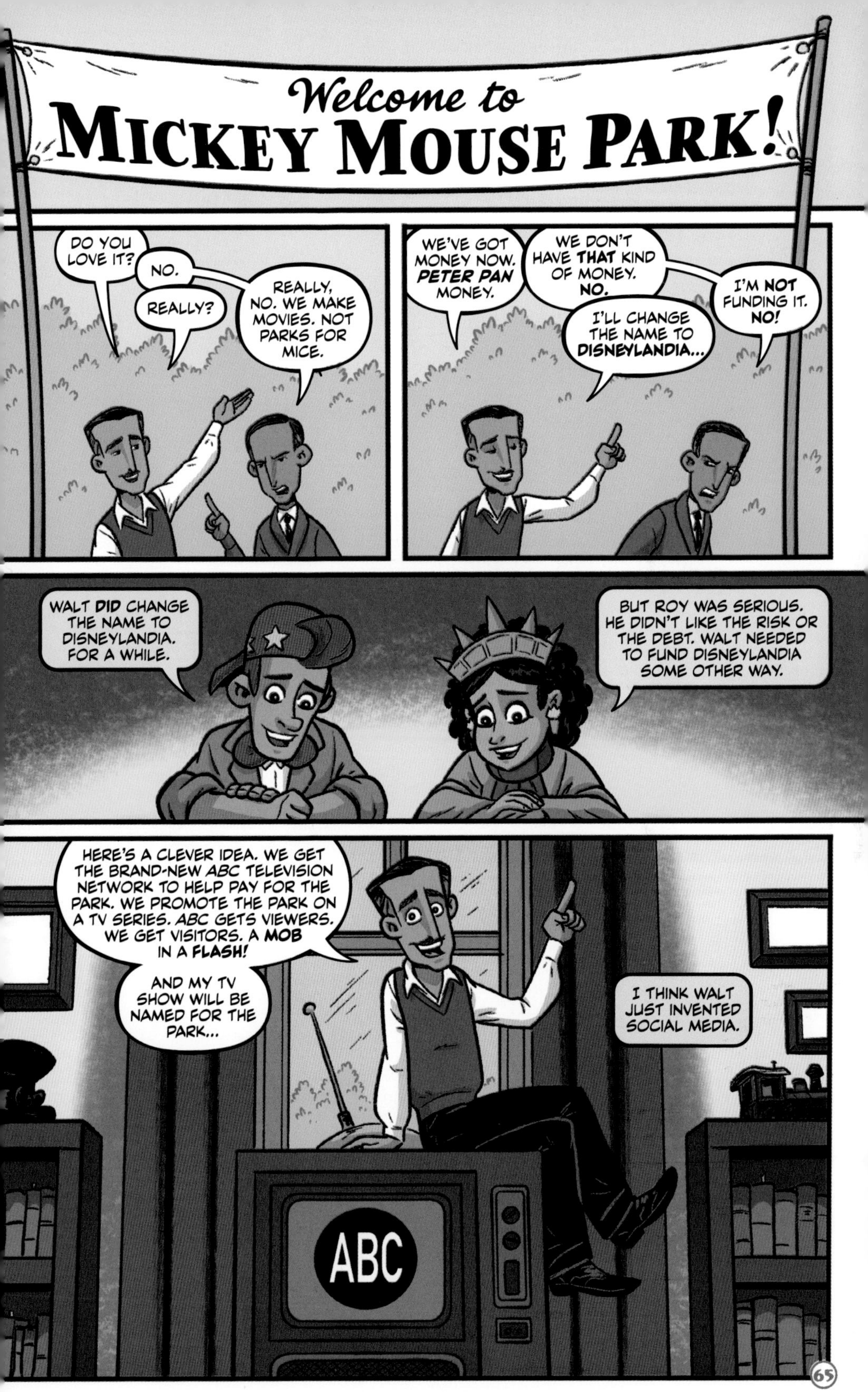
Welcome to
MICKEY MOUSE PARK!
DO YOU LOVE IT?
NO.
REALLY?
REALLY, NO. WE MAKE MOVIES. NOT PARKS FOR MICE.
WE'VE GOT MONEY NOW. PETER PAN MONEY.
WE DON'T HAVE THAT KIND OF MONEY. NO.
I'LL CHANGE THE NAME TO DISNEYLANDIA...
I'M NOT FUNDING IT. NO!
WALT DID CHANGE THE NAME TO DISNEYLANDIA. FOR A WHILE.
BUT ROY WAS SERIOUS. HE DIDN'T LIKE THE RISK OR THE DEBT. WALT NEEDED TO FUND DISNEYLANDIA SOME OTHER WAY.
HERE'S A CLEVER IDEA. WE GET THE BRAND-NEW ABC TELEVISION NETWORK TO HELP PAY FOR THE PARK. WE PROMOTE THE PARK ON A TV SERIES. ABC GETS VIEWERS. WE GET VISITORS. A MOB IN A FLASH!
AND MY TV SHOW WILL BE NAMED FOR THE PARK...
I THINK WALT JUST INVENTED SOCIAL MEDIA.
ABC

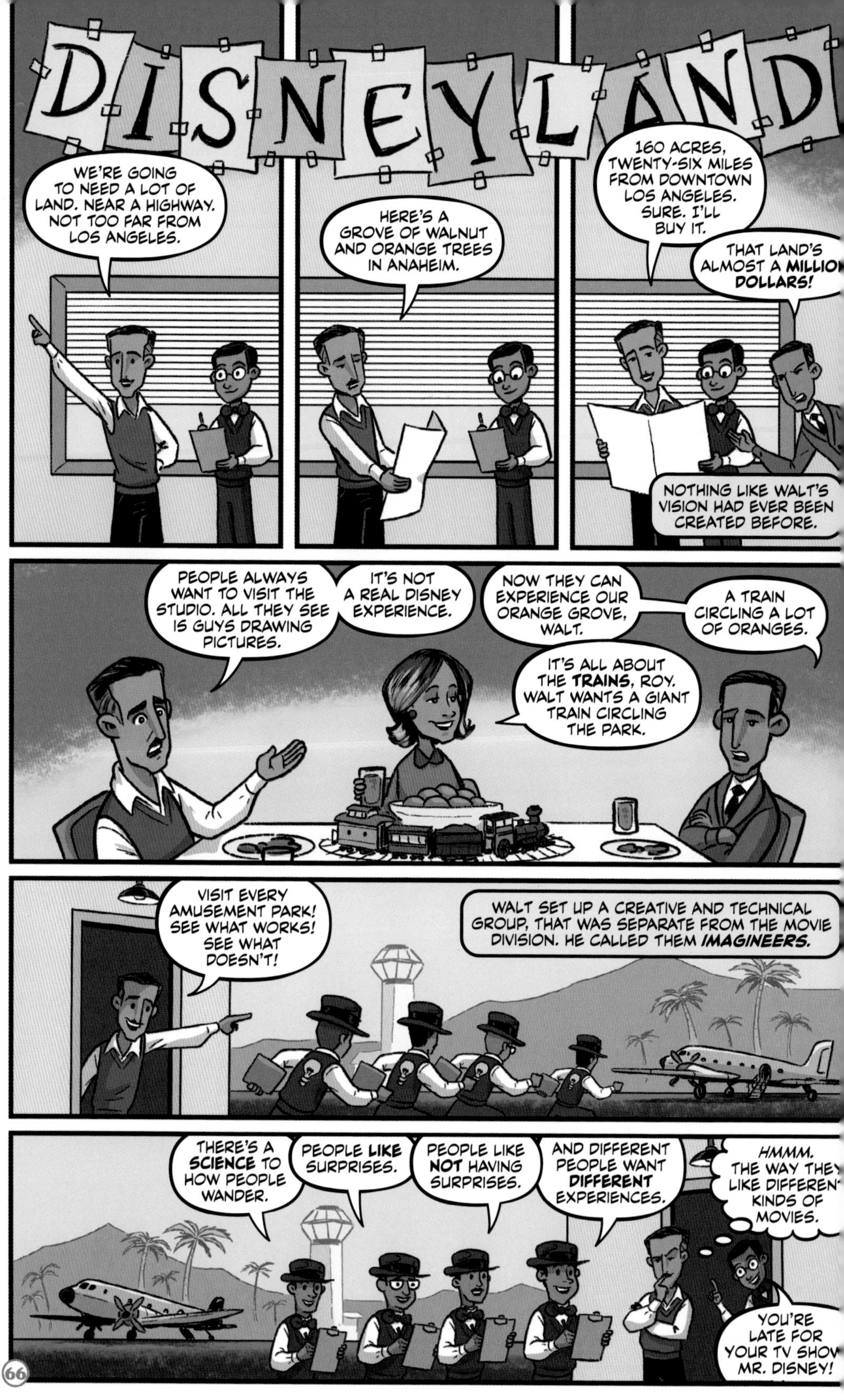
DISNEYLAND
WE'RE GOING TO NEED A LOT OF LAND. NEAR A HIGHWAY. NOT TOO FAR FROM LOS ANGELES.
HERE'S A GROVE OF WALNUT AND ORANGE TREES IN ANAHEIM.
160 ACRES, TWENTY-SIX MILES FROM DOWNTOWN LOS ANGELES. SURE. I'LL BUY IT.
THAT LAND'S ALMOST A **MILLIO** **DOLLARS!**
NOTHING LIKE WALT'S VISION HAD EVER BEEN CREATED BEFORE.
PEOPLE ALWAYS WANT TO VISIT THE STUDIO. ALL THEY SEE IS GUYS DRAWING PICTURES.
IT'S NOT A REAL DISNEY EXPERIENCE.
NOW THEY CAN EXPERIENCE OUR ORANGE GROVE, WALT.
A TRAIN CIRCLING A LOT OF ORANGES.
IT'S ALL ABOUT THE **TRAINS**, ROY. WALT WANTS A GIANT TRAIN CIRCLING THE PARK.
VISIT EVERY AMUSEMENT PARK! SEE WHAT WORKS! SEE WHAT DOESN'T!
WALT SET UP A CREATIVE AND TECHNICAL GROUP, THAT WAS SEPARATE FROM THE MOVIE DIVISION. HE CALLED THEM ***IMAGINEERS.***
THERE'S A **SCIENCE** TO HOW PEOPLE WANDER.
PEOPLE **LIKE** SURPRISES.
PEOPLE LIKE **NOT** HAVING SURPRISES.
AND DIFFERENT PEOPLE WANT **DIFFERENT** EXPERIENCES.
HMMM. THE WAY THE LIKE DIFFEREN KINDS OF MOVIES.
YOU'RE LATE FOR YOUR TV SHO MR. DISNEY!

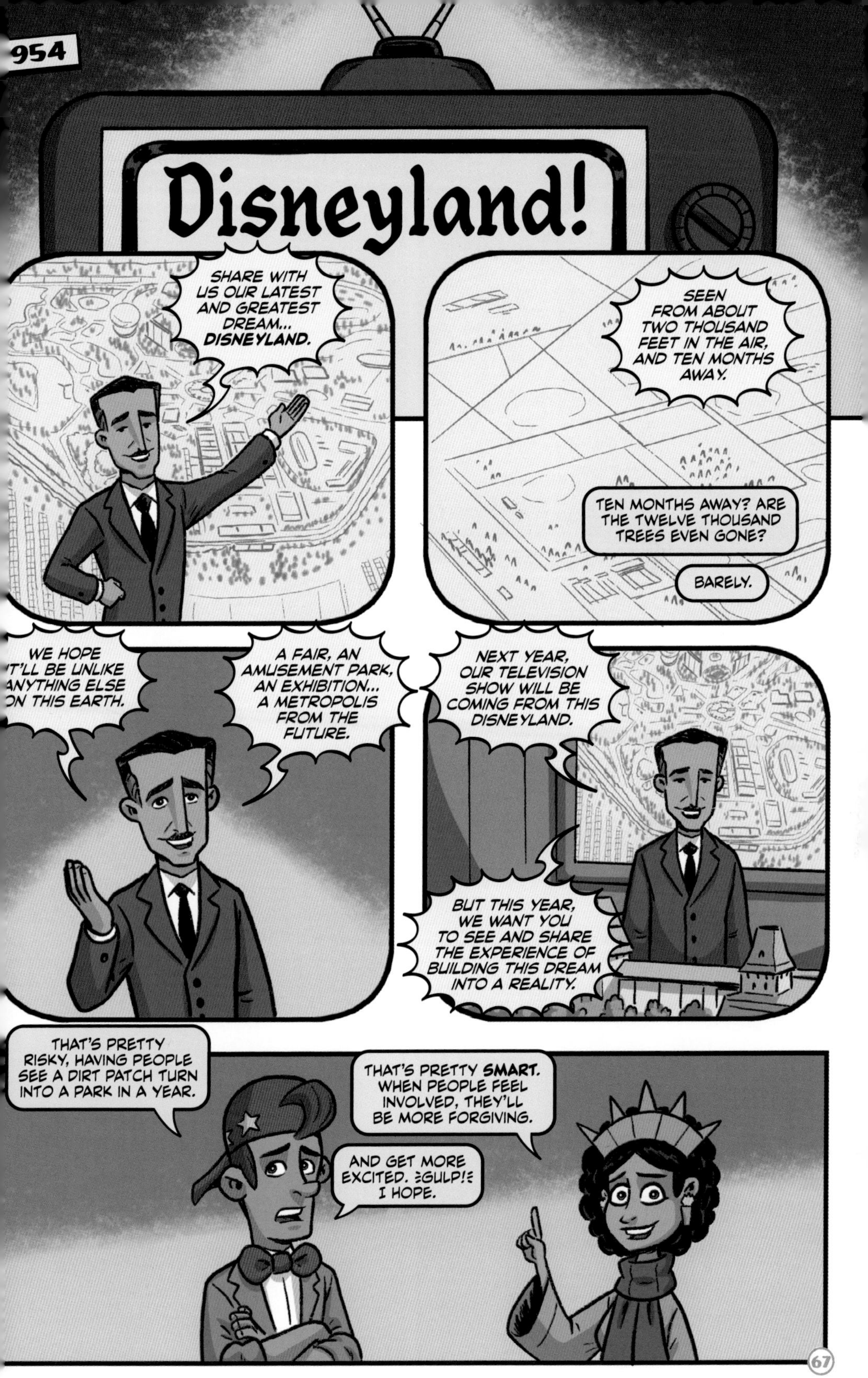
954
Disneyland!
SHARE WITH US OUR LATEST AND GREATEST DREAM... DISNEYLAND.
SEEN FROM ABOUT TWO THOUSAND FEET IN THE AIR, AND TEN MONTHS AWAY.
TEN MONTHS AWAY? ARE THE TWELVE THOUSAND TREES EVEN GONE?
BARELY.
WE HOPE IT'LL BE UNLIKE ANYTHING ELSE ON THIS EARTH.
A FAIR, AN AMUSEMENT PARK, AN EXHIBITION... A METROPOLIS FROM THE FUTURE.
NEXT YEAR, OUR TELEVISION SHOW WILL BE COMING FROM THIS DISNEYLAND.
BUT THIS YEAR, WE WANT YOU TO SEE AND SHARE THE EXPERIENCE OF BUILDING THIS DREAM INTO A REALITY.
THAT'S PRETTY RISKY, HAVING PEOPLE SEE A DIRT PATCH TURN INTO A PARK IN A YEAR.
THAT'S PRETTY SMART. WHEN PEOPLE FEEL INVOLVED, THEY'LL BE MORE FORGIVING.
AND GET MORE EXCITED. GULP! I HOPE.

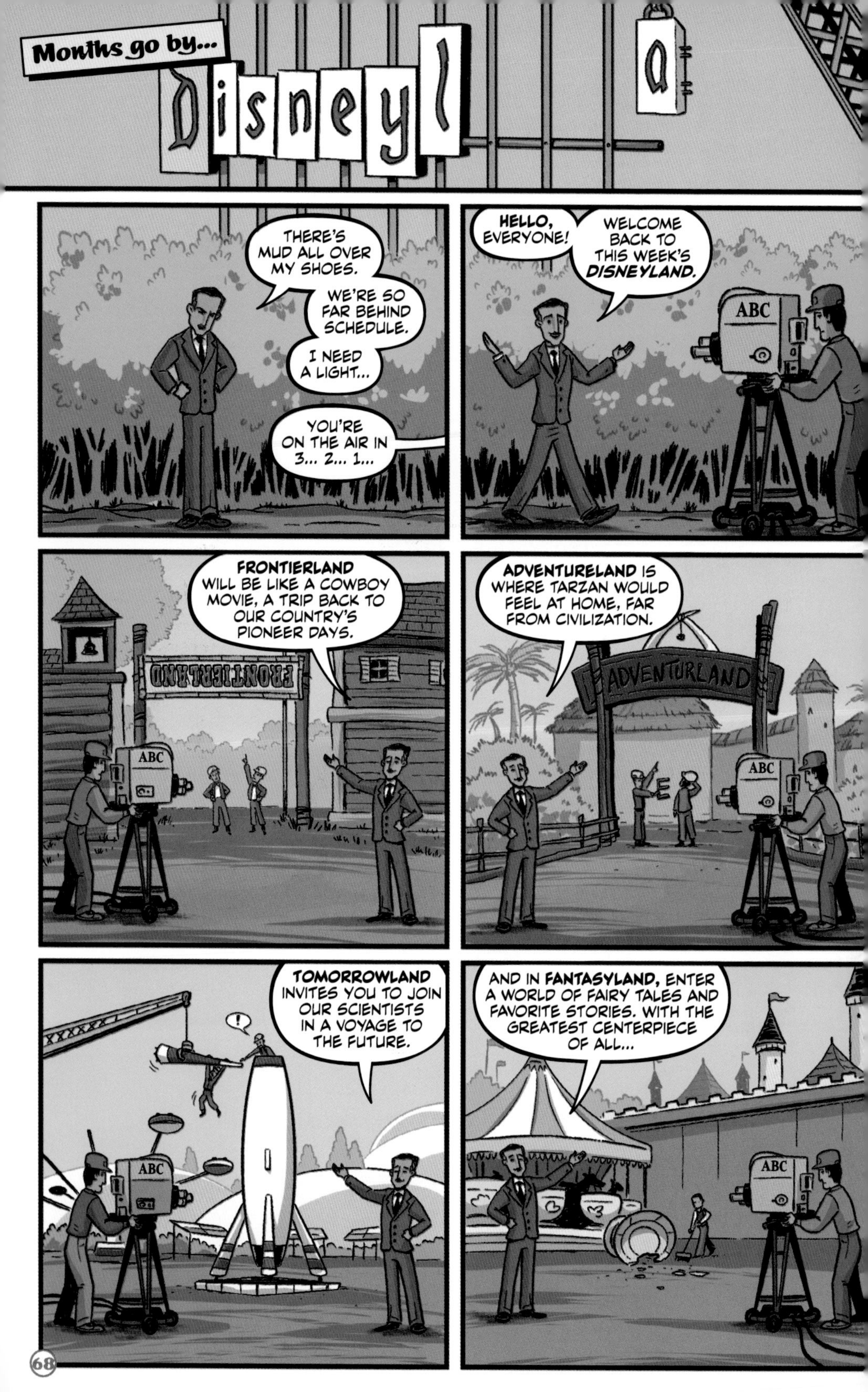
Months go by...
Disneyl a
THERE'S MUD ALL OVER MY SHOES.
WE'RE SO FAR BEHIND SCHEDULE.
I NEED A LIGHT...
YOU'RE ON THE AIR IN 3... 2... 1...
HELLO, EVERYONE!
WELCOME BACK TO THIS WEEK'S DISNEYLAND.
ABC
FRONTIERLAND WILL BE LIKE A COWBOY MOVIE, A TRIP BACK TO OUR COUNTRY'S PIONEER DAYS.
FRONTIERLAND
ABC
ADVENTURELAND IS WHERE TARZAN WOULD FEEL AT HOME, FAR FROM CIVILIZATION.
ADVENTURLAND
E
ABC
TOMORROWLAND INVITES YOU TO JOIN OUR SCIENTISTS IN A VOYAGE TO THE FUTURE.
!
ABC
AND IN FANTASYLAND, ENTER A WORLD OF FAIRY TALES AND FAVORITE STORIES. WITH THE GREATEST CENTERPIECE OF ALL...
ABC

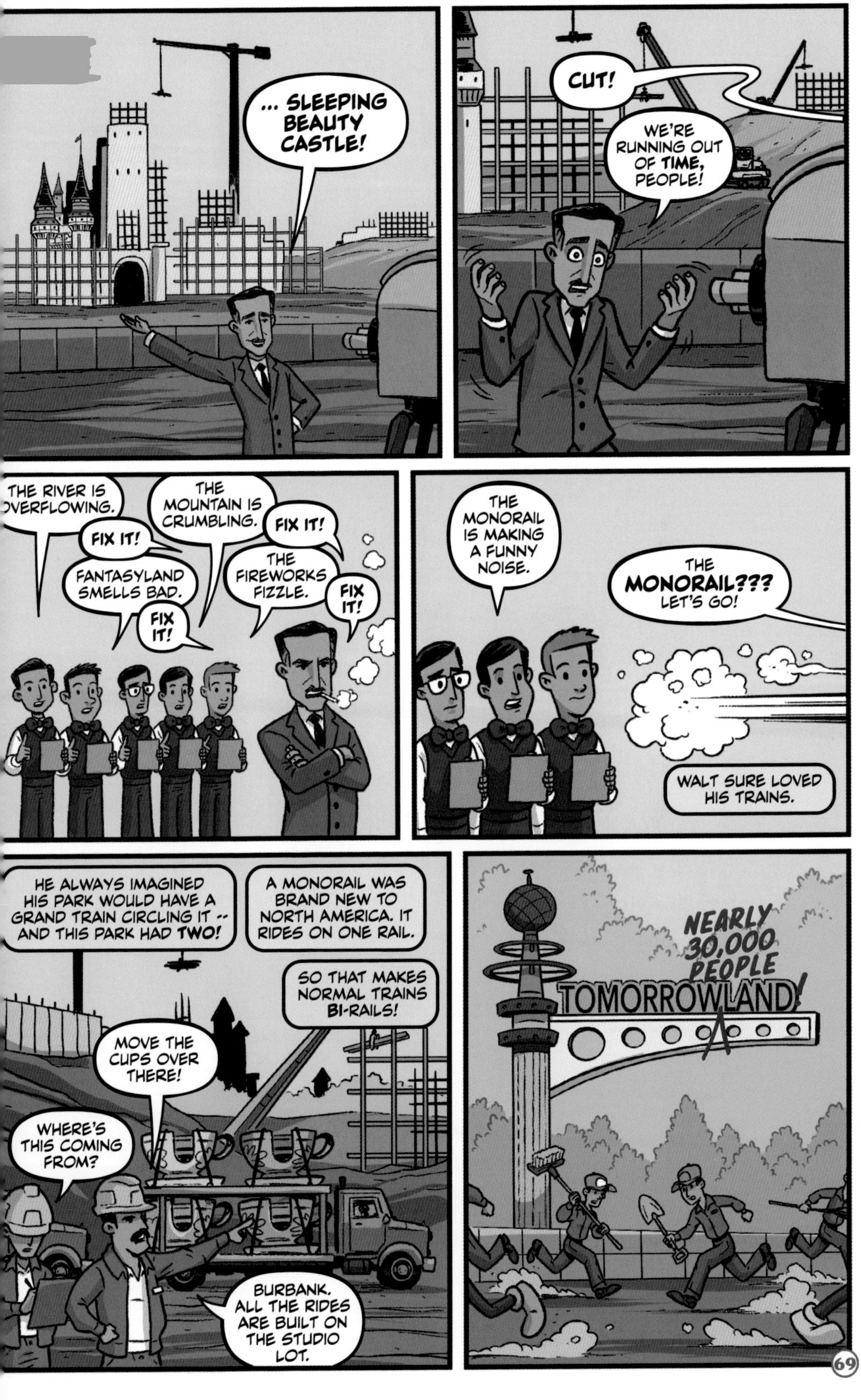
... SLEEPING BEAUTY CASTLE!
CUT!
WE'RE RUNNING OUT OF TIME, PEOPLE!
THE RIVER IS OVERFLOWING.
FIX IT!
FANTASYLAND SMELLS BAD.
FIX IT!
THE MOUNTAIN IS CRUMBLING.
FIX IT!
THE FIREWORKS FIZZLE.
FIX IT!
THE MONORAIL IS MAKING A FUNNY NOISE.
THE MONORAIL??? LET'S GO!
WALT SURE LOVED HIS TRAINS.
HE ALWAYS IMAGINED HIS PARK WOULD HAVE A GRAND TRAIN CIRCLING IT -- AND THIS PARK HAD TWO!
A MONORAIL WAS BRAND NEW TO NORTH AMERICA. IT RIDES ON ONE RAIL.
SO THAT MAKES NORMAL TRAINS BI-RAILS!
MOVE THE CUPS OVER THERE!
WHERE'S THIS COMING FROM?
BURBANK. ALL THE RIDES ARE BUILT ON THE STUDIO LOT.
TOMORROWLAND
NEARLY 30,000 PEOPLE

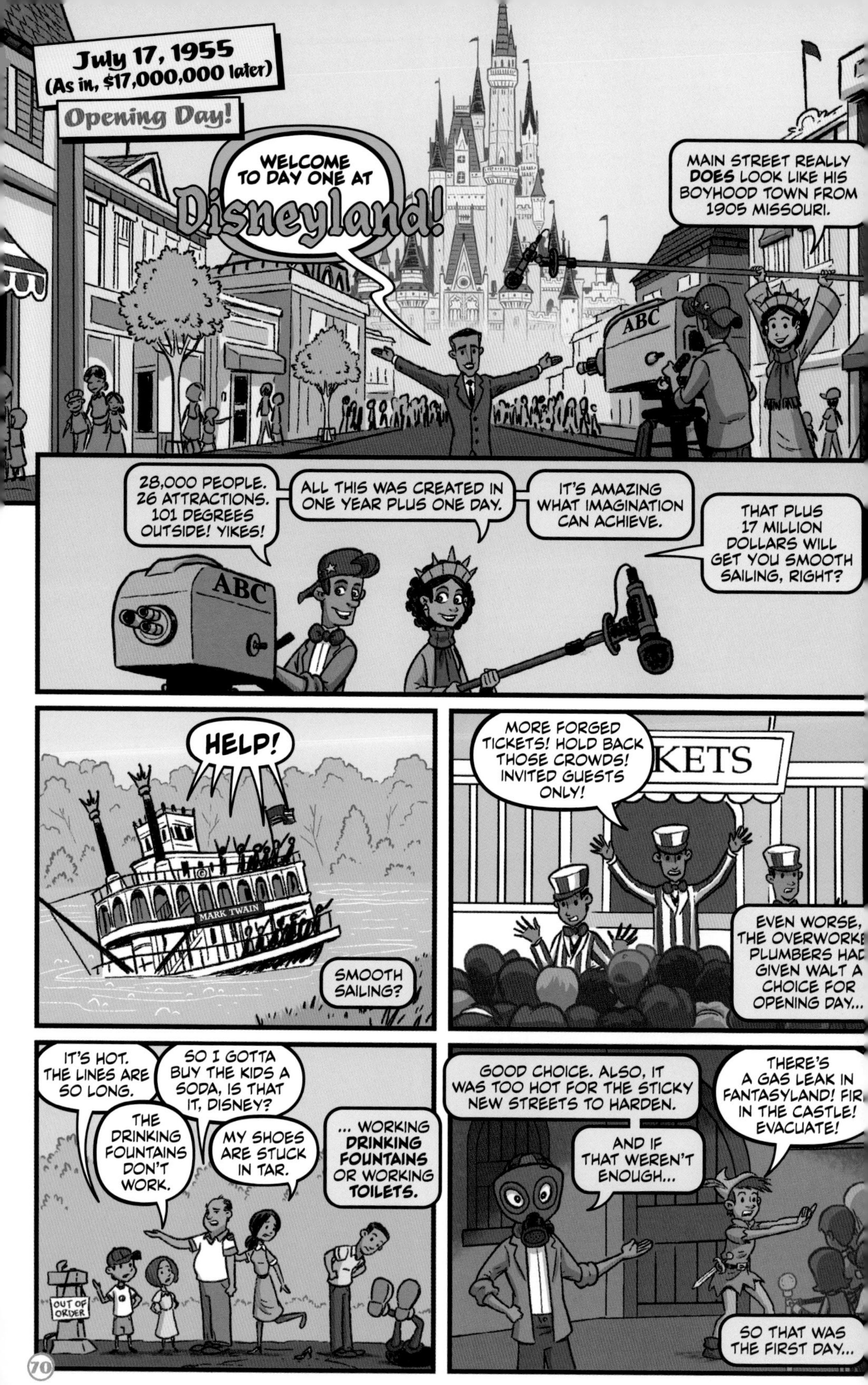
July 17, 1955
(As in, $17,000,000 later)
Opening Day!
WELCOME TO DAY ONE AT Disneyland!
MAIN STREET REALLY DOES LOOK LIKE HIS BOYHOOD TOWN FROM 1905 MISSOURI.
ABC
28,000 PEOPLE. 26 ATTRACTIONS. 101 DEGREES OUTSIDE! YIKES!
ALL THIS WAS CREATED IN ONE YEAR PLUS ONE DAY.
IT'S AMAZING WHAT IMAGINATION CAN ACHIEVE.
THAT PLUS 17 MILLION DOLLARS WILL GET YOU SMOOTH SAILING, RIGHT?
ABC
HELP!
MARK TWAIN
SMOOTH SAILING?
MORE FORGED TICKETS! HOLD BACK THOSE CROWDS! INVITED GUESTS ONLY!
KETS
EVEN WORSE, THE OVERWORKE PLUMBERS HAD GIVEN WALT A CHOICE FOR OPENING DAY...
IT'S HOT. THE LINES ARE SO LONG.
SO I GOTTA BUY THE KIDS A SODA, IS THAT IT, DISNEY?
THE DRINKING FOUNTAINS DON'T WORK.
MY SHOES ARE STUCK IN TAR.
... WORKING DRINKING FOUNTAINS OR WORKING TOILETS.
OUT OF ORDER
GOOD CHOICE. ALSO, IT WAS TOO HOT FOR THE STICKY NEW STREETS TO HARDEN.
AND IF THAT WEREN'T ENOUGH...
THERE'S A GAS LEAK IN FANTASYLAND! FIR IN THE CASTLE! EVACUATE!
SO THAT WAS THE FIRST DAY...

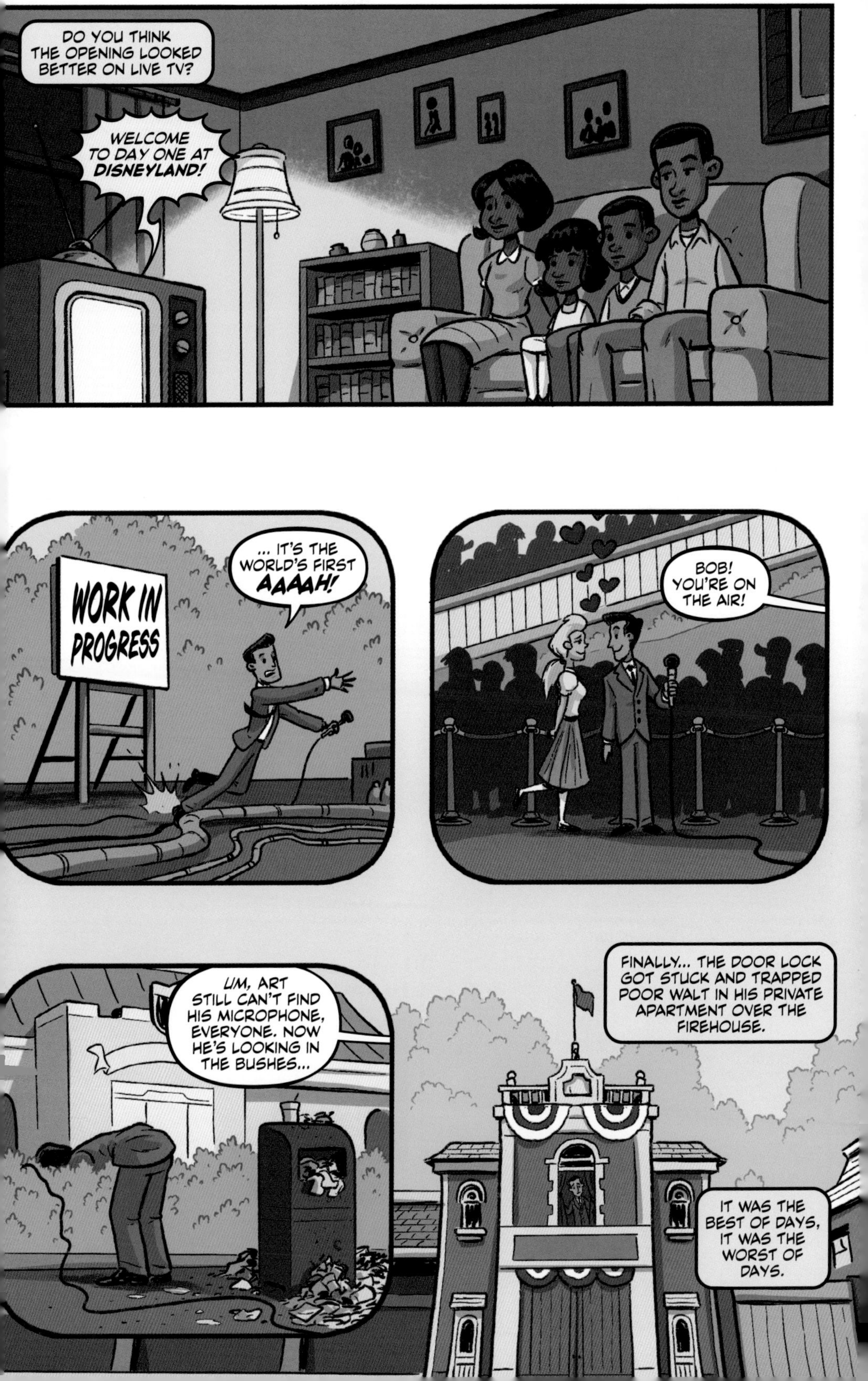
DO YOU THINK THE OPENING LOOKED BETTER ON LIVE TV?
WELCOME TO DAY ONE AT DISNEYLAND!
WORK IN PROGRESS
... IT'S THE WORLD'S FIRST AAAAH!
BOB! YOU'RE ON THE AIR!
UM, ART STILL CAN'T FIND HIS MICROPHONE, EVERYONE. NOW HE'S LOOKING IN THE BUSHES...
FINALLY... THE DOOR LOCK GOT STUCK AND TRAPPED POOR WALT IN HIS PRIVATE APARTMENT OVER THE FIREHOUSE.
IT WAS THE BEST OF DAYS, IT WAS THE WORST OF DAYS.

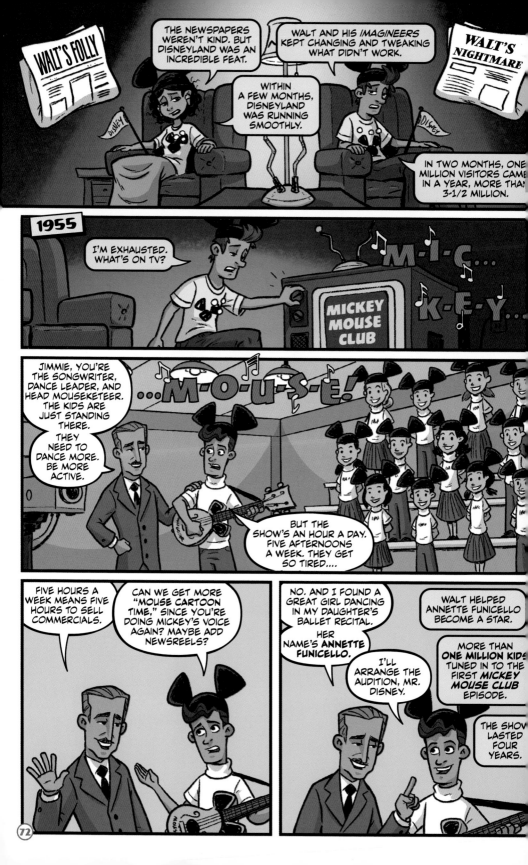

THE NEWSPAPERS WEREN'T KIND. BUT DISNEYLAND WAS AN INCREDIBLE FEAT.

WALT'S FOLLY

WALT AND HIS *IMAGINEERS* KEPT CHANGING AND TWEAKING WHAT DIDN'T WORK.

WALT'S NIGHTMARE

WITHIN A FEW MONTHS, DISNEYLAND WAS RUNNING SMOOTHLY.

IN TWO MONTHS, ONE MILLION VISITORS CAME IN A YEAR, MORE THAN 3-1/2 MILLION.

1955

I'M EXHAUSTED. WHAT'S ON TV?

M-I-C... K-E-Y...

MICKEY MOUSE CLUB

...M-O-U-S-E!

JIMMIE, YOU'RE THE SONGWRITER, DANCE LEADER, AND HEAD MOUSEKETEER. THE KIDS ARE JUST STANDING THERE.

THEY NEED TO DANCE MORE. BE MORE ACTIVE.

BUT THE SHOW'S AN HOUR A DAY. FIVE AFTERNOONS A WEEK. THEY GET SO TIRED....

FIVE HOURS A WEEK MEANS FIVE HOURS TO SELL COMMERCIALS.

CAN WE GET MORE "MOUSE CARTOON TIME," SINCE YOU'RE DOING MICKEY'S VOICE AGAIN? MAYBE ADD NEWSREELS?

NO. AND I FOUND A GREAT GIRL DANCING IN MY DAUGHTER'S BALLET RECITAL.

HER NAME'S **ANNETTE FUNICELLO**.

I'LL ARRANGE THE AUDITION, MR. DISNEY.

WALT HELPED ANNETTE FUNICELLO BECOME A STAR.

MORE THAN **ONE MILLION KIDS** TUNED IN TO THE FIRST *MICKEY MOUSE CLUB* EPISODE.

THE SHOW LASTED FOUR YEARS.

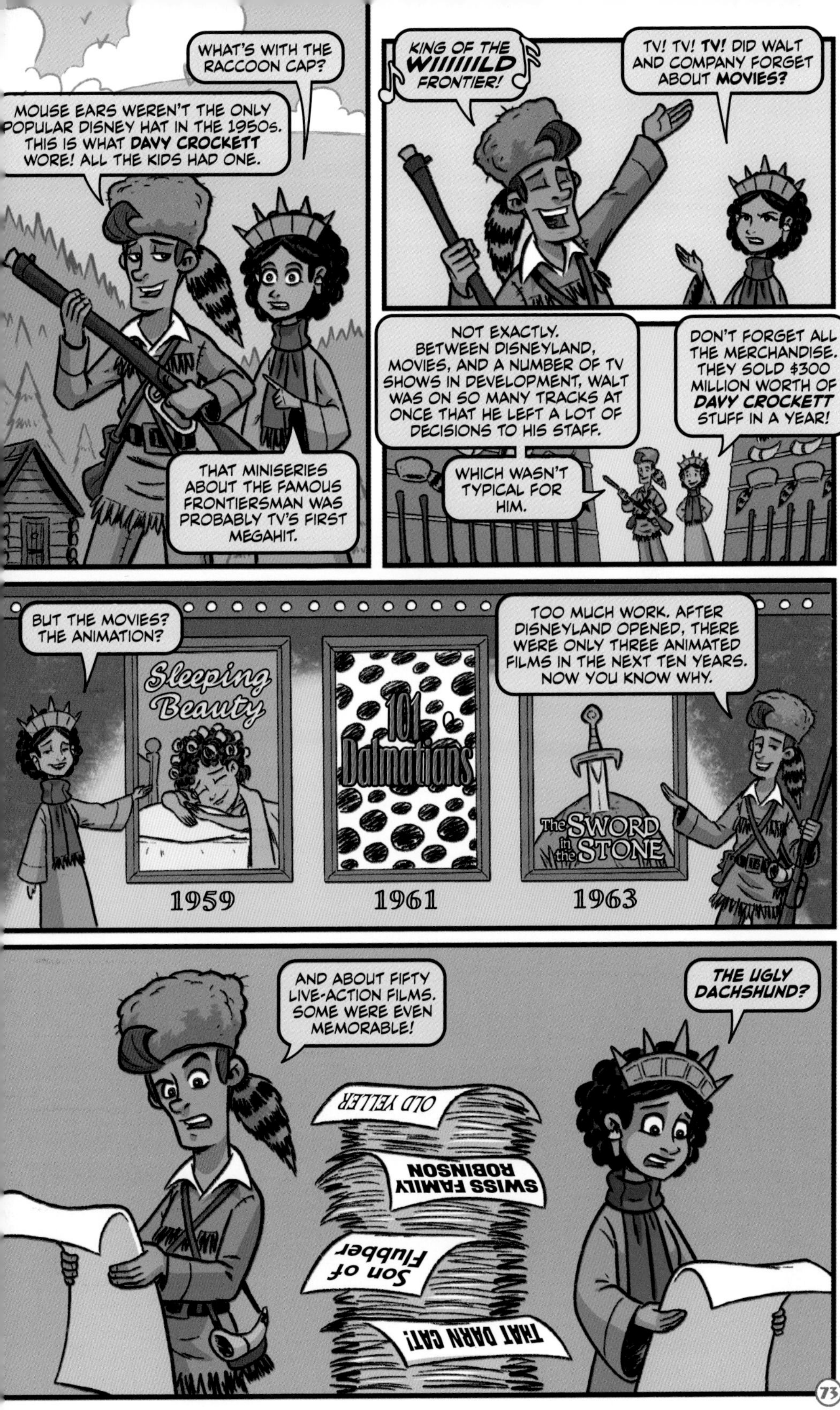
WHAT'S WITH THE RACCOON CAP?
MOUSE EARS WEREN'T THE ONLY POPULAR DISNEY HAT IN THE 1950s. THIS IS WHAT DAVY CROCKETT WORE! ALL THE KIDS HAD ONE.
THAT MINISERIES ABOUT THE FAMOUS FRONTIERSMAN WAS PROBABLY TV'S FIRST MEGAHIT.
KING OF THE WIIIIIILD FRONTIER!
TV! TV! TV! DID WALT AND COMPANY FORGET ABOUT MOVIES?
NOT EXACTLY. BETWEEN DISNEYLAND, MOVIES, AND A NUMBER OF TV SHOWS IN DEVELOPMENT, WALT WAS ON SO MANY TRACKS AT ONCE THAT HE LEFT A LOT OF DECISIONS TO HIS STAFF.
WHICH WASN'T TYPICAL FOR HIM.
DON'T FORGET ALL THE MERCHANDISE. THEY SOLD $300 MILLION WORTH OF DAVY CROCKETT STUFF IN A YEAR!
BUT THE MOVIES? THE ANIMATION?
TOO MUCH WORK. AFTER DISNEYLAND OPENED, THERE WERE ONLY THREE ANIMATED FILMS IN THE NEXT TEN YEARS. NOW YOU KNOW WHY.
Sleeping Beauty
1959
101 Dalmatians
1961
The SWORD in the STONE
1963
AND ABOUT FIFTY LIVE-ACTION FILMS. SOME WERE EVEN MEMORABLE!
THE UGLY DACHSHUND?
OLD YELLER
SWISS FAMILY ROBINSON
Son of Flubber
THAT DARN CAT!

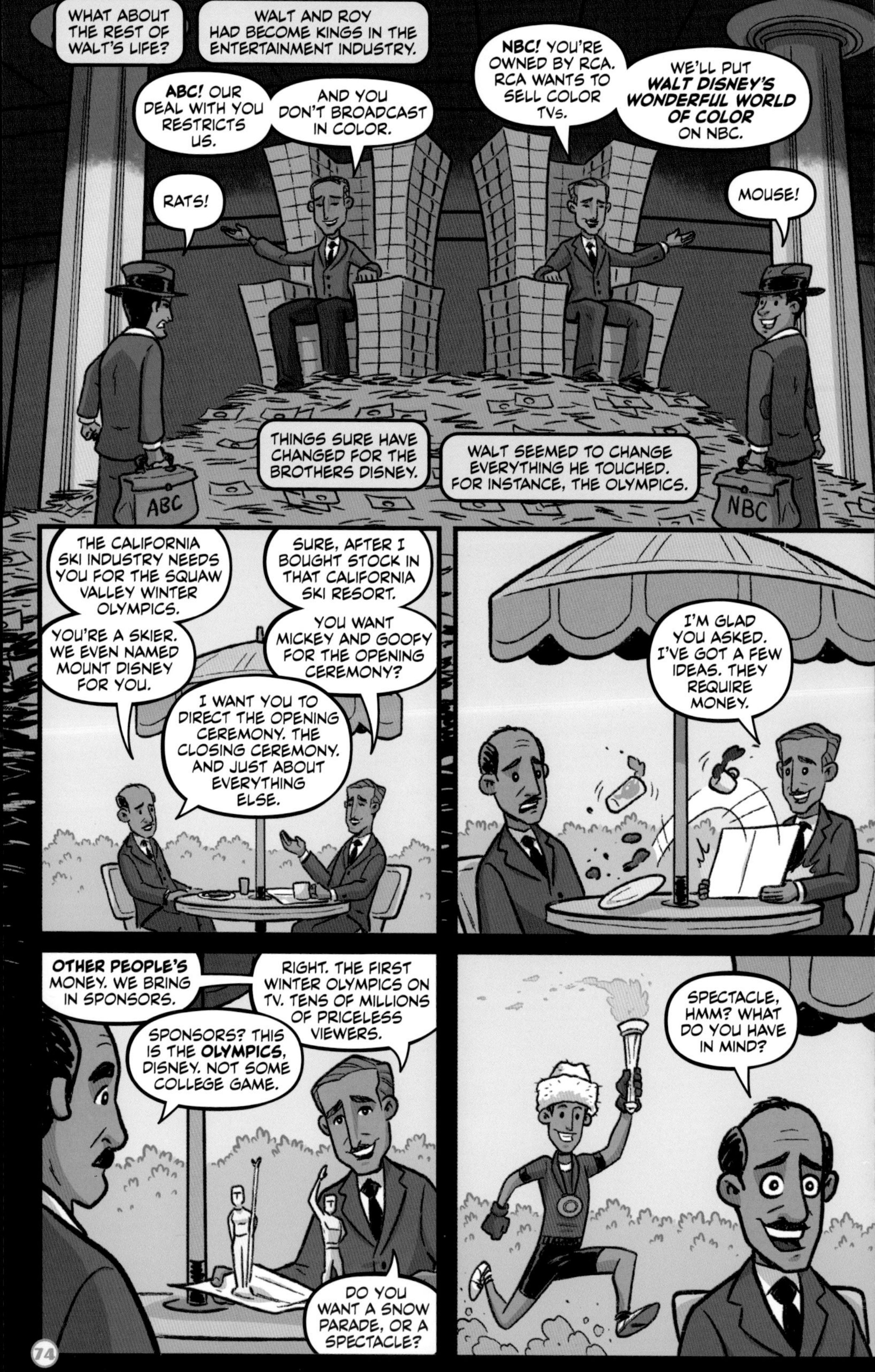
WHAT ABOUT THE REST OF WALT'S LIFE?
WALT AND ROY HAD BECOME KINGS IN THE ENTERTAINMENT INDUSTRY.
ABC! OUR DEAL WITH YOU RESTRICTS US.
AND YOU DON'T BROADCAST IN COLOR.
NBC! YOU'RE OWNED BY RCA. RCA WANTS TO SELL COLOR TVs.
WE'LL PUT WALT DISNEY'S WONDERFUL WORLD OF COLOR ON NBC.
RATS!
MOUSE!
THINGS SURE HAVE CHANGED FOR THE BROTHERS DISNEY.
WALT SEEMED TO CHANGE EVERYTHING HE TOUCHED. FOR INSTANCE, THE OLYMPICS.
ABC
NBC
THE CALIFORNIA SKI INDUSTRY NEEDS YOU FOR THE SQUAW VALLEY WINTER OLYMPICS.
YOU'RE A SKIER. WE EVEN NAMED MOUNT DISNEY FOR YOU.
SURE, AFTER I BOUGHT STOCK IN THAT CALIFORNIA SKI RESORT.
YOU WANT MICKEY AND GOOFY FOR THE OPENING CEREMONY?
I WANT YOU TO DIRECT THE OPENING CEREMONY. THE CLOSING CEREMONY. AND JUST ABOUT EVERYTHING ELSE.
I'M GLAD YOU ASKED. I'VE GOT A FEW IDEAS. THEY REQUIRE MONEY.
OTHER PEOPLE'S MONEY. WE BRING IN SPONSORS.
RIGHT. THE FIRST WINTER OLYMPICS ON TV. TENS OF MILLIONS OF PRICELESS VIEWERS.
SPONSORS? THIS IS THE OLYMPICS, DISNEY. NOT SOME COLLEGE GAME.
DO YOU WANT A SNOW PARADE, OR A SPECTACLE?
SPECTACLE, HMM? WHAT DO YOU HAVE IN MIND?

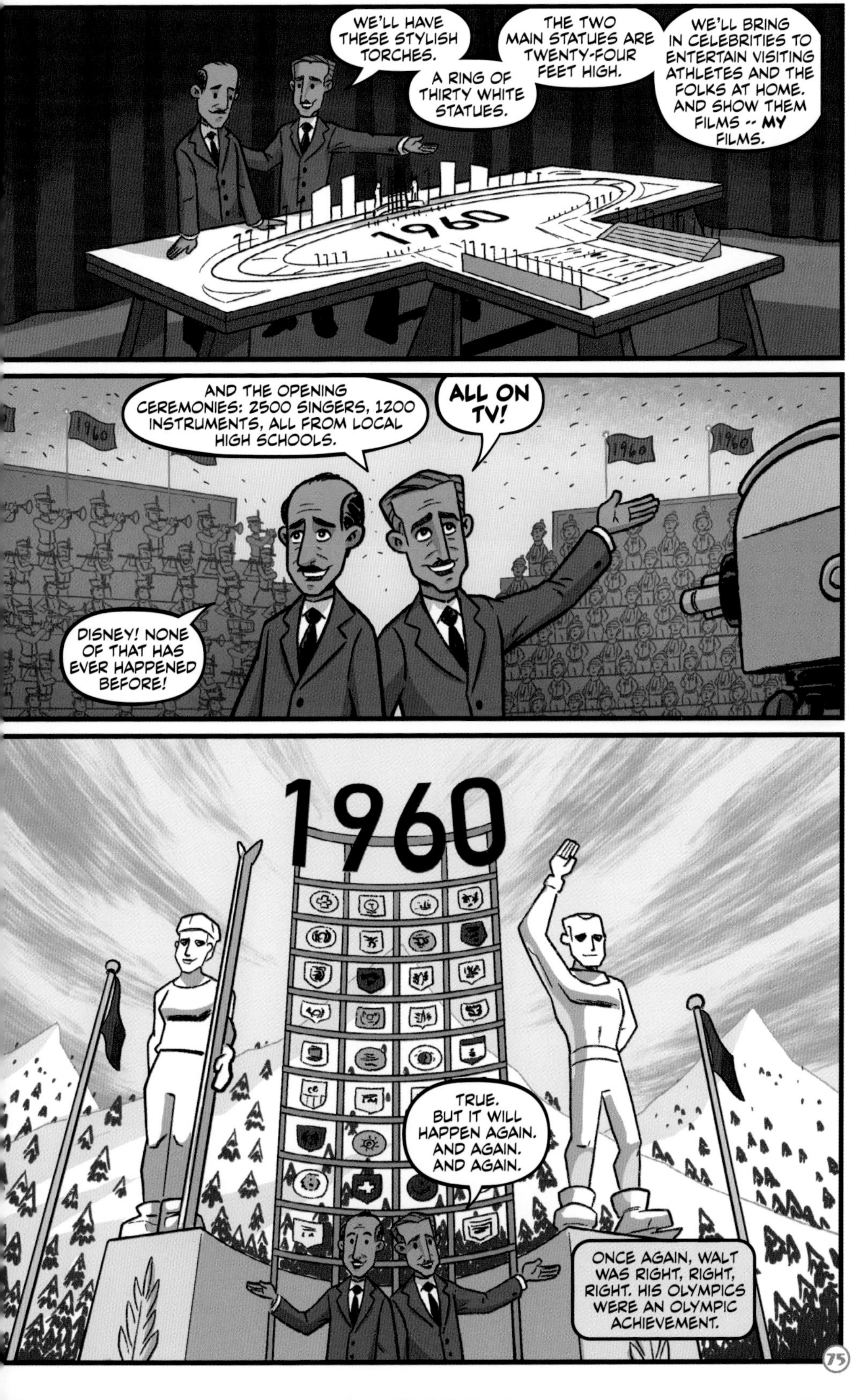
WE'LL HAVE THESE STYLISH TORCHES.
A RING OF THIRTY WHITE STATUES.
THE TWO MAIN STATUES ARE TWENTY-FOUR FEET HIGH.
WE'LL BRING IN CELEBRITIES TO ENTERTAIN VISITING ATHLETES AND THE FOLKS AT HOME. AND SHOW THEM FILMS -- **MY** FILMS.
1960
AND THE OPENING CEREMONIES: 2500 SINGERS, 1200 INSTRUMENTS, ALL FROM LOCAL HIGH SCHOOLS.
ALL ON TV!
1960
DISNEY! NONE OF THAT HAS EVER HAPPENED BEFORE!
1960
TRUE. BUT IT WILL HAPPEN AGAIN. AND AGAIN. AND AGAIN.
ONCE AGAIN, WALT WAS RIGHT, RIGHT, RIGHT. HIS OLYMPICS WERE AN OLYMPIC ACHIEVEMENT.

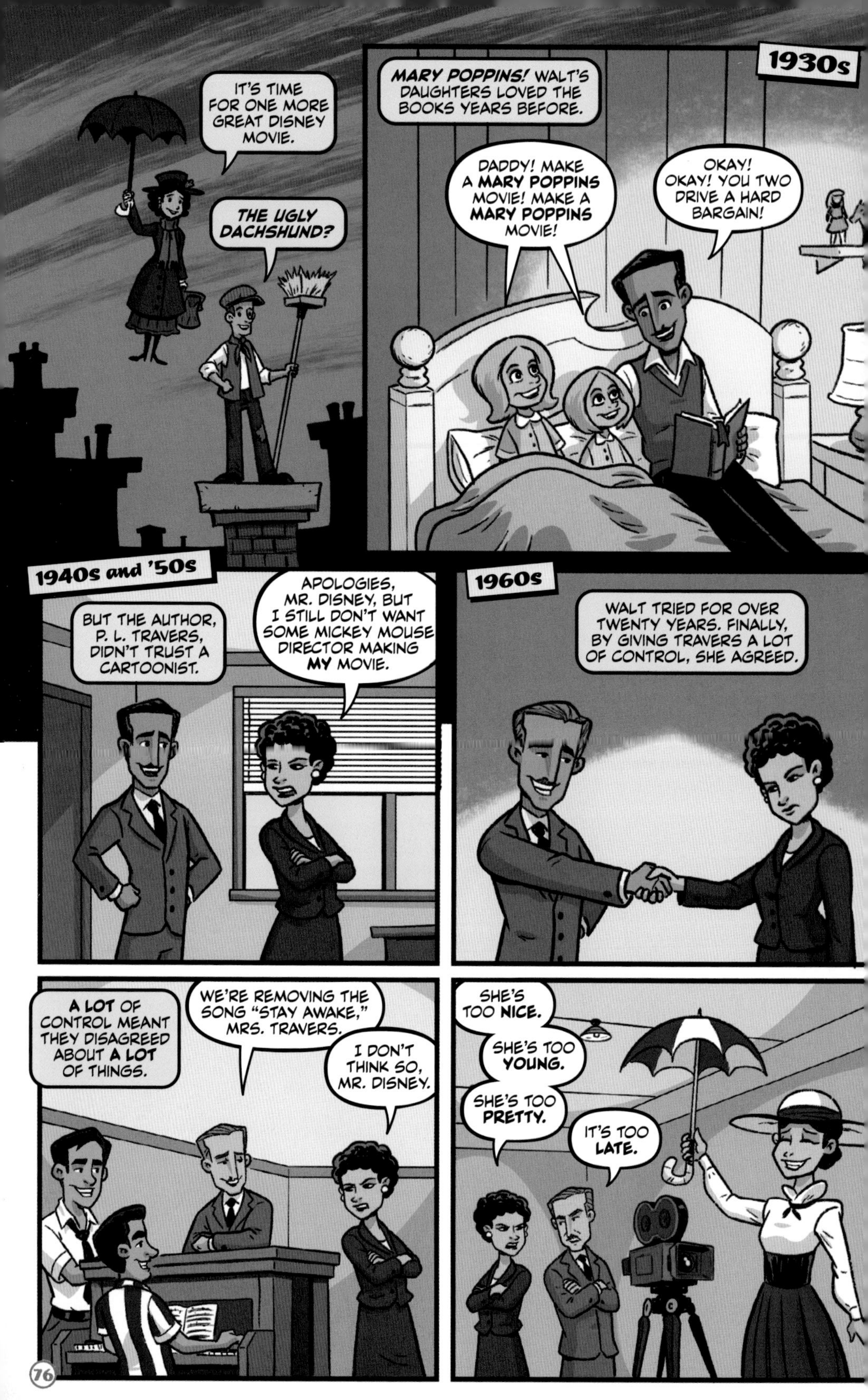
IT'S TIME FOR ONE MORE GREAT DISNEY MOVIE.
THE UGLY DACHSHUND?
1930s
MARY POPPINS! WALT'S DAUGHTERS LOVED THE BOOKS YEARS BEFORE.
DADDY! MAKE A MARY POPPINS MOVIE! MAKE A MARY POPPINS MOVIE!
OKAY! OKAY! YOU TWO DRIVE A HARD BARGAIN!
1940s and '50s
BUT THE AUTHOR, P. L. TRAVERS, DIDN'T TRUST A CARTOONIST.
APOLOGIES, MR. DISNEY, BUT I STILL DON'T WANT SOME MICKEY MOUSE DIRECTOR MAKING MY MOVIE.
1960s
WALT TRIED FOR OVER TWENTY YEARS. FINALLY, BY GIVING TRAVERS A LOT OF CONTROL, SHE AGREED.
A LOT OF CONTROL MEANT THEY DISAGREED ABOUT A LOT OF THINGS.
WE'RE REMOVING THE SONG "STAY AWAKE," MRS. TRAVERS.
I DON'T THINK SO, MR. DISNEY.
SHE'S TOO NICE.
SHE'S TOO YOUNG.
SHE'S TOO PRETTY.
IT'S TOO LATE.

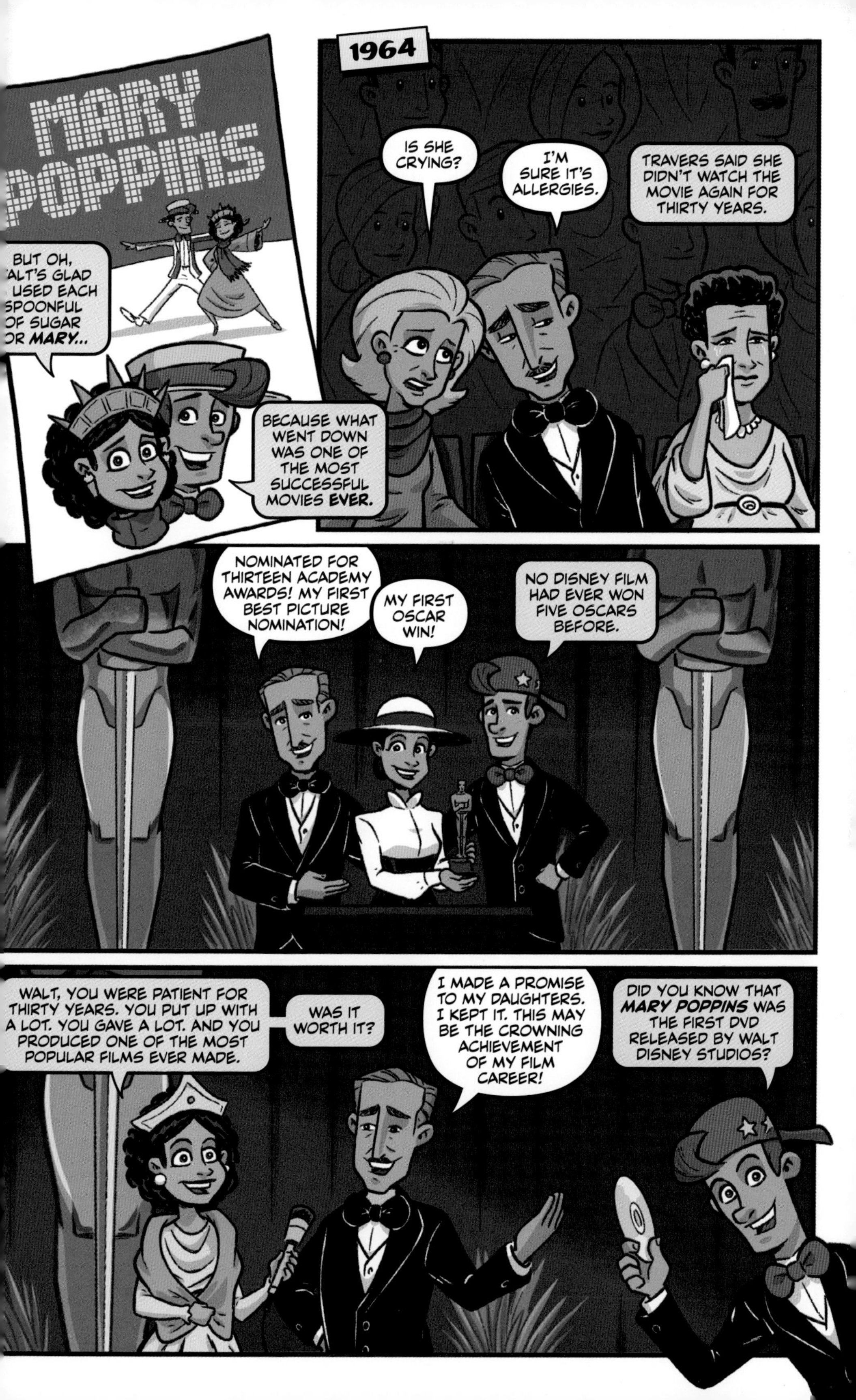
MARY POPPINS
BUT OH, ALT'S GLAD USED EACH SPOONFUL OF SUGAR OR MARY...
BECAUSE WHAT WENT DOWN WAS ONE OF THE MOST SUCCESSFUL MOVIES EVER.
1964
IS SHE CRYING?
I'M SURE IT'S ALLERGIES.
TRAVERS SAID SHE DIDN'T WATCH THE MOVIE AGAIN FOR THIRTY YEARS.
NOMINATED FOR THIRTEEN ACADEMY AWARDS! MY FIRST BEST PICTURE NOMINATION!
MY FIRST OSCAR WIN!
NO DISNEY FILM HAD EVER WON FIVE OSCARS BEFORE.
WALT, YOU WERE PATIENT FOR THIRTY YEARS. YOU PUT UP WITH A LOT. YOU GAVE A LOT. AND YOU PRODUCED ONE OF THE MOST POPULAR FILMS EVER MADE.
WAS IT WORTH IT?
I MADE A PROMISE TO MY DAUGHTERS. I KEPT IT. THIS MAY BE THE CROWNING ACHIEVEMENT OF MY FILM CAREER!
DID YOU KNOW THAT MARY POPPINS WAS THE FIRST DVD RELEASED BY WALT DISNEY STUDIOS?

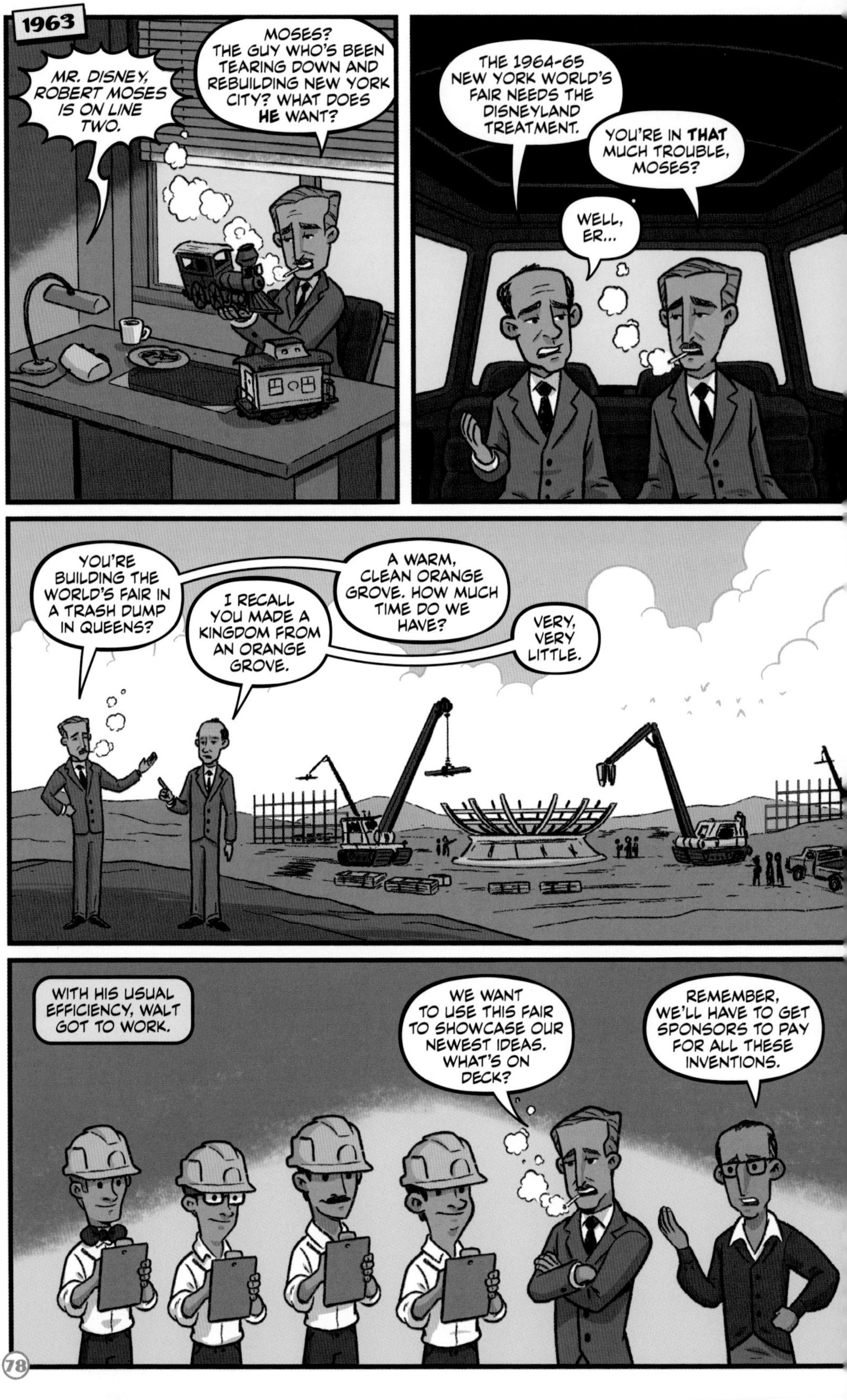
1963
MR. DISNEY, ROBERT MOSES IS ON LINE TWO.
MOSES? THE GUY WHO'S BEEN TEARING DOWN AND REBUILDING NEW YORK CITY? WHAT DOES **HE** WANT?
THE 1964-65 NEW YORK WORLD'S FAIR NEEDS THE DISNEYLAND TREATMENT.
YOU'RE IN **THAT** MUCH TROUBLE, MOSES?
WELL, ER...
YOU'RE BUILDING THE WORLD'S FAIR IN A TRASH DUMP IN QUEENS?
I RECALL YOU MADE A KINGDOM FROM AN ORANGE GROVE.
A WARM, CLEAN ORANGE GROVE. HOW MUCH TIME DO WE HAVE?
VERY, VERY LITTLE.
WITH HIS USUAL EFFICIENCY, WALT GOT TO WORK.
WE WANT TO USE THIS FAIR TO SHOWCASE OUR NEWEST IDEAS. WHAT'S ON DECK?
REMEMBER, WE'LL HAVE TO GET SPONSORS TO PAY FOR ALL THESE INVENTIONS.

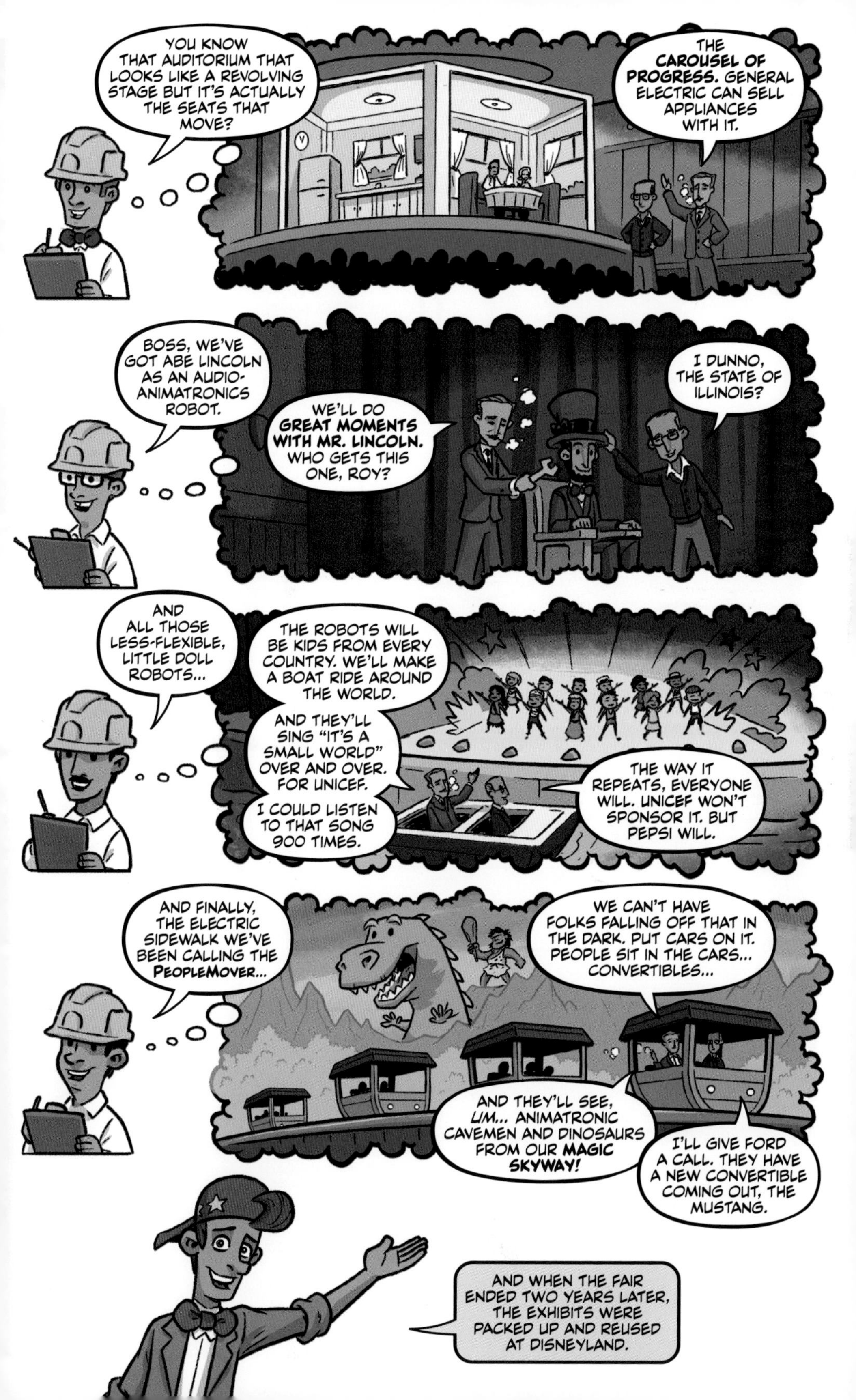
YOU KNOW THAT AUDITORIUM THAT LOOKS LIKE A REVOLVING STAGE BUT IT'S ACTUALLY THE SEATS THAT MOVE?
THE CAROUSEL OF PROGRESS. GENERAL ELECTRIC CAN SELL APPLIANCES WITH IT.
BOSS, WE'VE GOT ABE LINCOLN AS AN AUDIO-ANIMATRONICS ROBOT.
WE'LL DO GREAT MOMENTS WITH MR. LINCOLN. WHO GETS THIS ONE, ROY?
I DUNNO, THE STATE OF ILLINOIS?
AND ALL THOSE LESS-FLEXIBLE, LITTLE DOLL ROBOTS...
THE ROBOTS WILL BE KIDS FROM EVERY COUNTRY. WE'LL MAKE A BOAT RIDE AROUND THE WORLD.
AND THEY'LL SING "IT'S A SMALL WORLD" OVER AND OVER. FOR UNICEF.
I COULD LISTEN TO THAT SONG 900 TIMES.
THE WAY IT REPEATS, EVERYONE WILL. UNICEF WON'T SPONSOR IT. BUT PEPSI WILL.
AND FINALLY, THE ELECTRIC SIDEWALK WE'VE BEEN CALLING THE PEOPLEMOVER...
WE CAN'T HAVE FOLKS FALLING OFF THAT IN THE DARK. PUT CARS ON IT. PEOPLE SIT IN THE CARS... CONVERTIBLES...
AND THEY'LL SEE, UM... ANIMATRONIC CAVEMEN AND DINOSAURS FROM OUR MAGIC SKYWAY!
I'LL GIVE FORD A CALL. THEY HAVE A NEW CONVERTIBLE COMING OUT, THE MUSTANG.
AND WHEN THE FAIR ENDED TWO YEARS LATER, THE EXHIBITS WERE PACKED UP AND REUSED AT DISNEYLAND.

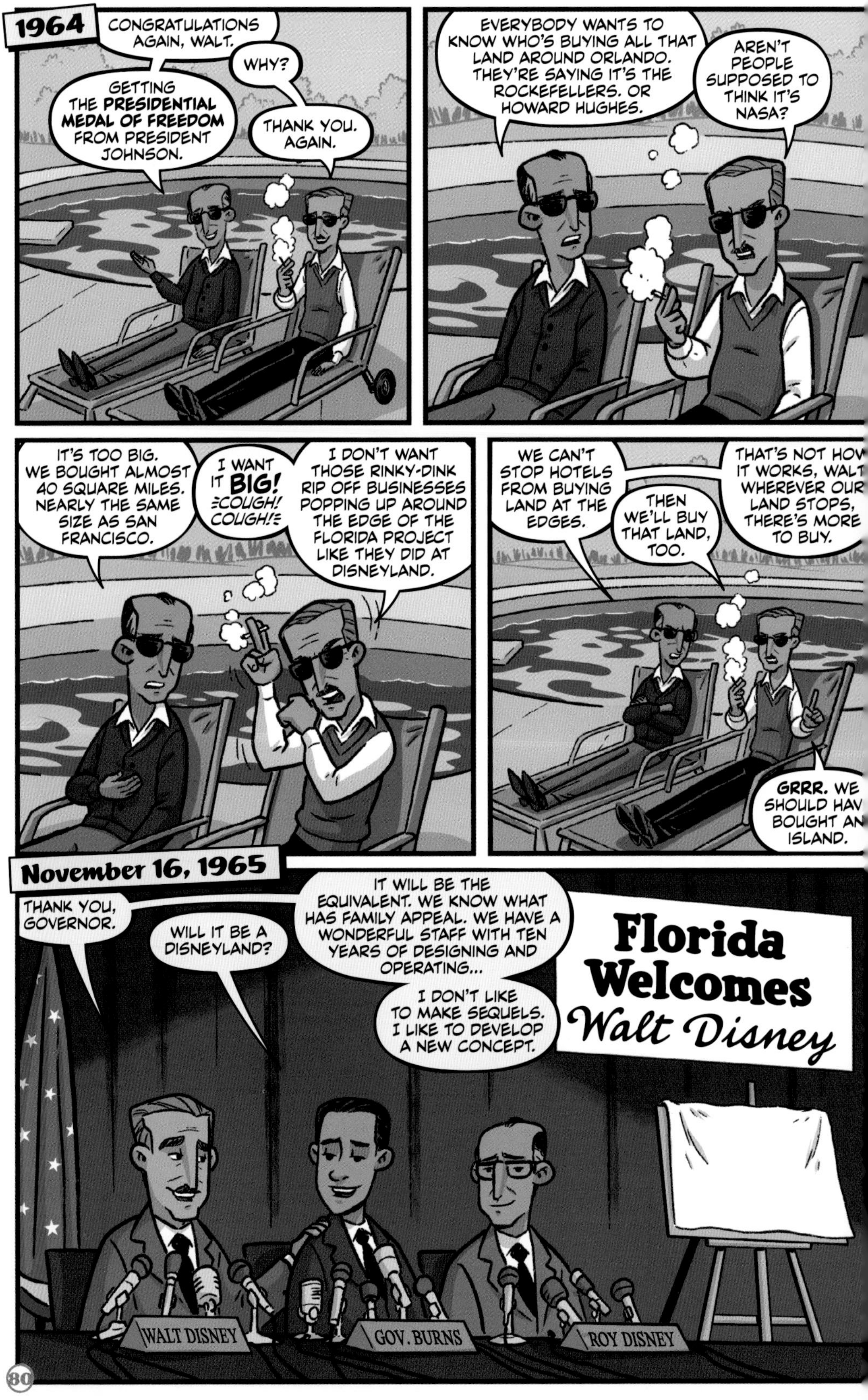
1964
CONGRATULATIONS AGAIN, WALT.
WHY?
GETTING THE **PRESIDENTIAL MEDAL OF FREEDOM** FROM PRESIDENT JOHNSON.
THANK YOU. AGAIN.
EVERYBODY WANTS TO KNOW WHO'S BUYING ALL THAT LAND AROUND ORLANDO. THEY'RE SAYING IT'S THE ROCKEFELLERS. OR HOWARD HUGHES.
AREN'T PEOPLE SUPPOSED TO THINK IT'S NASA?
IT'S TOO BIG. WE BOUGHT ALMOST 40 SQUARE MILES. NEARLY THE SAME SIZE AS SAN FRANCISCO.
I WANT IT **BIG!** COUGH! COUGH!
I DON'T WANT THOSE RINKY-DINK RIP OFF BUSINESSES POPPING UP AROUND THE EDGE OF THE FLORIDA PROJECT LIKE THEY DID AT DISNEYLAND.
WE CAN'T STOP HOTELS FROM BUYING LAND AT THE EDGES.
THEN WE'LL BUY THAT LAND, TOO.
THAT'S NOT HOW IT WORKS, WALT. WHEREVER OUR LAND STOPS, THERE'S MORE TO BUY.
GRRR. WE SHOULD HAVE BOUGHT AN ISLAND.
November 16, 1965
THANK YOU, GOVERNOR.
WILL IT BE A DISNEYLAND?
IT WILL BE THE EQUIVALENT. WE KNOW WHAT HAS FAMILY APPEAL. WE HAVE A WONDERFUL STAFF WITH TEN YEARS OF DESIGNING AND OPERATING...
I DON'T LIKE TO MAKE SEQUELS. I LIKE TO DEVELOP A NEW CONCEPT.
Florida Welcomes Walt Disney
WALT DISNEY
GOV. BURNS
ROY DISNEY

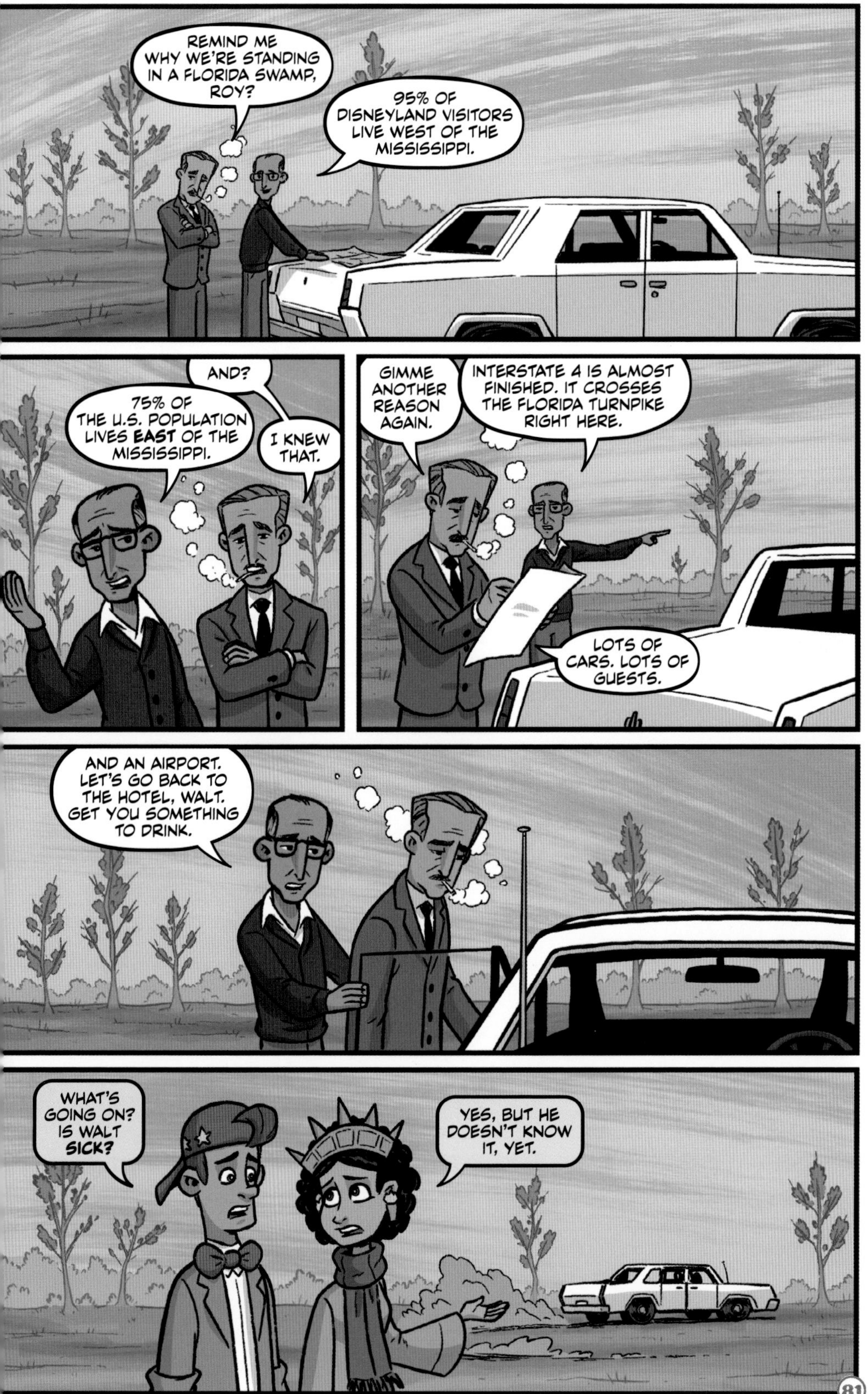
REMIND ME WHY WE'RE STANDING IN A FLORIDA SWAMP, ROY?
95% OF DISNEYLAND VISITORS LIVE WEST OF THE MISSISSIPPI.
75% OF THE U.S. POPULATION LIVES **EAST** OF THE MISSISSIPPI.
AND?
I KNEW THAT.
GIMME ANOTHER REASON AGAIN.
INTERSTATE 4 IS ALMOST FINISHED. IT CROSSES THE FLORIDA TURNPIKE RIGHT HERE.
LOTS OF CARS. LOTS OF GUESTS.
AND AN AIRPORT. LET'S GO BACK TO THE HOTEL, WALT. GET YOU SOMETHING TO DRINK.
WHAT'S GOING ON? IS WALT **SICK?**
YES, BUT HE DOESN'T KNOW IT, YET.

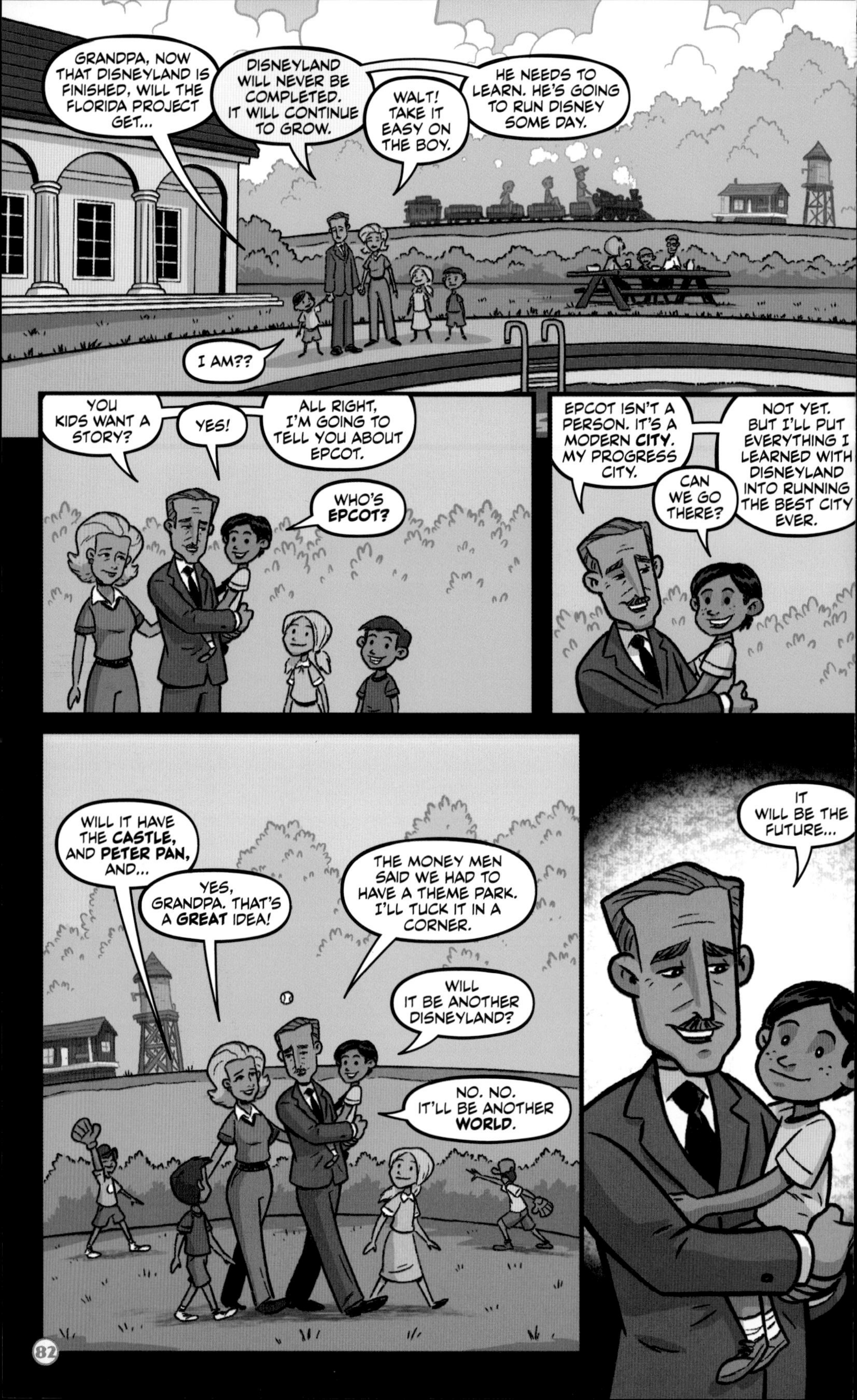

GRANDPA, NOW THAT DISNEYLAND IS FINISHED, WILL THE FLORIDA PROJECT GET...
DISNEYLAND WILL NEVER BE COMPLETED. IT WILL CONTINUE TO GROW.
WALT! TAKE IT EASY ON THE BOY.
HE NEEDS TO LEARN. HE'S GOING TO RUN DISNEY SOME DAY.
I AM??
YOU KIDS WANT A STORY?
YES!
ALL RIGHT, I'M GOING TO TELL YOU ABOUT EPCOT.
WHO'S **EPCOT?**
EPCOT ISN'T A PERSON. IT'S A MODERN **CITY**. MY PROGRESS CITY.
CAN WE GO THERE?
NOT YET. BUT I'LL PUT EVERYTHING I LEARNED WITH DISNEYLAND INTO RUNNING THE BEST CITY EVER.
WILL IT HAVE THE **CASTLE,** AND **PETER PAN,** AND...
YES, GRANDPA. THAT'S A **GREAT** IDEA!
THE MONEY MEN SAID WE HAD TO HAVE A THEME PARK. I'LL TUCK IT IN A CORNER.
WILL IT BE ANOTHER DISNEYLAND?
NO. NO. IT'LL BE ANOTHER **WORLD**.
IT WILL BE THE FUTURE...

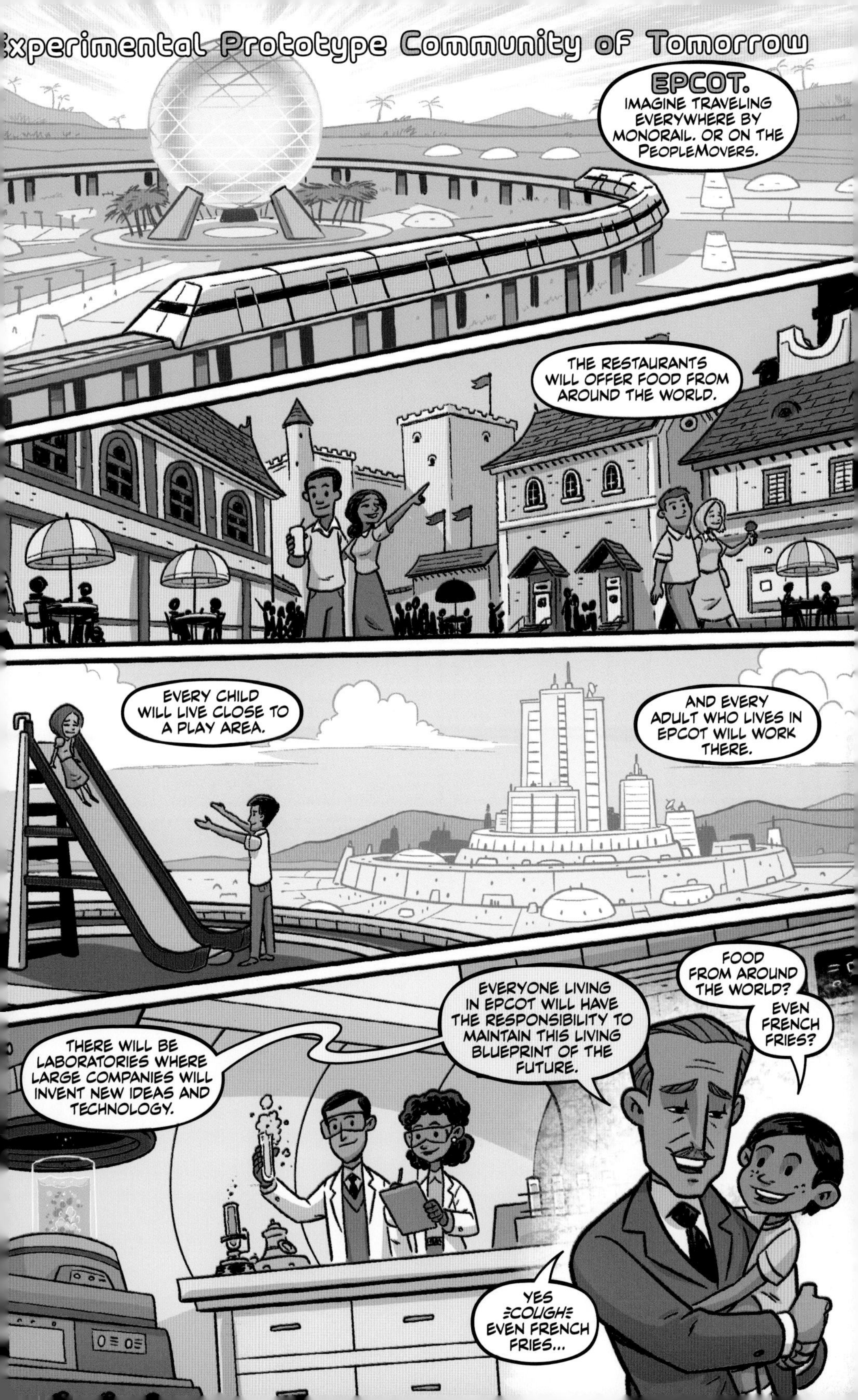
Experimental Prototype Community of Tomorrow
EPCOT. IMAGINE TRAVELING EVERYWHERE BY MONORAIL. OR ON THE PEOPLEMOVERS.
THE RESTAURANTS WILL OFFER FOOD FROM AROUND THE WORLD.
EVERY CHILD WILL LIVE CLOSE TO A PLAY AREA.
AND EVERY ADULT WHO LIVES IN EPCOT WILL WORK THERE.
THERE WILL BE LABORATORIES WHERE LARGE COMPANIES WILL INVENT NEW IDEAS AND TECHNOLOGY.
EVERYONE LIVING IN EPCOT WILL HAVE THE RESPONSIBILITY TO MAINTAIN THIS LIVING BLUEPRINT OF THE FUTURE.
FOOD FROM AROUND THE WORLD?
EVEN FRENCH FRIES?
YES COUGH EVEN FRENCH FRIES...

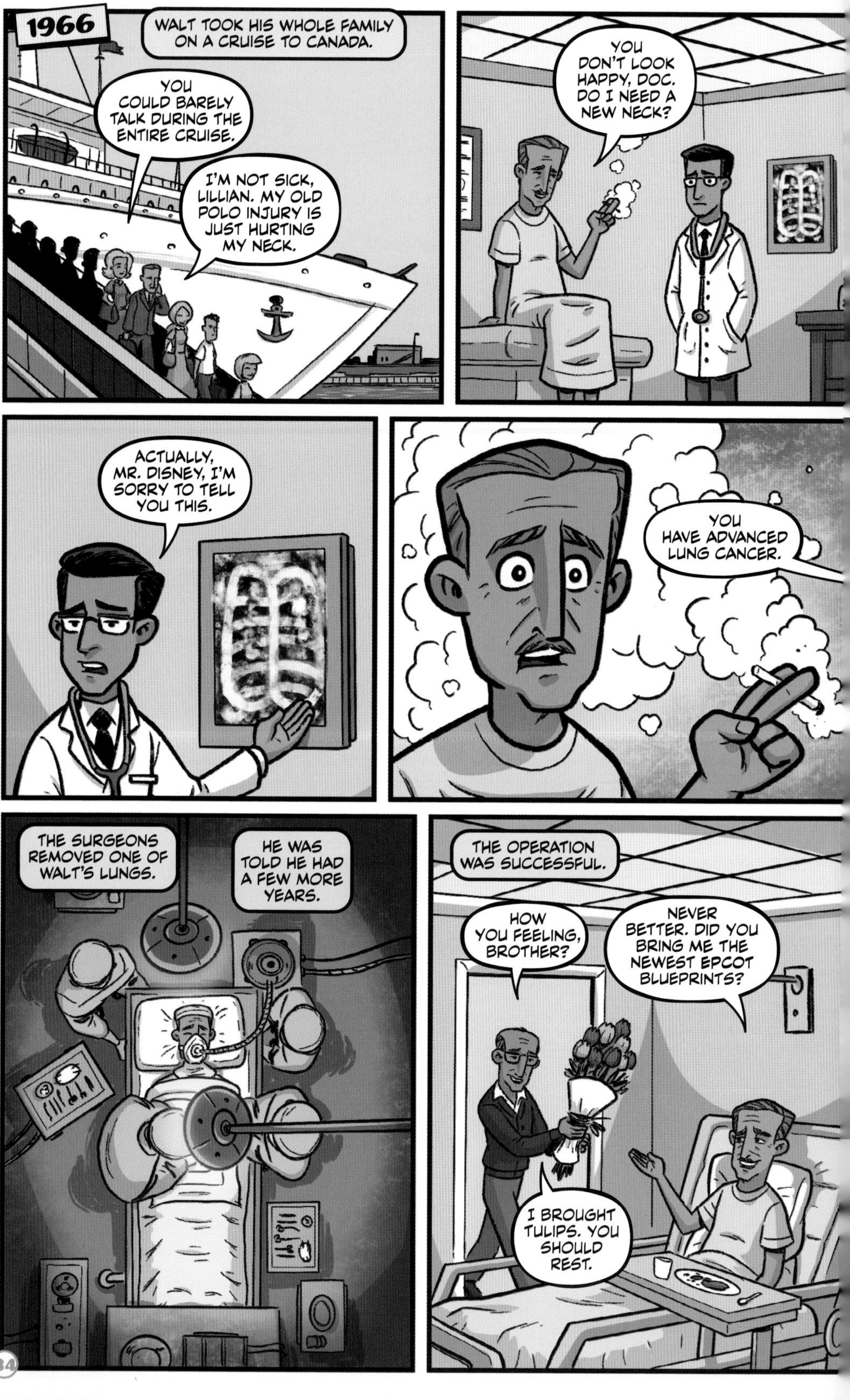
1966
WALT TOOK HIS WHOLE FAMILY ON A CRUISE TO CANADA.
YOU COULD BARELY TALK DURING THE ENTIRE CRUISE.
I'M NOT SICK, LILLIAN. MY OLD POLO INJURY IS JUST HURTING MY NECK.
YOU DON'T LOOK HAPPY, DOC. DO I NEED A NEW NECK?
ACTUALLY, MR. DISNEY, I'M SORRY TO TELL YOU THIS.
YOU HAVE ADVANCED LUNG CANCER.
THE SURGEONS REMOVED ONE OF WALT'S LUNGS.
HE WAS TOLD HE HAD A FEW MORE YEARS.
THE OPERATION WAS SUCCESSFUL.
HOW YOU FEELING, BROTHER?
NEVER BETTER. DID YOU BRING ME THE NEWEST EPCOT BLUEPRINTS?
I BROUGHT TULIPS. YOU SHOULD REST.

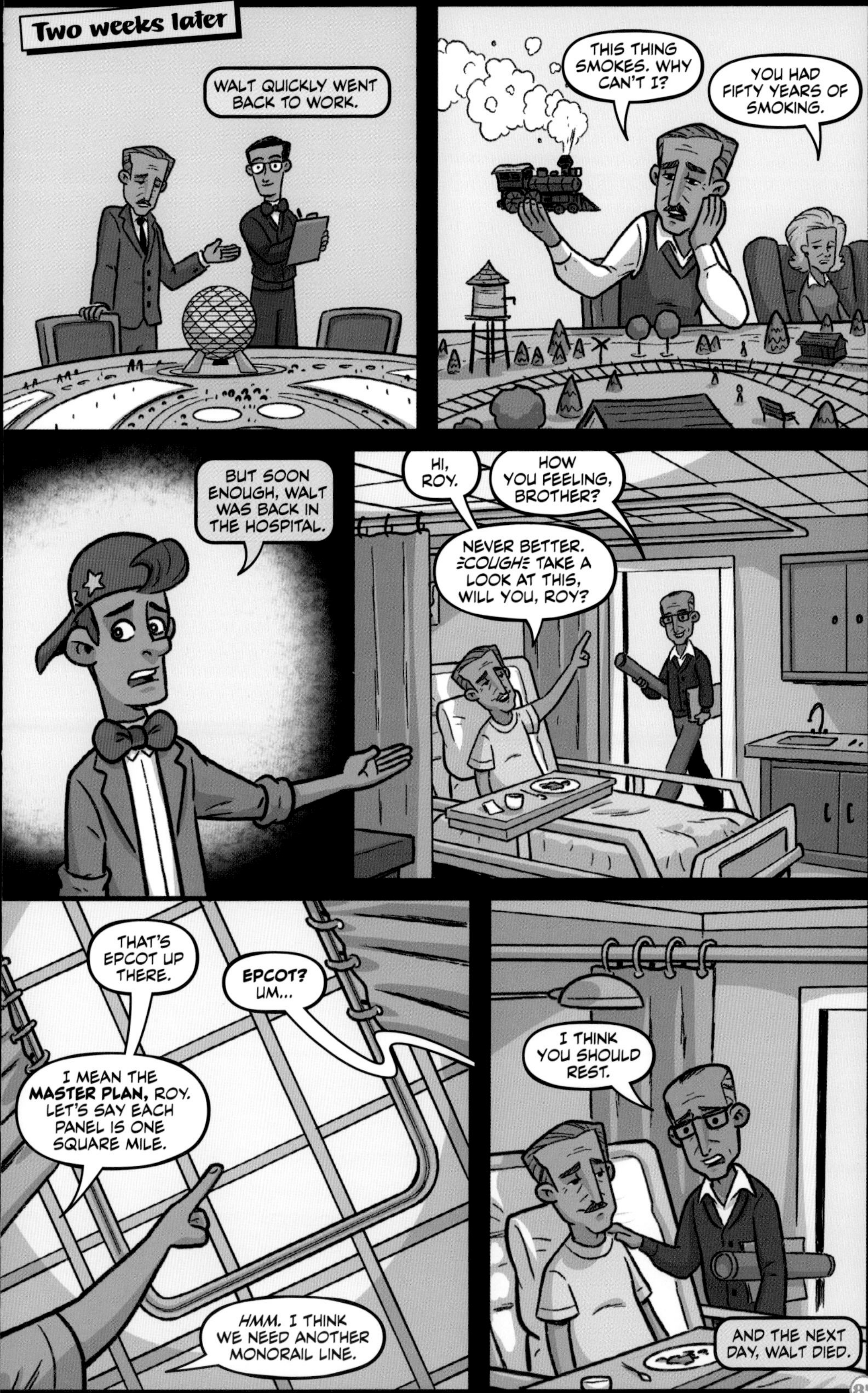

Two weeks later
WALT QUICKLY WENT BACK TO WORK.
THIS THING SMOKES. WHY CAN'T I?
YOU HAD FIFTY YEARS OF SMOKING.
BUT SOON ENOUGH, WALT WAS BACK IN THE HOSPITAL.
HI, ROY.
HOW YOU FEELING, BROTHER?
NEVER BETTER. *COUGH* TAKE A LOOK AT THIS, WILL YOU, ROY?
THAT'S EPCOT UP THERE.
EPCOT? UM...
I MEAN THE MASTER PLAN, ROY. LET'S SAY EACH PANEL IS ONE SQUARE MILE.
HMM. I THINK WE NEED ANOTHER MONORAIL LINE.
I THINK YOU SHOULD REST.
AND THE NEXT DAY, WALT DIED.

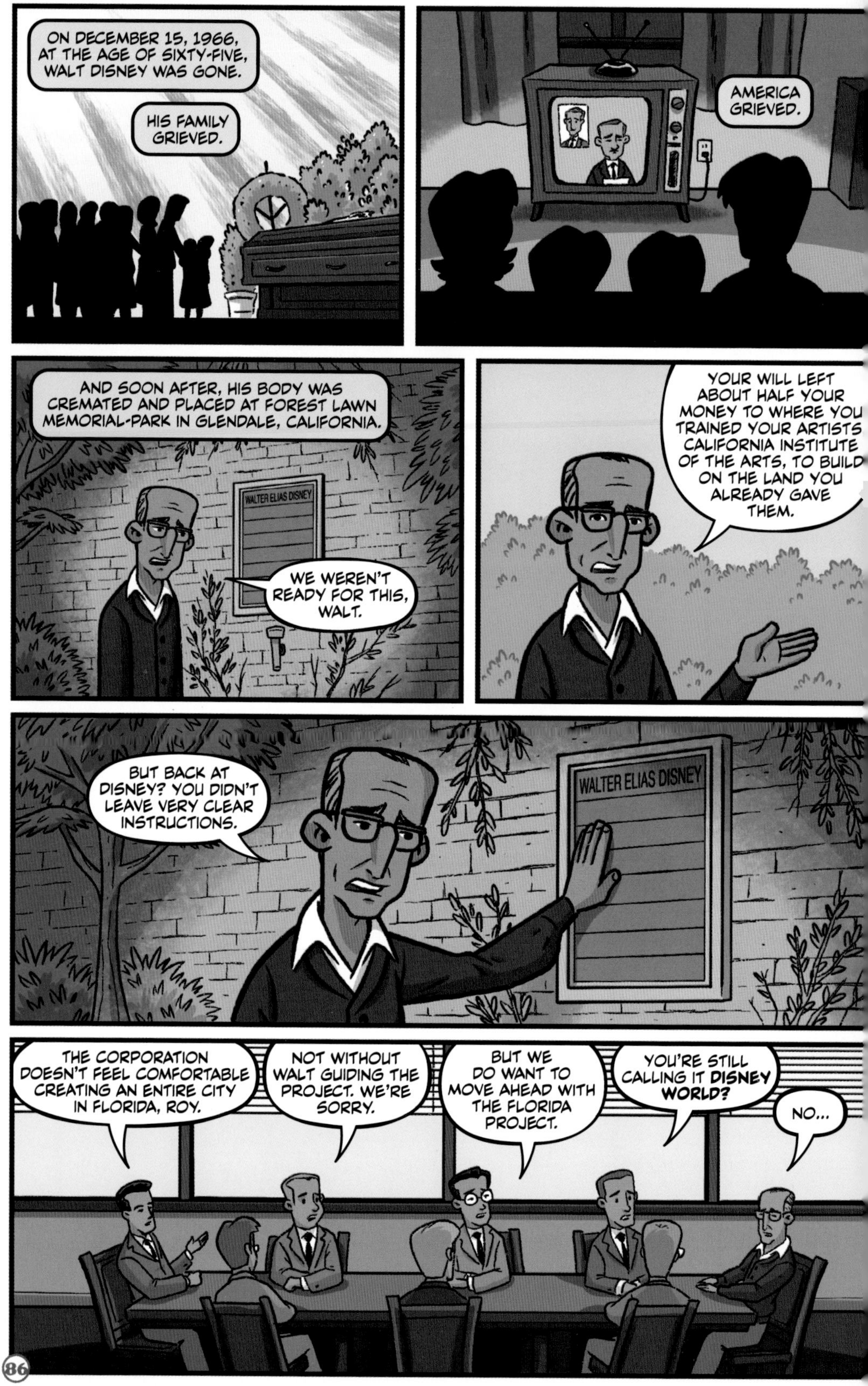
ON DECEMBER 15, 1966, AT THE AGE OF SIXTY-FIVE, WALT DISNEY WAS GONE.
HIS FAMILY GRIEVED.
AMERICA GRIEVED.
AND SOON AFTER, HIS BODY WAS CREMATED AND PLACED AT FOREST LAWN MEMORIAL-PARK IN GLENDALE, CALIFORNIA.
WALTER ELIAS DISNEY
WE WEREN'T READY FOR THIS, WALT.
YOUR WILL LEFT ABOUT HALF YOUR MONEY TO WHERE YOU TRAINED YOUR ARTISTS CALIFORNIA INSTITUTE OF THE ARTS, TO BUILD ON THE LAND YOU ALREADY GAVE THEM.
BUT BACK AT DISNEY? YOU DIDN'T LEAVE VERY CLEAR INSTRUCTIONS.
WALTER ELIAS DISNEY
THE CORPORATION DOESN'T FEEL COMFORTABLE CREATING AN ENTIRE CITY IN FLORIDA, ROY.
NOT WITHOUT WALT GUIDING THE PROJECT. WE'RE SORRY.
BUT WE DO WANT TO MOVE AHEAD WITH THE FLORIDA PROJECT.
YOU'RE STILL CALLING IT **DISNEY WORLD?**
NO...

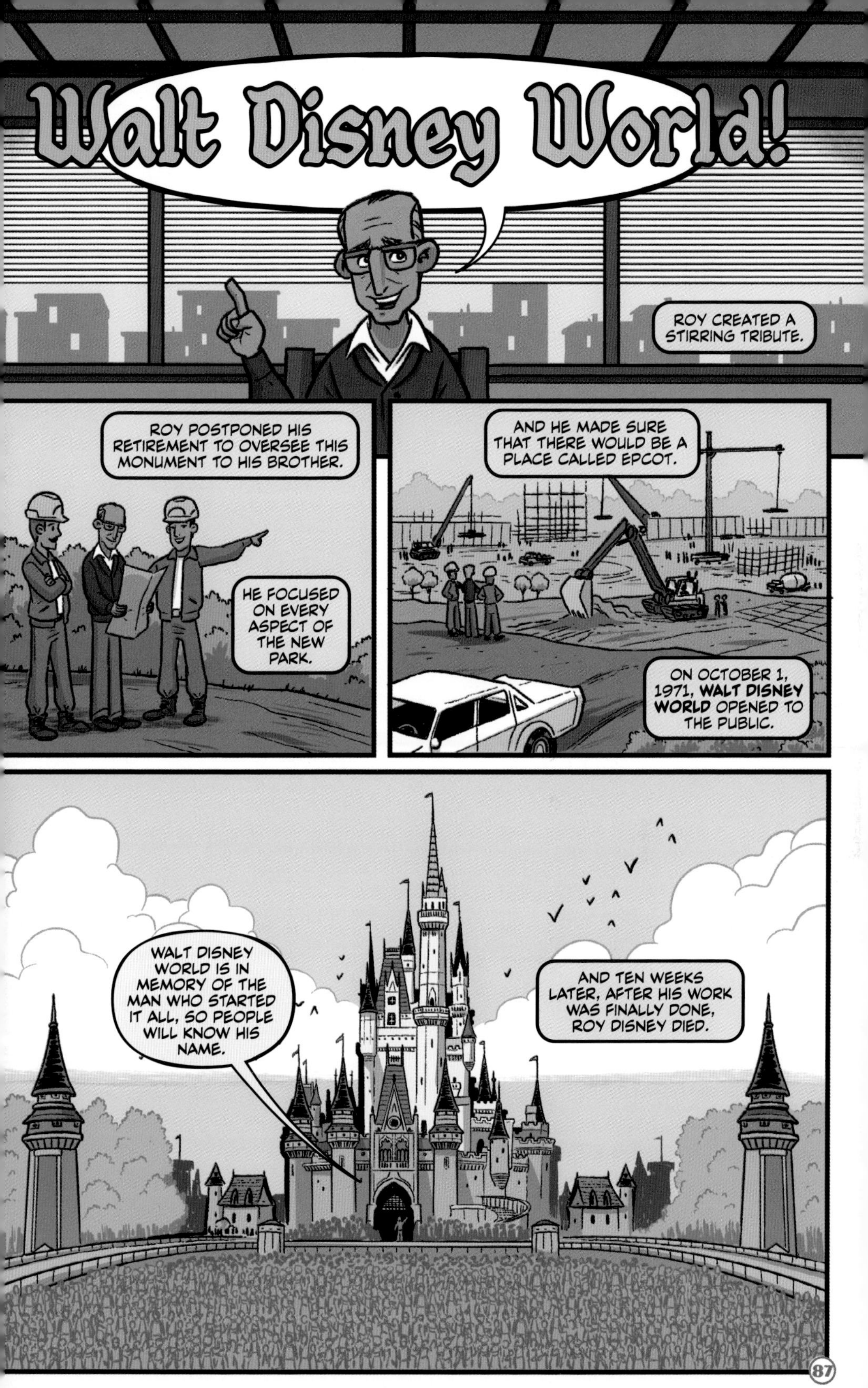
Walt Disney World!
ROY CREATED A STIRRING TRIBUTE.
ROY POSTPONED HIS RETIREMENT TO OVERSEE THIS MONUMENT TO HIS BROTHER.
HE FOCUSED ON EVERY ASPECT OF THE NEW PARK.
AND HE MADE SURE THAT THERE WOULD BE A PLACE CALLED EPCOT.
ON OCTOBER 1, 1971, **WALT DISNEY WORLD** OPENED TO THE PUBLIC.
WALT DISNEY WORLD IS IN MEMORY OF THE MAN WHO STARTED IT ALL, SO PEOPLE WILL KNOW HIS NAME.
AND TEN WEEKS LATER, AFTER HIS WORK WAS FINALLY DONE, ROY DISNEY DIED.

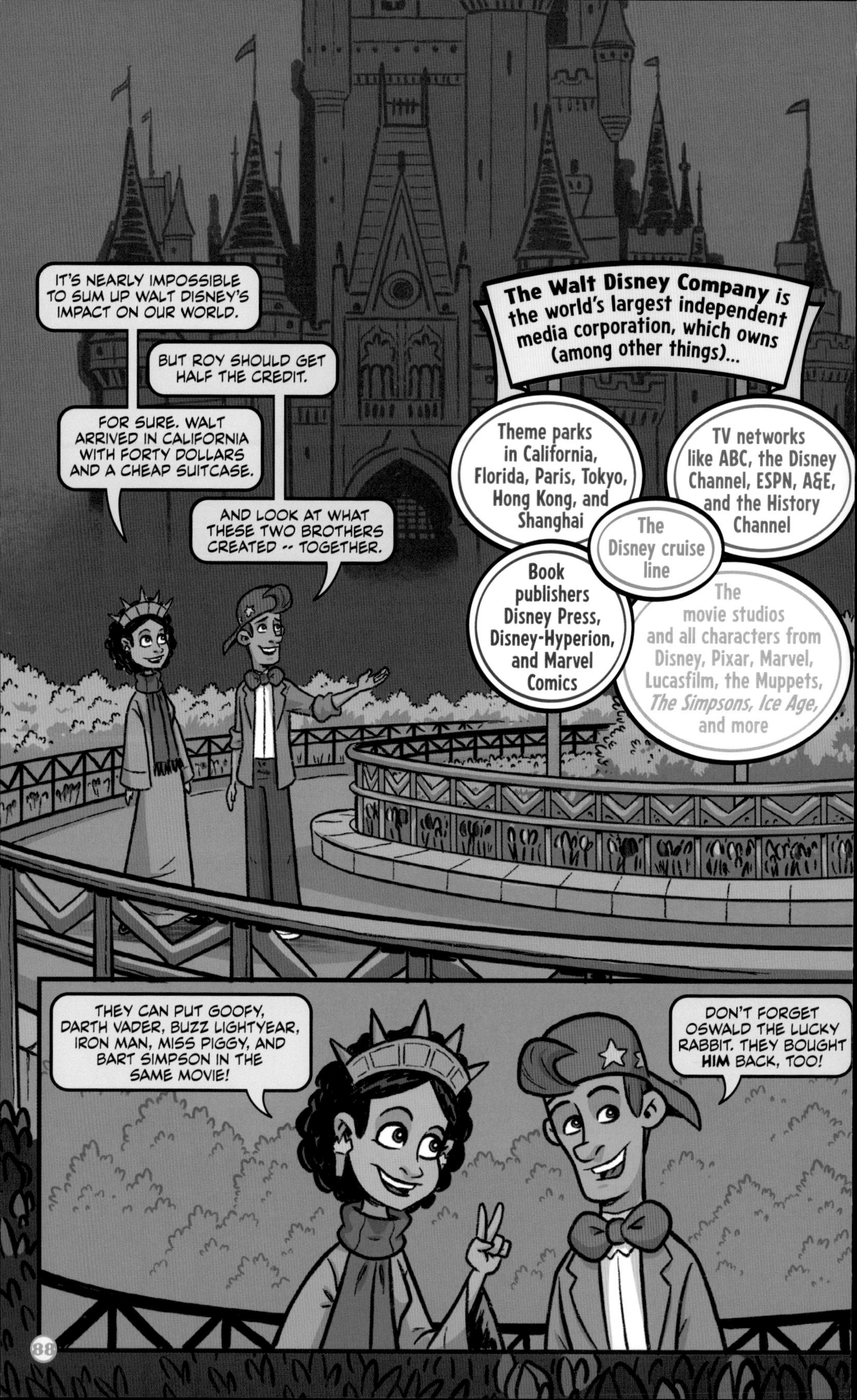

IT'S NEARLY IMPOSSIBLE TO SUM UP WALT DISNEY'S IMPACT ON OUR WORLD.
BUT ROY SHOULD GET HALF THE CREDIT.
FOR SURE. WALT ARRIVED IN CALIFORNIA WITH FORTY DOLLARS AND A CHEAP SUITCASE.
AND LOOK AT WHAT THESE TWO BROTHERS CREATED -- TOGETHER.
The Walt Disney Company is the world's largest independent media corporation, which owns (among other things)...
Theme parks in California, Florida, Paris, Tokyo, Hong Kong, and Shanghai
TV networks like ABC, the Disney Channel, ESPN, A&E, and the History Channel
The Disney cruise line
Book publishers Disney Press, Disney-Hyperion, and Marvel Comics
The movie studios and all characters from Disney, Pixar, Marvel, Lucasfilm, the Muppets, *The Simpsons, Ice Age,* and more
THEY CAN PUT GOOFY, DARTH VADER, BUZZ LIGHTYEAR, IRON MAN, MISS PIGGY, AND BART SIMPSON IN THE SAME MOVIE!
DON'T FORGET OSWALD THE LUCKY RABBIT. THEY BOUGHT **HIM** BACK, TOO!

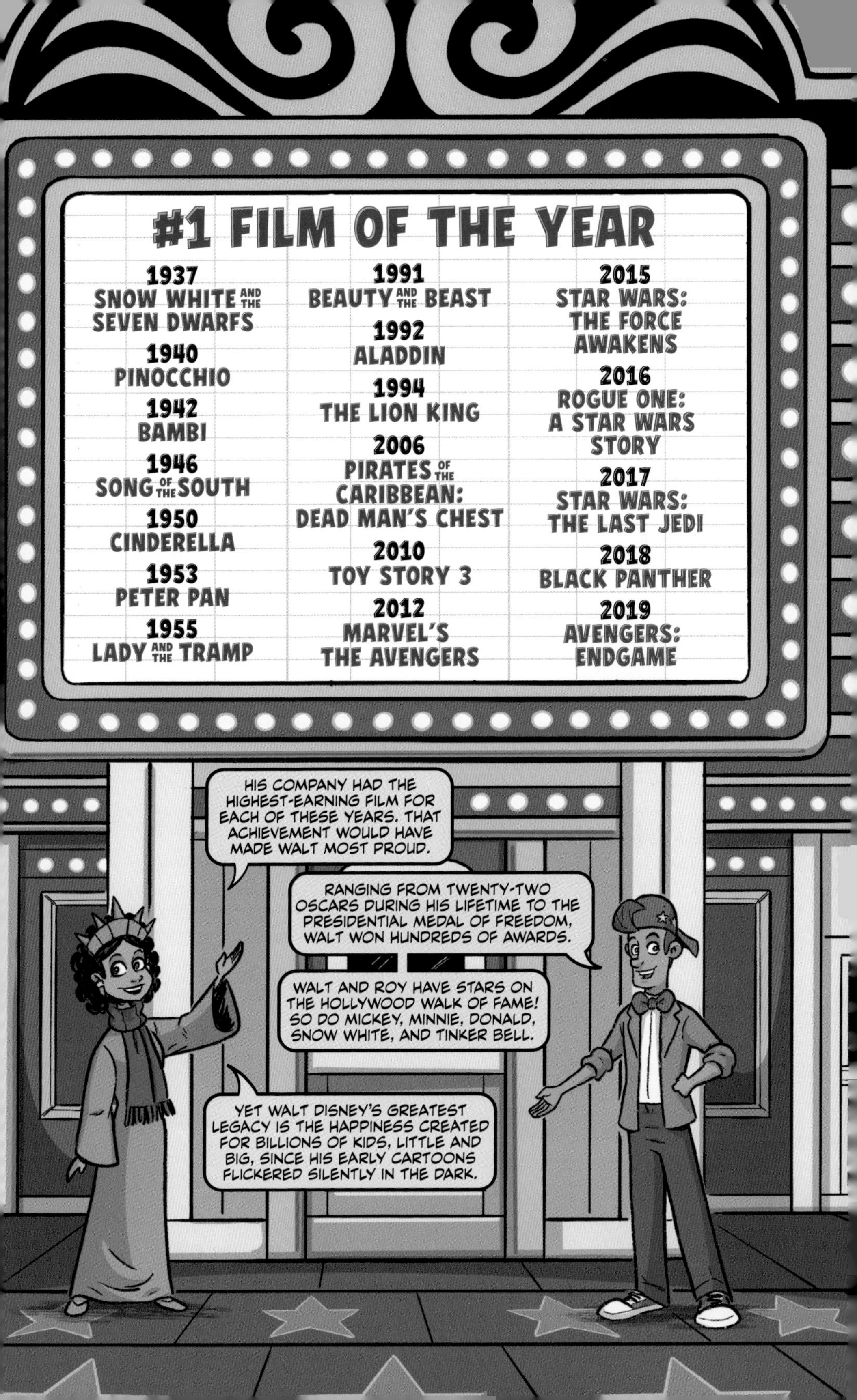
#1 FILM OF THE YEAR
1937 SNOW WHITE AND THE SEVEN DWARFS
1940 PINOCCHIO
1942 BAMBI
1946 SONG OF THE SOUTH
1950 CINDERELLA
1953 PETER PAN
1955 LADY AND THE TRAMP
1991 BEAUTY AND THE BEAST
1992 ALADDIN
1994 THE LION KING
2006 PIRATES OF THE CARIBBEAN: DEAD MAN'S CHEST
2010 TOY STORY 3
2012 MARVEL'S THE AVENGERS
2015 STAR WARS: THE FORCE AWAKENS
2016 ROGUE ONE: A STAR WARS STORY
2017 STAR WARS: THE LAST JEDI
2018 BLACK PANTHER
2019 AVENGERS: ENDGAME
HIS COMPANY HAD THE HIGHEST-EARNING FILM FOR EACH OF THESE YEARS. THAT ACHIEVEMENT WOULD HAVE MADE WALT MOST PROUD.
RANGING FROM TWENTY-TWO OSCARS DURING HIS LIFETIME TO THE PRESIDENTIAL MEDAL OF FREEDOM, WALT WON HUNDREDS OF AWARDS.
WALT AND ROY HAVE STARS ON THE HOLLYWOOD WALK OF FAME! SO DO MICKEY, MINNIE, DONALD, SNOW WHITE, AND TINKER BELL.
YET WALT DISNEY'S GREATEST LEGACY IS THE HAPPINESS CREATED FOR BILLIONS OF KIDS, LITTLE AND BIG, SINCE HIS EARLY CARTOONS FLICKERED SILENTLY IN THE DARK.

FAMOUS ANIMATORS

HERE ARE SOME OTHER TALENTED ARTISTS WHO BROUGHT INNOVATION TO ANIMATION.

WINSOR McCAY: Known mostly for early newspaper comics such as *Little Nemo in Slumberland*, McCay pioneered early animation with *Gertie the Dinosaur* (1914), and the first animated documentary, *The Sinking of the Lusitania* (1918).

MAX FLEISCHER: This early animation superstar brought Popeye, Superman, and Betty Boop to the screen. He invented the Rotoscope, which let animators trace images from live action films. Superman used to jump until Fleischer made him fly.

LILLIAN FRIEDMAN: She was the first female animator within the major studio system in the 1930s. Friedman became the first-ever woman Head Animator, and worked on at least 13 Fleischer Studios films.

RAY HARRYHAUSEN: The first great stop-motion model animator, his Dynamation technique brought a giant gorilla to life (*Mighty Joe Young*), Cyclops battling a dragon (*The 7th Voyage of Sinbad*), a skeleton swordfight (*Clash of the Titans*), and much more -- all before computers.

CHUCK JONES & TEX AVERY: They animated Bugs Bunny, Daffy Duck, Porky Pig, and the Road Runner in the *Looney Tunes* and *Merrie Melodies* animated series for Warner Bros. Later, for TV, Jones created the original animated special, *How the Grinch Stole Christmas!*

WILLIAM HANNA & JOSEPH BARBERA: They led TV animation from the 1950s to the 1980s, with hit shows like *The Flintstones*, *The Jetsons*, *Scooby-Doo, Where Are You!*, and the *Smurfs*. Their vision and techniques paved the way for modern TV cartoons.

HAYAO MIYAZAKI: This legendary Japanese manga artist and master storyteller created lavish paintings and timeless heroes in *My Neighbor Totoro* and *Howl's Moving Castle*. His *Spirited Away* is the most successful Japanese film ever released in the United States.

NICK PARK: In the era of computer-generated animation, he revived old-fashioned, painstaking clay animation for the beloved *Wallace and Gromit* series.

WALT DISNEY TIMELINE

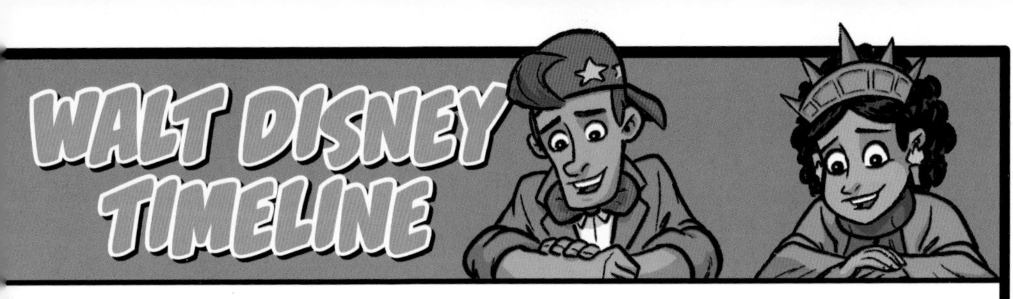

1901 Walt is born on December 5th in Chicago.

1906-1910 The family moves to Marceline, Missouri. Walt eventually models Disneyland's Main Street USA after his home town.

1910-1917 Walt's family moves to Kansas City, MO, where he falls in love with movies; then back to Chicago, where he wants to be a cartoonist.

1918 Walt forges papers to join World War I as an ambulance driver, since he is underage. Arrives in Paris after the war is over.

1919-1922 In Kansas City, Walt works as a commercial artist. He partners with Ub Iwerks, and their art studio quickly fails. They learn basic animation for early commercials, then start Laugh-O-Gram Studio to make funny short cartoons.

1923 Bankrupt, Walt joins brother Roy in Hollywood to start Disney Brothers' Studio. Always an innovator, Walt's *Alice in Cartoonland* comedies put a live girl in an animated world.

1927 Walt and Ub create *Oswald the Lucky Rabbit*, a successful cartoon series. The distributor ends up taking Oswald and most of Walt's animators. Walt's response: Mickey Mouse.

1928 *Steamboat Willie*, the first talking cartoon, is a hit. The Mickey Mouse Club and merchandise explode.

1932 The Great Depression grips the country, and people flock to movies to forget their troubles. Walt introduces Technicolor to his films and begins winning Academy Awards.

1938 *Snow White and the Seven Dwarfs*, the world's first full-length animated film, is a financial success after three years of make-or-break production.

1941-1945 The studio dedicates itself to making World War II films, and the password for the D-Day strike was "Mickey Mouse." Animators go on strike, and join the *Screen Cartoonists Guild*.

1948 Walt testifies in Congress, in front of the House Un-American Activities Committee.

1955 Walt envisions Disneyland, betting the shop on the first-ever theme park. It's partly funded by the TV programs *Disneyland* and the *Mickey Mouse Club*.

1960 As the head of pageantry for the Winter Olympics, Walt redefines ceremonies for TV.

1964-1965 *Mary Poppins* becomes the most successful Disney film to this point. Disney buys forty square miles of land near Orlando, Florida to build a city of tomorrow.

1966 After a lifetime of smoking, Walt Disney dies of lung cancer on December 15th, at age sixty-five.

GLOSSARY

ANIMATION: Individual cels filmed in sequence to give the illusion of motion.

CEL: A clear sheet of celluloid plastic with a character or scene painted on it, used as a single frame of an animation.

COMMUNISTS: Believers in central control of society and its property, who are against private wealth. In Disney's time, the Communist U.S.S.R. (centered in Russia) was the enemy of the United States.

FASCISTS: Governments with a dictator or leaders who have complete power, and stop any opposition. During World War II, Germany and Italy were fascist nations.

INTELLECTUAL PROPERTY: An image, character, story, or other concept that comes from someone's original creative thought and is protected by law.

LABOR UNIONS: Groups of workers who officially organize together to protect their rights and make agreements with their employers.

MULTIPLANE CAMERA: A camera that moves different cels past the camera at different speeds and distances to make action and backgrounds seem more lifelike.

NEWSREEL: Short current events films seen in movie theaters, in the days before television and TV news.

PROPAGANDA: Intentionally misleading, one-sided messages, ideas, facts and sometimes lies, created to support one cause and to harm the opposite cause.

STOP ACTION: An early film animation method in which objects or puppets are filmed one frame at a time, and then moved slightly, to give the final film the illusion of motion.

STRIKE: A way for employees to protest their employers and change working conditions by stopping work as an organized group.

TECHNICOLOR: A patented process for making color movies by combining images filmed in red, yellow/green, and blue into a single, full-color print.

UNICEF: The United Nations International Children's Emergency Fund is an arm of the UN whose chief focus is aiding children in poor or war-torn countries.

FIND OUT MORE

BOOKS

Gabler, Neal. *Walt Disney: The Triumph of the American Imagination.* New York: Knopf, 2006.

Goldberg, Aaron H. *The Disney Story: Chronicling the Man, the Mouse & the Parks.* Royal Oak, Michigan: Quaker Scribe, 2016.

Norwich, Grace. *I Am Walt Disney.* I Am series. New York: Scholastic, 2014.

Scollon, Bill. *Walt Disney: Drawn from Imagination.* New York: Disney Press, 2014.

Stewart, Whitney. *Who Was Walt Disney?* Who Was? series. New York: Penguin Group, 2009.

Sutcliffe, Jane. *Walt Disney.* History Maker Bios series. Minneapolis, Minnesota: Lerner Publishing, 2009.

VIDEOS

Hancock, John Lee, dir. *Saving Mr. Banks.* Burbank, CA: Walt Disney Studios, 2013.

Le, Khoa, dir. *Walt Before Mickey.* Calabasas, CA: Mission Pictures Int'l, 2015.

SHOW ME HISTORY!

COLLECT EVERY BOOK IN THE SERIES AND FIND THE *STORY* IN HISTORY!

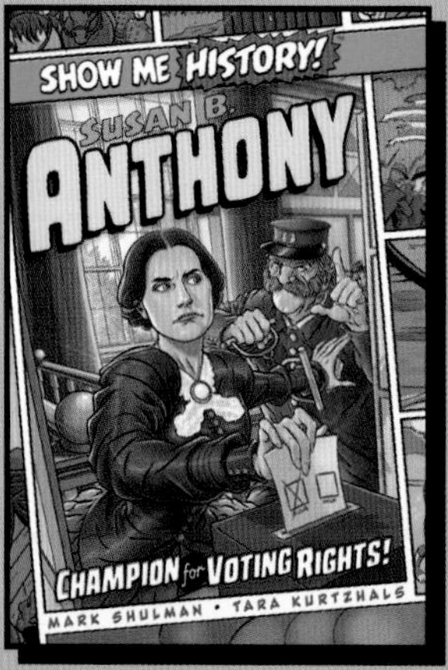
SHOW ME HISTORY!
SUSAN B. ANTHONY
CHAMPION for VOTING RIGHTS!
MARK SHULMAN • TARA KURTZHALS

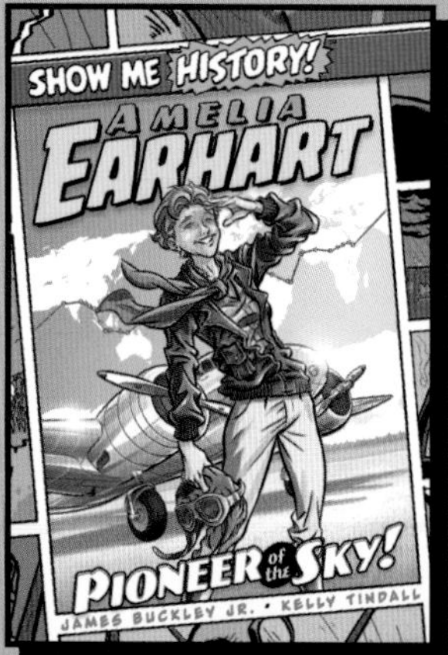
SHOW ME HISTORY!
AMELIA EARHART
PIONEER of the SKY!
JAMES BUCKLEY JR. • KELLY TINDALL

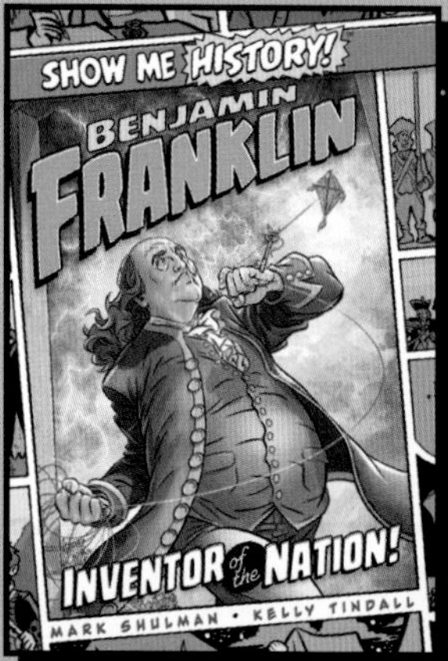
SHOW ME HISTORY!
BENJAMIN FRANKLIN
INVENTOR of the NATION!
MARK SHULMAN • KELLY TINDALL

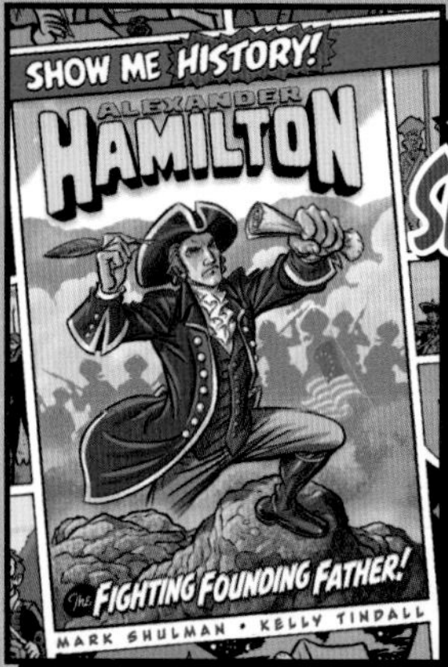
SHOW ME HISTORY!
ALEXANDER HAMILTON
The FIGHTING FOUNDING FATHER!
MARK SHULMAN • KELLY TINDALL

PARENTS AND TEACHERS: VISIT OUR WEBSITE FOR MORE *SHOW ME HISTORY!* FUN:

SHOWMEHISTORY.COM

Learn more about the authors and illustrators.

Download a free preview of each book.

Sign up for our email newsletter.

Access our *Show Me History! Reading Guide*, perfect for teachers, librarians, homeschoolers, and parents.

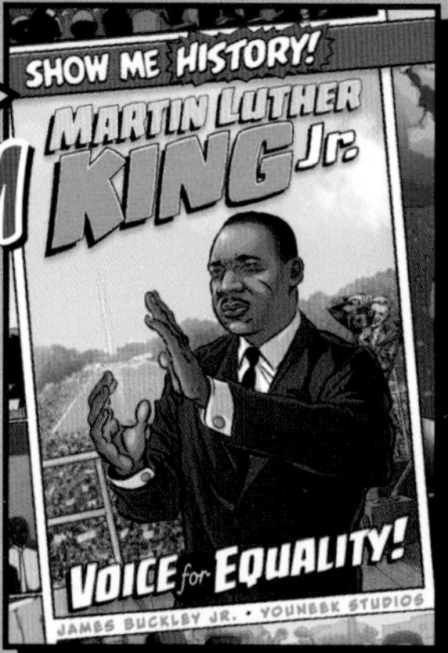
SHOW ME HISTORY!
MARTIN LUTHER KING Jr.
VOICE for EQUALITY!
JAMES BUCKLEY JR. • YOUNEEK STUDIOS

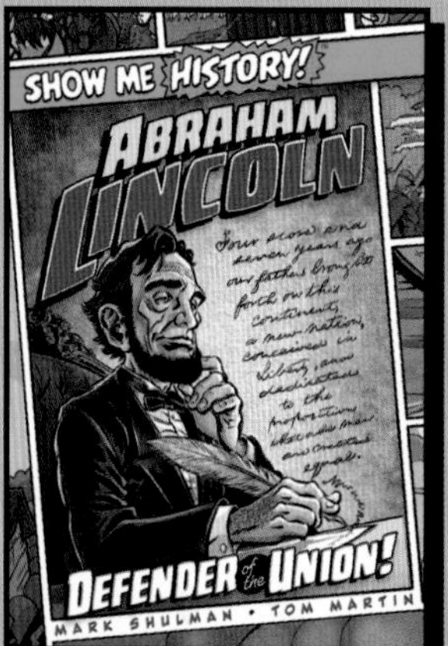
SHOW ME HISTORY!
ABRAHAM LINCOLN
DEFENDER of the UNION!
MARK SHULMAN • TOM MARTIN

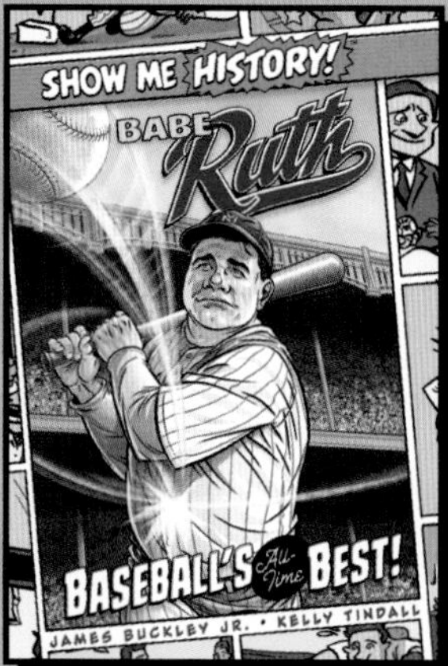
SHOW ME HISTORY!
BABE Ruth
BASEBALL'S All-Time BEST!
JAMES BUCKLEY JR. • KELLY TINDALL

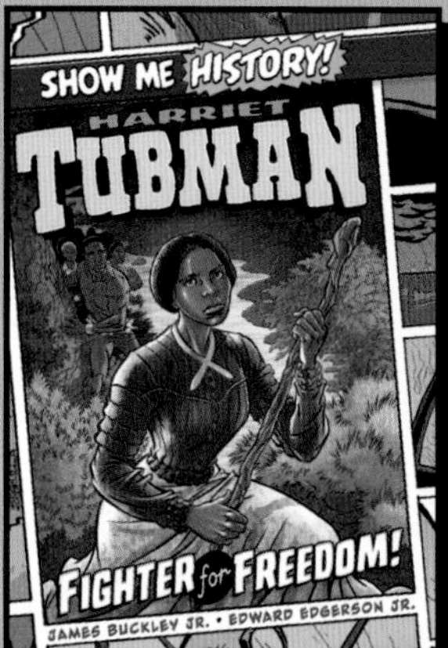
SHOW ME HISTORY!
HARRIET TUBMAN
FIGHTER for FREEDOM!
JAMES BUCKLEY JR. • EDWARD EDGERSON JR.

FOLLOW US ON SOCIAL MEDIA:

www.facebook.com/portablepress

www.pinterest.com/portablepress

@portablepress

@portablepress

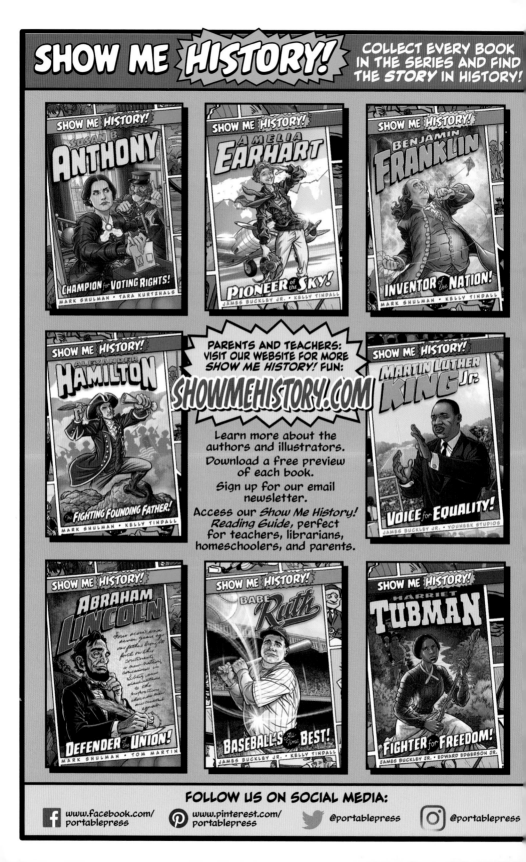

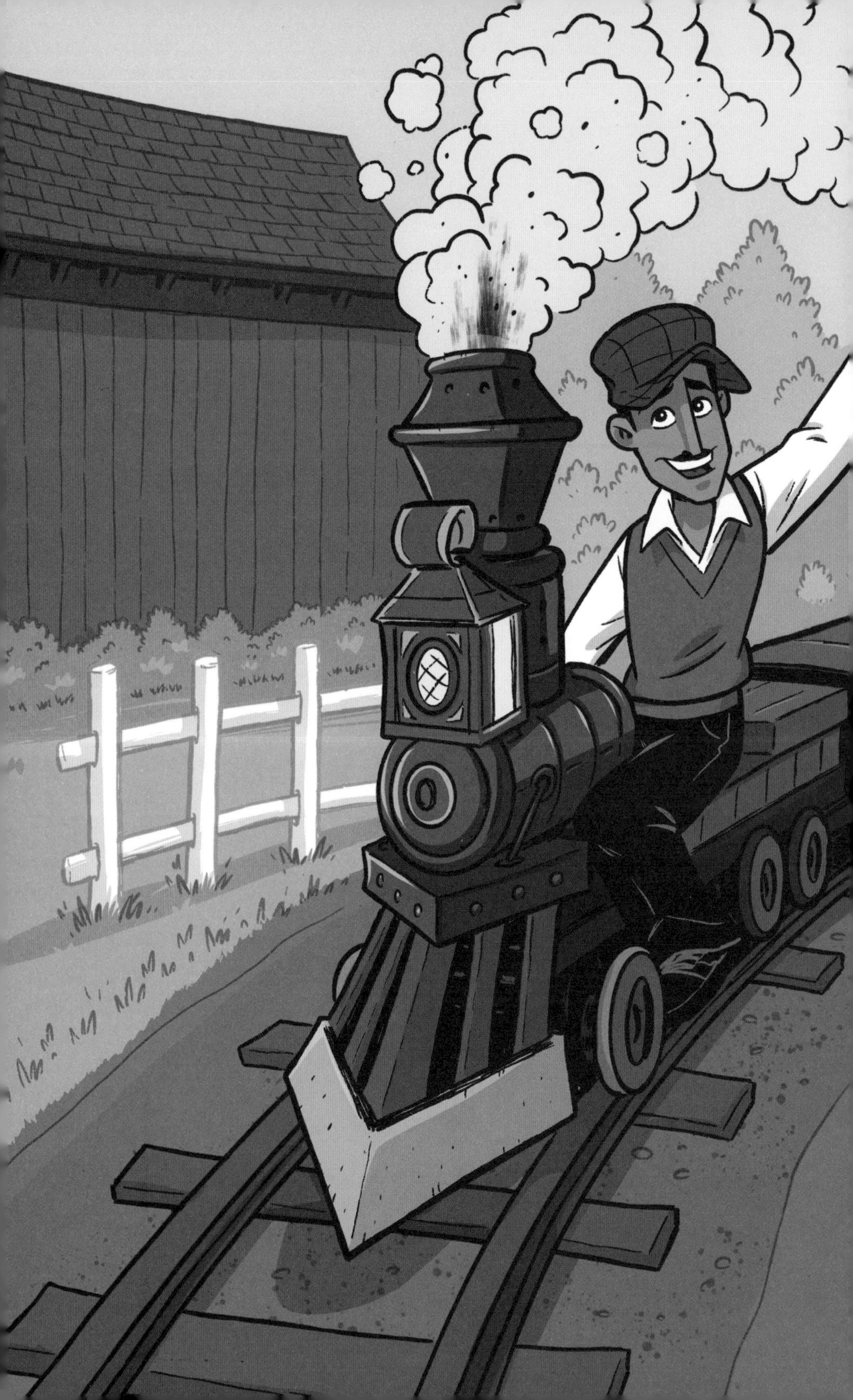